THE WORK

THE WORK

A JIGSAW MEMOIR

ZACHARY SKLAR

OLIVE PRESS

The Work: A Jigsaw Memoir © 2022 by Zachary Sklar

Paperback ISBN 978-1-954744-96-7
eBook ISBN 978-1-954744-97-4

Library of Congress Control Number 2022921595

Published by Olive Press
olivepress.thework@gmail.com

Distributed by Epigraph Books
22 East Market Street, Suite 304
Rhinebeck, NY 12572
(845) 876-4861
epigraphps.com

Cover design by Simi Nallaseth
Author photo by Jennifer May
Reservoir photo by Sarah Plant

Dedicated to my parents

Miriam Blecher Sklar (1912-1979)

George Sklar (1908-1988)

CONTENTS

Introduction

I grew up among writers. My father was a playwright and novelist. My godmother Vera Caspary and most of my parents' friends were writers. My older sister Judy is a journalist, book editor, and author of non-fiction books. My older brother Daniel is a playwright, author, and creator of Playmaking, his innovative method of teaching playwriting.

It's hardly a surprise that I, too, caught the writing bug. Starting in junior high, I followed my sister's path into journalism, editing the school newspaper. After college, Woodward and Bernstein's Watergate reporting inspired me. I got a master's degree from Columbia Graduate School of Journalism and began my career first as an all-night proofreader at *Time* magazine, then as a freelance reporter, later as a magazine and book editor and journalism teacher. Eventually, via a fluke revealed in the essay *Bill and Ellen vs. the CIA*, I shifted into writing screenplays and advising at screenwriting workshops.

I never set out to write a memoir. But over the years I wrote a number of personal essays about people, places, and experiences that had a profound effect on me. Some of the pieces were long, some short. Some published, some not. In the last couple of years, I realized that these essays, when put together like a jigsaw puzzle, added up to an informal collective memoir.

The pieces were written at different times. The urgency of the *contra* war in 1984 demanded that I write *Report from Nicaragua's Coffee Fields* in the heat of the moment. But it took 15 years before I could face the painful emotions described in *Nyoko*. And I couldn't begin to understand the impact of what had happened to me on Daufuskie Island in 1969 until five decades later when I finally put words on paper.

Reconstructing the past, I relied whenever possible on my primary source, the diary I kept for years. In it, I had recorded, for example, some of the rich Gullah language quoted in *A Winter on Daufuskie Island*. But most of the dialogue in these pages is not literal. Instead it conveys the essence of what people said.

I have also relied on my memories of people and events. Where I had no direct experience, or memory had faded, I filled the gaps and assured accuracy by consulting books, magazine and newspaper articles, and the internet. Most important, I recorded in-depth interviews with the extraordinary people portrayed here. Their recollections, and those of their families and friends, were invaluable. If there are any factual errors in these pages, however, I alone am responsible.

Each of the essays in this collection is, in its own way, a love letter. Most of the events I've written about took place long ago. Many of the places have changed beyond recognition. Some of the people have died. But in my memory, and now in the pages of this loving tribute, they all live on, defying time.

THE WORK

Well, while I'm here I'll
              do the work—
and what's the Work?
                    To ease the pain of living.
Everything else, drunken
                    dumbshow.

—*Allen Ginsberg*, Memory Gardens

Miriam Blecher Sklar, my mother as a young
modern dancer in New York, early 1930s

George Sklar, my father, circa 1960

CHILD OF THE BLACKLIST

The Hollywood blacklist began in 1947. Fifty years later, as the film community took a soul-searching look back at the blacklist era, I wrote an essay describing what it was like for me, the son of a black-listed writer, to grow up in Hollywood amid fear and hysteria during that terrible time. The essay was published in *Scenario: The Magazine of Screenwriting Art* in Winter 1997, Vol. 3, No. 4.

AUGUST 1957. I'M NINE YEARS OLD, sprawled on the living room floor, reading the sports section of the *L.A. Mirror News.* It's late afternoon, four days into a heat wave, temperature pushing 100, smog not stirring, but as usual all the windows are locked, curtains drawn. My father, a short man in his late 40s, with hairy arms and wire-rimmed spectacles, emerges from his study, writing finished for the day. He lies down in his customary place on the couch and begins reading *The New York Times.*

A car engine stops in front. Then footsteps on the porch. I get up to answer the door, but my father waves me away. He peers through a crack in a side window curtain, then takes off his shoes.

"Don't answer," he whispers emphatically. "Do you understand? Stay here, don't make any noise. When they're gone, come get me."

I nod and watch my father tiptoe toward the back porch. With a sink-ing sensation in my stomach, I kneel on the floor. The doorbell buzzes long and hard—once, twice, three times. Crawling over to the side win-dow, I peek out. Two strangers, tall men in suits and ties and brown hats, briefcases at their sides.

I sit perfectly still on the floor, wondering if they can hear my breath-ing. The air feels thick in my throat. I swallow hard to keep from coughing.

Finally the buzzing stops, footsteps go down the stairs, an engine starts. I look again through the crack and see two hats sticking up in the front seat of a dark blue car as it disappears around a corner.

I run to the backyard and find my father hiding behind the playhouse. "They're gone." I put my hand in his. We're both trembling.

All these years later, the fear lingers. I still don't know who those men were. I assume, as my father did at the time, that they were FBI agents—minor characters in an ongoing nightmare that had begun in 1947 when the House Un-American Activities Committee launched an investigation into alleged Communist subversion in Hollywood. Led by Chairman J. Parnell Thomas and a publicity-seeking freshman representative named Richard Nixon, the Committee visited Hollywood in May 1947 and then subpoenaed 19 witnesses to testify at public hearings in Washington in October, just a month or so before I was conceived. If my parents had known what would happen over the next couple of decades, I surely would not be walking the planet today.

The Hollywood blacklist began when ten of the 19 refused to cooperate with the Committee. They were asked about their own political beliefs and associations: Are you a member of the Screenwriters Guild? Are you or have you ever been a member of the Communist Party? The privacy of such perfectly legal associations is, of course, protected by the First Amendment, and the Hollywood Ten stood their ground. They knew the rules of this game were that if you answered such questions about yourself, you would then be obliged to answer questions about others—to name names of fellow members of the Guild or of the Communist Party. The ten chose not to. Cited for contempt of Congress, they each were sentenced to a year in federal penitentiary.

Unfortunately, there were many others in Hollywood who were willing to discard the First Amendment and name names before the Committee. Although the producers' association briefly made a fuss about censorship and government intrusion, they quickly succumbed to pressure from the Committee and its fervent anti-Communist supporters in such organizations as the American Legion and the Veterans of Foreign Wars. The Committee, spurred on by the headlines, held more hearings. *Red Channels* published an ever-growing list of people accused of being Communists. Those named never got jobs in the movies again—unless they "cleared" themselves by appearing before HUAC and naming others.

The blacklist lasted from 1947 till 1960, when one of the Hollywood Ten, Dalton Trumbo, finally received onscreen credits for writing *Exodus* and *Spartacus*. Others followed, and several of them made it back to the top of their profession—Waldo Salt with *Midnight Cowboy*, Frank Tarloff with *Father Goose*, Ring Lardner, Jr. with *M*A*S*H*, all Oscar winners.

But those storybook endings were not typical. For most of the several hundred named writers, actors, directors and others in the industry, the blacklist endured late into the 1960s or never ended at all. They survived any way they could. Some wrote under pseudonyms at cut rates. Michael Wilson, for example, co-wrote *The Bridge on the River Kwai* and *Lawrence of Arabia* this way. Some got people to "front" for them, as Walter Bernstein shows in his film of that name. Some took their savings and moved to Mexico or Europe, seeking work and hoping to wait it out. Some, while writing on the side, took other jobs. Robert Lees, who co-wrote many of the Abbott and Costello comedies, became a maitre d' for awhile.

My father, George Sklar, blacklisted after being named three times before the Committee, weighed all these options. He had been a playwright in New York and had already published a bestselling novel that a film studio had bought. So he decided to write another novel on spec. During the blacklist years he published three moderately successful novels, but of course none could be sold to the movies. Money was a problem. My mother, Miriam Blecher Sklar, a former Martha Graham dancer and a founder of the New Dance Group in New York, went back to teaching modern dance part-time. We lived frugally in a small Spanish-style house in the Fairfax area of Los Angeles. In the 1940s, my parents had frequently dined at Musso and Frank's, where other writers gathered, but I don't recall them ever going out to any restaurant all through the 1950s. Partly this was because eating out cost too much, but it was also because they didn't want to run into an informer. My father always said if he saw a rat, he'd vomit because they made him sick. In retrospect, I'm sure he was afraid of the confrontation.

The blacklist evoked lots of feelings in my family—moral indignation, outrage at the injustice, contempt for the Committee and the informers. But the thing I remember most vividly was the fear that pervaded our lives. When I watched my father slip out the back door that August day in 1957, I was terrified. A boy of nine wants his father to face the enemy like the heroes in the movies. Instead, my father was crumbling before my eyes. He had withdrawn into our house, hiding behind locked doors, closed windows, drawn curtains. When I was younger, he walked all over the neighborhood. As the blacklist dragged on, he stopped taking those long walks. When he did go out and ran into an informer, he crossed to the other side of the street. Even at the theater, the one indulgence the family never gave up, he stayed in his seat at intermission rather than risk running into a rat. As the years passed, he seemed more and more preoccupied. He worked in his study or read on the couch. His bad back got worse, he developed a stomach ulcer, and he was taking sleeping pills for insomnia.

There was so much fear in the air that I didn't know what to do with it. When I was in junior high, I was terrified that a boy who lived around the block would somehow do something awful to me if he ever got his hands on me. Ray was bigger and stronger than I, and we may have had a minor run-in once. But I built up this conflict in my mind to the point where every time I glimpsed him in the neighborhood or school, I ran away. Ray thought it was a wonderful game, though I'm sure he had no idea why I was scared of him. I didn't know myself. I'd invented a demon I could see in order to vent the fear of the unseen that was all around me. I never spoke to my parents about Ray. They had problems enough of their own.

Not everyone reacted to the blacklist this way. If you read Dalton Trumbo's letters in his book *Additional Dialogue*, it's clear that his instinct was to fight back. He actually seemed to relish the combat. Normally, that would have been my mother's response, too. She was a tough street fighter from the Lower East Side of New York. But when my father withdrew, the burden of surviving the blacklist fell to her—making money, shopping, cooking, driving, raising kids—and she didn't have the strength to fight back by herself. When she saw *High Noon* for the first time, it was during the bleakest days of the blacklist. She identified with the Gary Cooper character, a sheriff trying to do the right thing, abandoned by all who at first encouraged him. When he stood alone to face the consequences, my mother was devastated. Suddenly she realized how isolated she was, how she had been stigmatized by the blacklist, abandoned by America. She felt Gary Cooper's aloneness, and she wept uncontrollably. Her faith in people had been shattered. Where were they? Scared off.

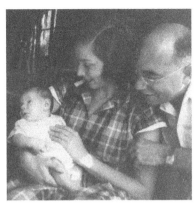

Sister Judy and brother Daniel with baby Zach, 1949

Baby Zach with parents Miriam and George just months after the blacklist began, 1948

The family in front of our house in Los Angeles, 1953

Of course people were afraid for a good reason. It would be easy to dismiss my father as agoraphobic and others as paranoid, cowardly or weak. But the fact is the country was in the grip of Cold War anti-Communist hysteria. Alger Hiss, longtime State Department official and first secretary-general of the United Nations, was sent to prison by Richard Nixon and a self-confessed liar (under oath) named Whittaker Chambers. The Rosenbergs were electrocuted, leaving two young sons. And FBI Director J. Edgar Hoover had a plan to round up all suspected reds and put them in concentration camps. (The Nixon administration's Huston plan for domestic espionage against radicals in the 1970s and Oliver North's plan to detain activists during civil unrest in the 1980s echoed Hoover's.)

Recently, using the Freedom of Information Act, I requested the FBI files on my parents. After a long wait, a packet with hundreds of pages arrived in the mail. To this day, the FBI is withholding more files on my father on grounds of national security, even though my father has been dead for nearly a decade. But from the few files that weren't blacked out, it's clear the FBI was watching our house, taking down license plate numbers of visitors, including guests at my birthday parties.

For me, perhaps the most frightening aspect of the blacklist was the way people suddenly disappeared from our lives. My father's best friend, Albert Maltz, with whom he'd collaborated on two plays, was taken away to federal prison, where he spent a year as one of the Hollywood Ten. After that, he moved to Mexico. My godmother, Vera Caspary, with whom my father had collaborated on the stage version of *Laura,* fled to Europe to avoid subpoena. These people were my extended family, and fortunately they returned years later.

But the informers, some of whom were also like aunts and uncles to me, never did. Several of my parents' closest friends, including a man who wanted my brother to say *kaddish* for him when he died, became informers. They were immediately banished from our home forever. My parents simply couldn't accept the idea that anyone could rat on his wife, his brother, or his friend to save his career. They never spoke to the rats again and never forgave them.

It wasn't easy for a child to understand these sudden disappearances. I was left with an abiding wariness about getting too close to people. My parents retreated into a circle-the-wagons mentality—a family under siege drawn in on itself. This had some positive aspects. Each summer we left L.A. (in part, to avoid subpoenas) and spent precious time together alone as a family at the beach. To this day, my sister Judy, my brother Daniel and I are as close as siblings can be. The community of blacklistees and their families also became a marvelous mutual support network. I've never been showered with such unearned love since. But it became increasingly difficult to trust anyone outside of this extended surrogate family. It was us vs. the rest of the world. Later, as I started to go out with women, I realized how deep my distrust ran. For years it prevented me from making any real or lasting connection.

If fear and distrust were primary legacies of the blacklist, secrecy was not far behind. When Albert Maltz went to prison, my parents didn't tell us kids. My father reasoned that if we knew, we might assume that he would be taken away next. When they finally told my sister and brother about the blacklist (I was still too little), my brother asked if they were Communists. They wouldn't say. That way, if anybody asked us, we could truthfully answer that we didn't know. In fact, my parents never did tell us directly that they had been Communists. I found out after my father died in 1988. (My mother had died in 1979.) I was clearing out books from the house when, from a musty old page, my father's Communist Party card dropped to the floor. So did my jaw as I gasped.

We kids led a double life. At school we were A students, jocks, editors of the paper, officers. But our parents told us not to discuss politics outside the house, not to talk to strangers, not to reveal anything on the phone. Still, each of us managed to find friends whose parents were also blacklisted, and we shared our secrets with them. My sister's small group even had a name—the Friendly Conspirators.

When we went off to college in the 1960s, our parents warned us not to get involved in the budding activist movements. HUAC came to San Francisco in 1960 and was met with demonstrations. My sister covered the story for her college paper and decided to write an investigative series on the Committee. My parents asked her to use a pseudonym. (She didn't. My mother later was ashamed of herself.) "Don't go to demonstrations," they urged me when I left for UC Santa Cruz in 1966. "Don't sign anything. Don't get your picture taken. We were hurt enough already. Let someone else do it."

This advice became a running joke among children of the blacklist as we marched in protests against the Vietnam War and pretended to shield our eyes from news (and FBI) cameras. The peace movement liberated me from my parents' residual blacklist fears. This was not a few hundred writers in the movie industry at the mercy of a reckless congressional committee. This was a vast movement of millions that I was part of. We had strength and broad support that the blacklistees, to America's shame, never enjoyed.

I became a political activist, rebelling not against my parents' political views but against their fear. Their silence made me all the more determined to speak out loud and clear. I organized, marched, and wrote for the college newspaper. Inspired by Woodward and Bernstein, I went to journalism school in New York, gravitated to leftish publishers, and became an editor at *The Nation* magazine and Sheridan Square Press.

Sheridan Square specialized in books by former CIA agents who'd turned against the Agency. It had a reputation as the CIA's public enemy number one. And that's why Jim Garrison, former District Attorney of New Orleans, sent his book on the Kennedy assassination to them. I was recruited to edit it, and I spent a year and a half working with Garrison to rewrite it. That book, *On the Trail of the Assassins*, was published in 1988. Because Garrison had been systematically smeared by the mainstream media, it received little attention.

However, the publishers, Ellen Ray and Bill Schaap, ran into Oliver Stone in an elevator at a film festival in Havana and handed him the book. He optioned it immediately, but because he was busy filming *Born on the Fourth of July*, he wanted someone who was familiar with the material to begin work on the screenplay. He hired me over the phone.

It had never occurred to me that I could be a screenwriter. Because of the blacklist and my father's experience, it seemed the last thing on Earth I would ever do. But by the late 1980s, times had changed. History had been kind to the blacklistees. They were no longer considered by most people to be villains. Quite the contrary, their tormentors were now disgraced––HUAC chairman J. Parnell Thomas convicted of corruption and sent to Danbury Federal Penitentiary, Richard Nixon forced to resign from the White House to avoid impeachment, Joe McCarthy synonymous with demagoguery.

And the victims were now heroes. Which was the way I had always thought of them. Despite my father's fears and weaknesses, I'd never seen him as either a coward or a victim. He may have had ulcers and a bad back, and he may have headed for the back door when the FBI arrived, but he kept his integrity. He never ratted on a friend, he never named a name, he never took a pseudonym, he never abandoned his home, he continued to write what he believed, and he was able to put enough money aside so that he and my mother could support our family through dire times. Most important, he was able to look at himself in the mirror every day and like what he saw.

My father didn't live to see *JFK,* but I think he would have been proud that it stirred so much controversy. And he would have been thrilled to know that Oliver Stone and I received nominations for both an Academy Award and a Writers Guild Award for best adapted screenplay. We didn't win, but the WGA awards dinner was one of the sweetest moments of my life. My family was there with me, and it was on this night that the Guild restored long-denied credits and Writers Guild awards to Albert Maltz for *Broken Arrow* and Dalton Trumbo for *Roman Holiday,* films they'd written during the blacklist. As their widows, Esther Maltz and Cleo Trumbo, accepted the posthumous awards on their husbands' behalf, the entire Beverly Hilton ballroom rose to its feet and gave them a thunderous ovation. My sister, my brother and I were all in tears. If you put that kind of homecoming in a movie, nobody would believe it.

Recently, the Guild has restored credit to many more blacklisted writers—most posthumously. And today, many of the children of blacklistees are not only accepted in the movie industry but are quite successful. For us, the blacklist is over.

Unfortunately, the story doesn't end there. Ever since the colonial era, America has always had periods of hysteria—witch hunts, massacres, lynchings, red scares, gay-bashing, internment camps—in which scapegoats were unjustly blamed for whatever was worrying people at the moment. People of color, gays, immigrants, women, communists, artists and intellectuals have all been—and continue to be—targets.

Could something like the blacklist happen again? Of course. The warning signs are everywhere. Bob Dole blasts Hollywood violence and immorality. The religious right, aided by Tipper Gore, tries to censor rap lyrics. Jesse Helms and his right-wing cohorts attack and gut the National Endowment for the Arts. First Oliver Stone, Ice-T, Karen Finley. Then, you and me.

The blacklist, ultimately, wasn't about a few hundred people losing their jobs in the movie industry. It was about democracy losing its voice, about freedom of speech becoming a moribund and empty phrase. Although today no congressional committee is dictating to Hollywood

World premiere of *JFK* in Los Angeles,
December 1991

Writers Guild Awards with niece Sonya Rasminsky and
longtime friend and fellow nominee Pat Conroy, 1992

whom it can hire and there is no Hays Office censoring films in the name of public morality, we face other dangers. The concentration of the entertainment industry into the hands of a few powerful media conglomerates threatens the diversity our democracy thrives on. The tyranny of the bottom line increasingly determines that movies appealing to the lowest common denominator will get made, and more offbeat, controversial films won't. So, writers and directors realize that if they want to work, they have to give the major distributors what they want. That is the plague that is upon us now. It's called self-censorship.

It is fifty years since the first HUAC hearings began the blacklist. Now a commemorative sculpture to the blacklistees is being created by Jenny Holzer on the USC campus. Its purpose is to remind future generations of the terrible things that happened in the past—and to encourage us to straighten out the mess we're in now.

If the blacklist has anything to teach us, it is that we must stick together and fight back—against the Doles and the Helmses and the religious right and the media conglomerates. We won't be able to do it alone, as Gary Cooper did in *High Noon*. But Dalton Trumbo, adapting Howard Fast's novel, suggested another way in the movie *Spartacus*. After a bloody battle, the Roman army captured the surviving rebel slaves and offered to spare them all if they would only turn over their leader, Spartacus. Sacrificing himself to save his men, Spartacus, played by Kirk Douglas, rose and said, "I'm Spartacus." All seemed lost. But then another man stood and said, "I'm Spartacus." And another, "I'm Spartacus." Until a whole field of Spartacuses were on their feet shouting back at the frustrated Roman commanders.

If we can learn that lesson of unity, the next time hysteria breaks out and another blacklist threatens, we will be ready.

We are all Spartacus.

Mrs. Viola Bryan. Photo by Edward Flaherty

A Winter on
Daufuskie Island

In 1969, as a 20-year-old college student, I lived for ten weeks on Daufuskie Island, one of the Sea Islands off the coast of South Carolina. Almost all of its approximately 100 residents were Gullah-speaking African-Americans whose extraordinary lives were revelations to a sheltered "California boy." Going to Daufuskie was such a moving and ineffable experience that it took me 52 years to write about it.

1.

WE WERE SOMEWHERE IN NEVADA, driving east on Highway 15. All you could see up ahead was flat, dry desert divided by a thin ribbon of asphalt. Not a car or a building or even a road sign. As the last rays of sun faded, the sky turned flaming orange, then pale yellow. The darkness of night descended like a black cloak decorated with pin points of twinkling starlight.

"So what the fuck is a field study, anyway?" asked Ed Flaherty, breaking the silence.

Ed was at the wheel, enjoying the speed and freedom of the open highway. Irish-American on both sides, 19 years old, he had dirty blond hair, wide muttonchops, and the powerful forearms of a high school wrestling champion from San Clemente, California.

Before this day in January 1969, I had never met Ed. But as part of the University of California Santa Cruz's new Extra-Mural Project,

I would be spending the next ten weeks with him on Daufuskie Island, South Carolina, the destination of our road trip. From mutual friends I'd heard he was smart and fun, but wild and unpredictable.

"I don't know," I said from my shotgun seat. "I just got into this at the last minute when someone dropped out. Didn't Professor Blake give you instructions?"

"Told me to shave my mustache." I could see a pale outline over Ed's mouth where his big handlebar had been. "Said we were supposed to 'serve the community'—whatever that means—and we'd learn a lot. What about you, Carol?"

In the back seat, Carol Dutton, 21, owner of the Datsun, stroked her bored, yappy chihuahua, Phoebe. Tall, blond, and reserved, Carol came from a modest family in Redding in the Sierra mountains. For the last several months Carol and Phoebe had lived in the communal house I shared with six students on Mission Street in Santa Cruz, but I can't say I knew her well.

"I'm supposed to do whatever Dr. Gatch wants," answered Carol. "And wear skirts and dresses and watch my language."

Carol, along with three other women from UCSC, would be working on the mainland near Daufuskie at a health clinic run by Dr. Donald Gatch—the man who'd almost singlehandedly brought hunger among the Black population of the South to public attention. He had recently been compared to Albert Schweitzer on the front page of the *New York Times* and in a long profile entitled "Let Us Now Praise Dr. Gatch" in *Esquire* magazine.

"For 15 credits, with no classes, I'd wear skirts and watch my language, too," said Ed. His blue eyes, framed by golden granny glasses, crinkled with delight. "Hey, either of you ever been down South?"

Carol and I both shook our heads. "You?" Carol asked.

"Shit, I been everywhere, man. Germany, Japan, Tallahassee, Florida, you name it, I been there. Air Force brat."

We'd started out that morning in Santa Cruz and made only one stop at Camp Roberts, a remote Army base in California. There Ed had disappeared into the PX while Carol and I filled up the Datsun's gas tank at the taxpayer-subsidized price of 26 cents per gallon. When Ed returned, he was carrying big bags brimming with junk food for the road.

"Perks of having a retired colonel for a dad," he said. "I can shop at any military base in the country—pay half the price you'd pay at a supermarket. Plus gas at cost, free health care, lifetime pension. Talk about socialism? Check out the U.S. military."

Ed switched on the radio. "We don't smoke marijuana in Muskogee," wailed Merle Haggard. "We don't take no trips on LSD; We don't burn no draft cards down on Main Street; We like livin' right, and bein' free... I'm proud to be an Okie from Muskogee..."

"You gotta be kidding," I said.

"Yeah, man," said Ed. "Welcome to America!"

Off in the distance, a faint glow appeared out of the darkness. As we approached Las Vegas, the glow grew bigger and brighter until, on the outskirts, it burst into spectacular color—a mosaic of flood lights beaming brilliant circles in the sky, blinking neon signs, casinos and garish hotels with exotic foreign themes, Olympic-size swimming pools, and fountains spraying precious desert water in every direction.

Ed drove slowly down the main strip, staring up at the neon extravaganza in awe, his eyes wide open, pupils dilated. "Whew," he said. "Can you believe this? Zappo!"

"What?" I said.

"Zappo, man, zappo, y'know, neon, plastic, garish, gaudy, outrageous..."

"You mean decadent?"

"Decadent, for sure. That's why we have to cruise up and down this strip and give an award to the most zappo place in Vegas."

"Are you stoned?" I asked.

"Well, I did eat a magic mushroom back at that last rest area."

I shook my head in disbelief.

"Y'know, Caesar's Palace isn't bad," said Ed, as we crawled past the ostentatious hotel. "The pink fountains, the Roman sculptures, so wildly out of harmony with the desert, the doormen and the parking guys in togas, that's a nice touch." Inching along, Ed pointed to the other side of the street. "On the other hand, the Sands has that sign—the lights blinking on and off like some giant sci-fi ray gun, the wave effect of the neon, the fuchsias and purples and reds, all total zap, not bad at all."

As we cruised up and down the main drag, Ed analyzed and compared the sights until finally Carol said, "Stop at that McDonald's on the right. Phoebe's starving."

Ed pulled in under the golden arch, and we sat in the car while Carol bought a couple of Big Macs. "Y'know, I gotta admit, I close my eyes and it's hard to picture any of that big hotel shit," Ed said. "The one that really sticks with me is this fucking golden arch—well, I guess it's really yellow, but it's classic, simple, unforgettably plastic. But somehow it feels welcoming, and the ever-changing 'Millions Sold' sign, that's the icing on the cake. Yeah, even against this stiff Vegas competition, I gotta give the zappo award to McDonald's."

"Well, Phoebe would agree with you," said Carol. The dog was chowing down on a Big Mac like this was her last meal.

We were all tired. Carol suggested we look for a cheap motel to get some sleep.

"I've got a plan for that," said Ed, pulling into the parking lot of The Little Chapel of the Bells. It was a small one-story building with vinyl siding, decorated with plastic vines and dust-covered fake roses.

Ed took Carol by the arm and motioned me to follow. "Let me do the talking."

We entered the empty chapel, a long, narrow room with a small altar at the back. Sally, the middle-aged, bleached-blond wedding officiant, greeted us. Her breath smelled of cheap whiskey. Ed introduced us and then made his pitch.

"You see, the little lady here and I are dying to get married." He gazed adoringly at Carol, who squirmed and looked uncomfortable. "And we brought our best friend as a witness. But the problem is, we don't have enough money to pay you for the wedding and then pay for a motel room too." He paused, batting his blue eyes, flashing the full, dimpled smile. He seemed to be able to come up with as many spontaneous lies as needed and then present himself as a picture of innocence. "So we're wondering if maybe you could put us up for the night, then you could marry us in the morning and we'd pay you then."

Sally was drunk, but she'd heard a thousand stories like this. She showed us the door. Undaunted, Ed had another plan. He dragged us into Circus Circus, the most conspicuously Mafioso casino on the strip. Claiming to have read a book with a surefire system for playing craps, he assured us we couldn't lose.

When we left the windowless casino, it was three in the morning. We'd blown our small budget for a motel room, and we'd had enough of Vegas anyway. Back in the car, Phoebe was curled up in a ball, asleep. Carol joined her in the back seat and closed her eyes. Ed volunteered to drive. He seemed to have boundless energy and no need for sleep.

I glared at him. "Ed, no more drugs on this trip, okay?"

"What? And miss all the fun?" he laughed.

"You can't drive when you're stoned out of your mind."

Ed floored it and laid a patch, the engine roaring as we pulled back onto the highway heading east. "Sure I can," he shouted. "I'm a California boy!"

Exhausted, my aching back cramped in the small seat, I looked out at the dotted white line stretching endlessly before us into the darkness. The tires of the '65 Datsun hummed on the pavement. How had I ended up here, driving through the middle of nowhere at 3:30 a.m. with a reckless madman, a reticent young woman from the boonies, and a high-strung chihuahua?

2.

I had no idea back then that I was at the beginning of a journey that would change my life forever. I was 20, a junior at the University of California at Santa Cruz, a fledgling progressive experiment in higher education that Republican State Superintendent of Public Instruction Max Rafferty called "a cross between a hippie pad and a brothel." The previous year, 1968, had been tumultuous for the world and for me personally. I was in a sophomore slump. The cockiness I'd flaunted as an award-winning high school newspaper editor and a freshman columnist for the college paper had vanished. I stopped writing because I didn't know what to write.

I was questioning everything about my life, in particular my views about politics, which I'd inherited from my parents. They'd been Communists during the Depression of the 1930s, but had left the party in the late 1940s. A few years later, as McCarthyism poisoned the land, my father, a writer, was named several times as a Communist before the House Un-American Activities Committee. As a result, he was black-listed and could no longer find work in the movie industry. Though in theory my parents maintained their allegiance to Marxist ideas, social justice, civil rights, labor unions, and world peace, McCarthyism had left them fearful. Not once in my entire childhood did they attend a demonstration or help any of the causes they still believed in.

I'd always been a political news junkie. With a combination of fascination, hope, and growing horror, I watched the unfolding turmoil of

1968, my emotions swinging wildly up and down from one day to the next. Elected as a peace candidate in 1964, President Lyndon Johnson had steadily escalated U.S. involvement in Vietnam, insisting there was "light at the end of the tunnel." From the beginning I'd joined the anti-war movement. This was a civil war in a country thousands of miles away that posed no threat to Americans. Millions of young white males, including me, had student deferments from the military draft, but 550,000 troops, a large portion of them poor and Black, weren't so lucky. They were now risking their own lives and killing others in Vietnam.

In spring of 1968, I'd taken "The Black Experience in America," a class taught by J. Herman Blake, a charismatic sociology professor in his early 30s. Blake was the only Black member of the UCSC faculty. Sporting a big Afro and a scraggly beard, he wore colorful dashikis and sunglasses even at night. Sometimes I'd see him punching a speed bag at the gym. His eloquent lectures delivered with the passion of a preacher inspired me, but I never had any real contact with the man.

Blake later co-authored the book *Revolutionary Suicide* with imprisoned Black Panther Party leader Huey Newton and, over the following decades, built an impressive academic career. He was the founding provost of Oakes College at UCSC, dedicated to racial, ethnic and cultural diversity, and then served as president of Tougaloo College in Mississippi and vice-chancellor of Indiana University. In his 70s, he returned to his South Carolina roots to become executive director of the Gullah Geechee Cultural Heritage Commission.

Blake's eye-opening class introduced me to a whole new world— James Baldwin's *The Fire Next Time*, Martin Luther King, Rosa Parks, Black Power, Stokely Carmichael, W.E.B. Dubois, Malcolm X's monumental autobiography, Angela Davis and George Jackson. We listened to recordings of Nina Simone's "I Wish I Knew How It Would Feel to Be Free" and Otis Redding's "Ole Man Trouble, leave me alone…" And the class culminated with a performance by the 50-strong Edwin Hawkins Singers who came down from Oakland and lifted their voices in a joyous gospel rendition of "Oh Happy Day," bringing all of us in the Cowell College dining hall to our feet, stomping and clapping and cheering. I couldn't get enough.

But shortly after that, on April 4, 1968, while I was reading Jonathan Kozol's *Death at an Early Age* in the Cowell library, a voice pierced the silence, shouting, "King's been shot!" Stunned, I flashed on the terrifying moment when the news of JFK's assassination had come over the loud speaker during my 10th-grade English class. Now, five years later, Martin Luther King, the foremost advocate of non-violent revolution in America, had been murdered in broad daylight on the balcony of the Lorraine Motel in Memphis. I watched on TV, feeling helpless, as uprisings broke out in scores of Black communities across the United States. Amid burning buildings, tanks rolled into Black residential neighborhoods, and thousands of heavily armed local police and National Guard troops patrolled the streets. I was far away, safe in an ivory tower surrounded by redwood trees. But like millions of Americans, I was shaken to the core.

That spring, student strikes at Columbia University and in Paris spread like wildfire around the globe. In Prague, students and workers danced in liberated streets and crowned Allen Ginsberg "King of May." On our bedroom walls, my friends and I tacked up posters of the beat poet, in his crazy Uncle Sam hat, hoisted on the shoulders of the Czech crowd. Change was in the air, and I allowed myself to believe that a peaceful phoenix might arise from the ashes of so much violence.

A month later on the night of June 5, I was glued to the TV in Cowell's student lounge, watching the returns of California's Democratic presidential primary. Demoralized by the North Vietnamese army's Tet offensive, President Lyndon Johnson had announced earlier in March he would not run again. When NBC declared Bobby Kennedy the winner in California on that June night, I felt optimistic and excited. It was clear to me that Bobby would win the nomination over the pro-war Vice President Hubert Humphrey and go on to be the next President. As Bobby spoke with quiet passion, surrounded by cheering supporters in the Ambassador Hotel, I felt his charisma. He had youth, momentum, the backing of the massive anti-war movement, and the magical Kennedy name. How could he lose?

And then, the shots rang out. Pandemonium broke loose at the hotel, but in our student lounge there was only stunned silence. In a few tragic seconds, the hopes of peace-loving people everywhere were crushed. Bobby Kennedy joined a list of young leaders cut down by assassins' bullets in just a few years—John Kennedy, Martin Luther King, Malcolm X, Medgar Evers—the most important leaders of an entire generation wiped out by violence that no longer could be written off as random.

The U.S. had always been violent, but it felt to me then that the country was on the verge of civil war. Angry Americans were pitted against each other over the war and race and just about everything else—the presidential election, Black Power, women's liberation, counterculture, hair, free love. At a teach-in, one of UCSC's radical young professors issued a blunt message to the students: "If you're serious about ending the violence, the Vietnam War, and the war against the Panthers, then go to San Francisco, chain yourselves to the federal building and shut it down."

I'd already taken baby steps toward activism, joining a weekly silent peace vigil started by a Quaker in my dorm. I'd marched with thousands of anti-war protesters at the Century City Hotel in L.A., shouting "Hey, hey, LBJ, how many kids did you kill today?" I'd barely escaped as a phalanx of 1,300 cops in riot gear smashed into our line of protesters trapped on a bridge, beating and bloodying hundreds with their nightsticks. In my mind, I could hear my parents whispering their warnings: don't sign anything, don't get your picture taken, don't get arrested, don't get hurt, we suffered enough during the blacklist.

That summer I did not chain myself to the federal building. But I shaved off my beard and long hair and volunteered for a peace caravan of the American Friends Service Committee. While radical young activists from the Yippies and Students for a Democratic Society chanted "The whole world is watching" at the Democratic Party convention as they were assaulted and tear-gassed by Chicago police, I was speaking to community groups, church congregations, and coffee houses about why we needed to stop the Vietnam War.

At the end of summer, I'd returned to Santa Cruz to begin my junior year. Around that time, Soviet tanks rolled into Czechoslovakia, destroying the dreams inspired by Prague Spring. Wanting to escape the roller coaster of world events, I moved into a communal house with friends and tried to focus on my studies. But one night in October, horrifying images were broadcast from Mexico City, where government soldiers fired on peaceful, protesting students, killing hundreds. It seemed to me that the entire world had lapsed into chaos, and there was no place to hide.

A few weeks later my housemates and I sat in our living room watching the presidential election returns on TV. My heart sank as Richard Nixon, one of the most notorious red-baiters responsible for the blacklist, won by a thin margin. On this one dreadful night, all the progress made by the civil rights movement, the anti-war movement, the women's liberation movement had been halted and rolled back. To me and my friends, the election of Nixon represented nothing short of a return to the repressed, violent, racist 1950s.

I descended into depression. Although I enjoyed my housemates, I was shy with women and was the only one with no girlfriend. My loneliness and search for something meaningful in my life had left me nearly paralyzed.

As the fall semester ended, Doug Brown, a dorm mate from my freshman year, found me in the Cowell College courtyard, gazing out at Monterey Bay, wondering what to do next. Doug had been one of the first two students Herman Blake had selected to spend a semester on Daufuskie Island as part of Cowell's Extra-Mural Project. Blake's father was born and raised on Johns Island, one of Daufuskie's neighboring South Carolina Sea Islands, so Herman had a deep personal connection to the area's Gullah/Geechee culture. He had started the extra-mural program as an experiment. Students would live in low-income communities of color. With no pre-conceived agenda, they would serve the community however it wanted. Herman believed this program would give Cowell students an opportunity to understand at a deeper level the poor Black communities where they worked, and would allow community residents to get to know white people in ways they had not often been able to.

Doug had gone to Daufuskie earlier that spring. He returned energized and transformed and spent a night regaling me with stories of his adventures. Now he told me that Herman was looking for someone to go to Daufuskie next semester. If I was interested, he'd recommend me, but I had to act fast—the two students would leave for South Carolina shortly after New Year's Day.

Doug's offer intrigued me. But I was terrified. I'd be going to the Deep South, far from home, where I knew not a soul. I was only too aware that not just Blacks, but white civil rights workers had been murdered in the South and that the Ku Klux Klan hated Jews almost as much as Blacks.

If I called my parents, I could predict what they would say: let someone else go and take the risks. Throughout my childhood, fear had dominated their lives and mine. Did I want to be like them, believing in ideals I was too frightened to fight for? The truth was, I'd been yearning to escape from the maze of academic abstractions. I wanted to experience life, to see, hear, smell, touch, and taste this vast, deeply troubled country I'd only read about, to work with my hands on something concrete, to get to know real people in the real world. And in the wake of Dr. King's assassination, I wanted to do my part, even a tiny part, to end racial injustice.

The choice was clear: overcome my fear or sink into a deeper depression. I knew that if I chose not to go to Daufuskie, I wouldn't be able to look in the mirror. I didn't call my parents. The next day, awestruck and intimidated, I met with Herman Blake. I don't remember anything he said. But I left the meeting feeling honored to be chosen by this man I respected so much. I was going to Daufuskie Island.

3.

Here we were, Ed at the wheel, speeding through the night. Uneasy about what lay ahead, I nodded off into a restless sleep. At dawn, with the sun inching up over powdery pink clouds, I awakened and drank in the rugged landscape of the Arizona desert—the white sand and rocky bluffs, striated layers of history painted in pastel golds, yellows, and reds. The stark beauty somehow calmed me.

My thoughts drifted away from what I'd left behind—my Jewish Communist home in L.A., my housemates on Mission Street in Santa Cruz, and the intellectual hippie bubble of the university. I could feel rising inside me the excitement of discovering a country that was foreign to me. The United States of early 1969 still had vestiges of an older America, the folkloric patchwork-quilt America of distinct regions, ethnicities, accents, religious sects, and off-the-beaten-path subcultures. America before TV, superhighways, the internet, shopping malls, and corporate chains homogenized it.

Around mid-morning, we stopped for gas at Two Guns, Arizona, a self-styled ghost town consisting of one dilapidated wooden building. Population: 4. The grizzled character drinking beer at the cash register, the mayor, claimed it had been a boom town with 30,000 people living there in the old days.

"What happened to them all?" asked Ed.

"That was back in 1870. Reckon they're all dead by now," said the deadpan mayor.

His gas pump wasn't working, but he tried to sucker us into buying a membership in his non-existent Chamber of Commerce. Two Guns, we found out when we got gas a few miles up the road, was just a good, old-fashioned Wild West scam like snake oil, a "ghost town" that had moved three times in the last decade, every time the highway changed its route.

Driving across country with Ed Flaherty was an unpredictable adventure, like a late '60s version of Kerouac's *On the Road.* Ed was my Neal Cassady. While I distrusted anyone outside my family—my legacy from the blacklist—Ed was friendly, open, fun-loving, charming, tireless, curious, and above all, fearless. He had a silver tongue and the absolute confidence that he could talk his way into or out of any situation.

Sometimes, the encounters Ed got us into were just kooky and harmless. Other times, his antics were downright dangerous. When he pilfered a small Confederate flag from a country store in rural Georgia, he came running out to the Datsun, the shotgun-wielding clerk in hot pursuit. As we sped away with Phoebe barking non-stop, I yelled at Ed, "Are you out of your fucking mind?" He just laughed. Carol didn't speak to him for two days. I was furious. Ed had been willing to risk our lives for a piece of cloth. Did he have no limits?

Still, I had to admit that I loved being on the road with Ed. I loved the open spaces, the feeling that anything could happen at any time. I loved the unexpected encounters with strangers, like the serendipitous one we stumbled into at the Rainbow Truckstop a few miles west of Las Cruces, New Mexico.

It was an ordinary diner with a blinking neon sign and formica tabletops. We'd been driving for several hours, hoping in vain to outrun an ominous thunderstorm moving toward us from the northwest. It was the only shelter for miles around.

We went inside, Carol cradling a trembling Phoebe, and joined a friendly crowd, all races, all ages, from every corner of the country, men and women drinking coffee, eating hamburgers and fries, laughing and swapping tales of the road and the weather. It was warm and the collective mood was jolly in the face of the impending storm, and nobody seemed to care that we might be hippies or that we had a dog with us. It was the kind of place where no matter who you were, you were welcome to stay as long as you wanted, the middle-aged waitress called you honey, and she never let your coffee get cold. We ate donuts, and everyone watched the forked bolts of lightning and the thunderheads rolling in while Loretta

Lynn belted from the jukebox "Don't come home a-drinkin' with lovin' on your mind." Ed chatted with the truckers, and I realized that this was the America I'd hoped was out there somewhere. And at this moment there was no place I'd rather be.

Though we drove hundreds of miles through endless flat prairie, boredom was not in Ed's lexicon. Even in the middle of the night, speeding through long stretches of West Texas, he would fiddle with the radio till he found an obscure soul or zydeco station from New Orleans, or he would fill up the emptiness with stories. His father, an Air Force colonel, and his mother, head nurse at Johns Hopkins University hospital in Baltimore, had met at the end of World II when he was recovering from a wound and she took care of him. More than 20 years later, both had retired and their divorce was in the works. Ed's family provided lots of material, and he could spin a yarn. A story about a visit to his mother, living as an expat in San Miguel de Allende, Mexico, and drinking too much, became a Cecil B. DeMille extravaganza that was both hilarious and poignant with Ed acting out all the parts while he drove.

But he could listen too. As curious about Carol and me as he was about everything else, he peppered us with questions. He coaxed Carol into telling us that she'd ended her romance with her high school sweetheart when he found Jesus and she'd now moved on to a new Mexican boyfriend. One night Ed asked me why I seemed nervous. "I'm... a little worried about going to Daufuskie," I said. "Y'know, a Jewish hippie activist in the Deep South. Remember what happened to Chaney, Goodman, and Schwerner."

"Hey, they were dirty commies," Ed said. "You're not a commie, right?"

Ed was joking, but the question made me uncomfortable. This was a subject I had been raised to avoid. "Let's just say my family was very, very, very, very far left."

Ed laughed. "Never met a real live commie before. You don't tend to run into 'em on Air Force bases."

There was not a hint of judgment in his voice. I found his acceptance touching and somehow liberating.

On our sixth day on the road, we drove through the night and ended up at dawn on a Cherokee reservation in the Great Smoky Mountains of North Carolina. A pamphlet we picked up at a visitor center recounted the 1838 "forced removal" of Cherokees from their own land to Indian Territory in Oklahoma. I had never heard of this. It wasn't taught in my high school American history course. More than 4,000 Cherokees had died on the grueling 1,000-mile march known as the Trail of Tears.

I couldn't stop thinking about it as we left the reservation and Ed steered us on winding dirt roads into the fog-bound hollers where the poor mountain people lived. A couple of days before in Memphis, we'd paid our respects at the site where Martin Luther King was gunned down, and the thought of what had occurred there made me sick to my stomach. Now as I thought about the Trail of Tears, I felt the same nausea returning.

We stopped at a rundown gas station to get something to eat. A balding white guy behind the cash register was explaining, "We ain't got no nigger problem..." when a news flash on the radio interrupted him. "Sam Quick, you know Sam, was shot by an Indian, Sam was foolin' around with some squaw, but he's okay. Got the bloodhounds out, had to shoot the Indian..."

The words, spoken in a matter-of-fact tone, slapped me in the face. The America I'd romanticized at the Rainbow diner, I was rudely reminded, was also the cruel, brutal America of slavery, assassination, and the Trail of Tears.

4.

On a chilly Sunday shortly before dusk, we arrived at Dr. Gatch's modest brick home just outside the small town of Bluffton, South Carolina, about 20 miles north of Savannah. It was one of three houses in an isolated compound in the heart of the Low Country—an intricate filigree of wetlands, swamps, rivers, and islands covered with tall grasses and ancient oaks laced with Spanish moss. The air was crisp, and as the sun set over the marshland bordering the house, we looked out across reeds that stretched to the horizon.

That moment of tranquility ended when the three Cowell students Carol was supposed to join came rushing out to greet us. Terry, Tree, and Fredi had arrived a few days before and had already settled in at the shabby wooden house behind Gatch's.

"Come and meet him," gushed Tree. "You're not gonna believe how fucking cool he is!"

Gatch's house seemed more like a college student's pad than the home of a 38-year-old doctor with a wife and two young kids. Though messy, it was clean enough. The housekeeper/nanny Malvena, a tall, heavy-set Black woman in her 50s who arrived every morning at dawn and stayed till late at night, kept it livable as she cooked, cleaned, and took care of Gatch's sons Eric, 3, and Rex, 1. But the living room had almost no furniture, just a couple of overstuffed sofas, a rug, and a few worn chairs that you might find at Goodwill.

Out of nowhere, like a silent wraith, Gatch appeared and welcomed us. His voice was measured, almost inaudible. Short and slight, he wore a rumpled shirt and jeans that looked baggy on his skinny frame. His pasty face was gaunt, and his glasses failed to cover the dark circles under his eyes. Malvena came out from the kitchen and offered us grits and eggs fried in bacon fat, but Gatch said he didn't have much appetite and waved her off. Though hungry, the rest of us were too polite to speak up.

The Cowell women were all eager to know what their jobs would be, but this was not a work day, and Gatch made it clear that he would rather talk about anything other than his medical practice. He asked about our studies, books that mattered to us, and he seemed most interested in history, philosophy and, in particular, politics. He wanted to know everything about Herman Blake and his connection to the Black Panthers.

As the evening wore on, the four young women gathered around Gatch in a semi-circle, hanging on every word he uttered, reverent, almost worshipful, the way many young people at that time devoted themselves to gurus like the orange-clad, Rolls-Royce-collecting Bhagwan Shree Rajneesh or the Beatles' favorite Maharishi Mahesh Yogi.

In a corner of the living room, I spotted Gatch's wife Anita, a pretty, 23-year-old British aristocrat Gatch had wooed away from Canadian/British publisher Lord Beaverbrook, according to rumors the Cowell women had heard. Gatch had met her at a radical-chic fundraiser in Savannah when she was 19 and swept her off her feet. Three weeks later, they'd married and had been living together in Bluffton for four years. Tiny, thin, and fragile, Anita couldn't have weighed more than 95 pounds. Food was not a high priority for anyone in the Gatch household.

Chain-smoking, saying nothing, Anita just watched her husband as he held forth, surrounded by four fresh, eager young college women from California. I imagine she was seething with jealousy. But the truth was, if Gatch was attracted to any of us, he seemed to have some special connection with Ed. They shared a voracious appetite for experience that knew no bounds, and they both liked nothing better than talking about the meaning of life.

"My philosophy comes down to three simple things," explained Gatch. "Freedom—you choose to do what you are doing because you think it's better than doing something else. Curiosity—a basic fascination with the way things are, an excitement and enjoyment of the world in all its infinite variety. And Arms Around—touching, embracing, feeling, communicating with all the senses, putting the intellect in perspective."

As Ed posed questions to Gatch, I felt like I was back at Santa Cruz in sophomore year. I started to tune out. But then Gatch said, "I've written it all down." He gestured for us to follow and led us to the smallest house in the compound.

The place was a mess. Apparently this was his home office. It was off limits to Anita, the kids, and anyone like Malvena who might impose some order. There was a desk in the middle of one room, but it was buried in papers stacked up almost to the ceiling. Books, files, magazines, and newspaper clippings covered the floor. If you wanted to get anywhere, you had to tiptoe and forge a narrow path through the piles. Gatch wandered around, picking up a file or a book or a clipping here and there. Maybe he had some vague idea where things might be, but it seemed to me that the clutter was completely random.

His eclectic library was scattered on the floor. The variety fascinated me—*The Rise and Fall of the Third Reich, Mein Kampf,* Sartre's *Anti-Semite and Jew,* Nietzsche's *Thus Spoke Zarathustra,* Michael Harrington's *The Other America: Poverty in the United States,* Richard Wright's *Native Son,* James Baldwin's *Giovanni's Room,* William Burroughs's *Naked Lunch,* Nabokov's *Lolita,* Masters & Johnson's *Human Sexual Response, The Warren Commission Report,* Mark Lane's *Rush to Judgment.* I had read almost none of these books, but clearly they focused on themes that obsessed Gatch— violence, Nazism, poverty, drug addiction, assassination, racism, sex.

"Some of my journals," Gatch said, pointing to a stack of loose-leaf notebooks. "Take a look." I opened one and started reading the hand-written scrawl. No daily chronicle of events here. The writing sounded like biblical prophecy. "Mankind has reached its judgment day. The world's peoples will wreak on us the vengeance of all mankind." I opened another. "I saw Hitler and his perverted crew come close to dominating the earth because they utilized an almost forgotten truth—that man is near superman in his strength and beauty and power and that if he wants he can destroy the meek, the poor, the desolate of the earth. But the truth of the Bible rose up to destroy him, for the meek and the poor and the humble shall inherit the earth."

"Here's a novel I've been working on," Gatch said, handing me a half-hand-scribbled, half-typed manuscript. "It's called *L.S.D. White,* explains who assassinated Kennedy. Maybe you can edit it."

I must have read for an hour or two. There was no story I could discern, not a single character of note, and not a single clue to the enduring mystery of the JFK assassination. But the prose was brilliant, muscular, inventive. More like crazy acid stream-of-consciousness jottings than a novel, the manuscript had plenty of imaginative ideas, apocalyptic predictions, bizarre theories, some of which seemed memorable at the time, but none of which I can recall now.

It was nearly three in the morning when I crashed on a couch in the Cowell women's living room, ignoring the sickening rotten-egg smell of the nearby swamp and the suffocating kerosene heater. Gatch and Ed were still yacking, feeding on each other's manic energy. I doubt either of them slept more than a couple of hours that night.

The next morning at 7, Carol shook me awake. Gatch had assigned her to be his driver. With Carol at the wheel of the doctor's Oldsmobile, Ed and I piled into the backseat. Gatch was waiting in the passenger front seat. To my surprise, he looked like a different man from the night before—showered, hair combed, he wore a clean white shirt, narrow tie, cheap polyester suit, medical bag at his side. It was Monday, and he was ready to go to work.

Gatch's clinic was located in the center of Bluffton. If you blinked, you could have missed this sleepy hamlet. There was a church, a post office, Bluffton Mercantile, a small general store owned by the Goodmans— locals called it "the Jew store"—a wooden dock at the end of town fronting on the May River, and not much else.

The clinic, a low-slung brick building, was nearly self-sufficient. After he'd testified before both state and federal legislative committees that 90 percent of the Black kids he treated had intestinal parasites and suffered from hunger and malnutrition, the local medical establishment had issued self-righteous denials and revoked his privileges at the biggest hospital in the county. To diagnose and treat patients on his own, he had equipped his full-service clinic with donated EKG and X-ray machines, as much sophisticated lab equipment as he could afford, and a free mini-pharmacy for patients who couldn't pay for drugs.

When we arrived, Gatch ushered us in to a private lab in the back. It was clean, but it was crowded with medical books and journals, vials of blood, urine and stool specimens, and petri dishes. Gatch led us directly to a microscope and told us to look into it and tell him what we saw.

"I think I've found a way to detect cancer cells at a very early stage," said Gatch in a secretive, barely audible voice. "If you look closely, you'll see some dark spots, and this could be a major breakthrough…" He rambled on about his research as Ed and I took turns at the microscope. Neither of us could see anything that resembled what he was describing. It was becoming clear that the quietly grandiose Dr. Gatch was either a true genius or a delusional madman—maybe both.

"The week hasn't even started, and you're already running late," interrupted the clinic's nurse, Helen. A heavy-set white woman in her 30s, she was in charge of the clinic's staff of five who were already scurrying around at 8 a.m.

The waiting room was packed with patients, all Black. It was always packed from morning till night, Helen explained. Nobody ever made appointments. They'd just show up and wait till Gatch could see them. He was the only doctor in the area who would treat Black patients. If they couldn't pay, he'd accept barter—eggs, canned goods, fruit, even chickens—or just treat people and give them medications for free. And if they were too sick to make it to the clinic, Gatch would go to them, day or night. Operating this way, Gatch's practice would never break even, let alone bring in the kind of money most doctors expected. The clinic and the Gatch family barely survived on donations and help from Anita's trust fund.

I'd never met anyone like Dr. Gatch. Though naive about what was going on in his private life, I couldn't help but be impressed with what I saw at his clinic. As I listened to the patients talk in the waiting room, it was obvious that in their eyes this gentle, soft-spoken white man was the best doctor in the world. He'd had an excellent medical education, interned and done his residency at an esteemed hospital in Savannah. He was smart, professional, sensitive, and worked hard for 12 to 18 hours a day. For poor Black patients whose health had been neglected for decades by local medical institutions, Gatch's clinic was a refuge and a godsend. Unlike other white doctors, he listened. He cared. He treated his patients with empathy, kindness, and respect. And for that, they loved him.

5.

The boat to Daufuskie left from Savannah. Carol dropped us off there, and we had a couple of hours to kill before our departure. Downtown Savannah's historic district was as pretty as a postcard—cobblestone streets, elegant Victorian homes, ornamental ironwork, lovely courtyards, and parks with manicured beds of colorful flowers.

But what stands out in my memory of Savannah was our lunch at Morrison's Cafeteria. The food, a wide variety of home-style Southern dishes, was tasty. Little did we know, however, that Morrison's was a chain founded in Mobile, Alabama by a staunch segregationist. It refused to serve Black customers. Apparently everyone in Savannah knew this except Ed and me. We looked around, and it was conspicuous that only white people were seated at tables. Yet all the waiters and busboys were Black men dressed in white shirts and black bow ties. One of them, a courteous, dignified Black man in his 50s, came to our table and said to Ed, "Suh, would you like something to drink?" When he repeated this question to me, I began to squirm with discomfort. In my entire life, I had never before been called "Sir."

After lunch, we headed toward the dock. An elderly gray-haired Black man with a cane was hobbling toward us on the sidewalk. As he approached, he looked down, avoiding our eyes, and stepped into the street while we passed. He did this, I realize now, not out of respect for a couple of 20-year-old white boys from California, but out of hard-earned experience that if he didn't show deference and instead continued to walk on the same sidewalk with two young white men, that could cause trouble for him. On television I'd seen much more extreme examples of racism and its consequences—the hosing of civil rights demonstrators in Alabama, the unleashing of dogs on civil rights workers in Mississippi. But somehow this brief incident remains vividly etched in my memory more than half a century later.

The Office of Economic Opportunity (OEO), the federal agency that administered Lyndon Johnson's War on Poverty programs in the

1960s, funded the boat that ran four times a week from Daufuskie to Savannah and once a week to Bluffton. A small World War II-era Navy vessel operated by a crew of three men from the island, it had room to carry about 10 people, their groceries, and some heavier supplies. Unlike neighboring Hilton Head Island, Daufuskie had no bridge, and for most of the approximately 100 poor Black island residents the *Miss Frances Jones*, named for a teacher at Daufuskie's elementary school, was their only lifeline to the mainland.

The 40-year-old captain, Willis Simmons, welcomed Ed and me onboard with a big smile. His slightly older first mate, Thomas Stafford, who limped on a clubfoot, shook my hand vigorously and the younger, slender second mate, Joe Bryan, helped swing our luggage onto the boat's stern.

Inside the cabin an elderly white couple introduced themselves as Henry and Rhea Netherton. Originally from England, Henry spoke with a British accent and had the puffy reddish face of a drinker. He wore khaki pants and a hunting cap that covered his ears and balding head. Wiry and white-haired with a no-nonsense, impatient manner, Rhea grew up on a farm in Illinois, but had married Henry many years before and shared a life with him in Berkeley, California. Over the roar of the engine, they explained that after Henry had spent 47 years importing whiskey—"most of which he consumed," said Rhea—they were ready for an adventure. Retired and in their late 60s, they volunteered for VISTA (Volunteers in Service to America), the domestic Peace Corps. They were assigned for a one-year stint to Daufuskie Island. They liked it so much that four years later, they were still there—no doubt setting the record for longest-serving VISTA workers in one location.

We climbed up on deck so we could see the waterways and marshes on the half-hour trip to the island. Henry liked to talk and enjoyed local gossip. First mate Thomas Stafford, he said, always wore sunglasses because his common-law wife had poked out one of his eyes with an icepick during a drunken squabble. Second mate Joe Bryan had fathered five children with Emily Miller, but his grandmother considered Emily beneath him and forbade him to marry her. Just as he began his dish on Captain Willis, Henry interrupted himself to point out Daufuskie, straight ahead. From a distance, even in the chill of January, it appeared lush and green, jungle-like, with gnarly oak trees laced with dusty Spanish moss growing wild everywhere you looked.

Henry explained that Daufuskie is a small island, five miles long by two miles wide, bounded by the Atlantic Ocean on the southeast shore, Calibogue Sound on the northeast, and the Cooper River and inter-coastal waterways on the west. It's shaped like a sharp feather, which is what "daufuskie" means in Muscogee, the language of the Native Americans who inhabited the island for centuries before the arrival of Europeans and Africans.

As we docked at the public landing, a couple of men bundled up in worn winter jackets and baseball caps helped with our luggage. Henry introduced us to a striking woman in her 40s, Albertha (usually called Bertha) Robinson, Thomas Stafford's wife. Warm and friendly, she welcomed us with a rush of words I couldn't sort out. I was having trouble following Gullah dialect. Thomas started loading supplies onto a wooden cart that Bertha had brought, pulled by her cow, Bobby. The island had no paved roads, Henry told us. To get around, most people walked the dirt pathways or used ox carts like Bertha's. Aside from the school bus and an OEO truck, the only usable vehicles on the island were a few beat-up pickup trucks from the 1950s. Coolie Grant, a taciturn, bespectacled 60-year-old in blue overalls, owned one of them. We piled into the cargo bed in back, and he drove us to our new home at Mrs. Viola Bryan's.

The white wooden house stood on a small plot of land out of sight of any neighbors. It had electricity, but no phone—there were no phones on the island until 1972—and no indoor plumbing or running water. Outside in the yard were a hand pump connected to a deep-water well—which assured us of clean drinking water—a tank for heating oil, an outhouse with a toilet that you "flushed" with a bucket of powdered lime, and a coop that housed eight chickens. A ragged wire fence in disrepair ran along the perimeter of the property, keeping out raccoons and possums and preventing Mrs. Bryan's four yappy mutts—Bea, Hardhead, Brownie, and Hobo—from running off.

Mrs. Bryan greeted us with a big, gold-toothy grin and a hug. Lively and fun, she looked just as Doug had described her—62 years old, just short of 5 foot 2, wide and heavyset, straightened gray hair parted in the middle and braided into pigtails. She asked how the four previous Cowell students who'd stayed with her were, all of whom she thought of as her "California boys." And we peppered her with questions. I was worried about snakes and bugs, but she assured us that in winter neither was a problem. Like a chirping songbird, she spoke very fast in a wee, high voice and a Gullah dialect I could barely decipher. I felt like a fool asking her to repeat herself, but she didn't seem to mind.

Dressed in a flower-print dress and an apron, she hoisted herself up from her chair. "C'mon leg, you and me born same time," she said, limping as she showed us around the house's small rooms. Mrs. Bryan had worked in service for many years in Savannah and though she suffered from diabetes and other physical problems, she worked hard and kept her house spotless. The simply furnished dining room, living room, kitchen, and her bedroom were all on the ground floor. She pointed up a flight of narrow, rickety stairs to a low-ceilinged semi-attic and told us we'd be sleeping up there.

"You boys must be hungry bad," she said and brought out plates piled high with fried chicken, steaming vegetables, and fresh-baked biscuits. We were paying minimal rent, but Mrs. Bryan would be spending most of it keeping us well fed. Before we dug in, Mrs. Bryan led us in the prayer we would say before every meal. "We thanks the Lord for what we are about to receive, to nourish the body from time to time. For Christ's sake, amen."

As we were finishing the delicious lunch, the dogs started barking outside and a dark-skinned Black man appeared at the kitchen door.

"Lordy, lordy, Doonie here now," said Mrs. Bryan. Lawrence Wiley, called Doonie, was 40 years old, skinny, wearing work clothes that needed washing. "Doonie, you drunk as a skunk?"

"Had my medicine this morning," Doonie said. He had a speech impediment, stuttered, and slurred his words like an alcoholic, but he spoke slowly so I could understand him. "Dr. Gatch say have one drink every morning, my medicine. Make you feel good. Dr. Gatch a good doctor."

"Dr. Gatch, Dr. Gatch, y'know I was first one to call him for my husband," said Mrs. Bryan. "He gimme some diet pills, I use 'em three days, made me all jittery like bedbugs, so I threw 'em over the fence. Now I go to the doctor in Savannah."

"Dr. Gatch say you gonna die, you die," said Doonie.

"I got one foot in the grave and the other one ain't got no business out. But if Dr. Gatch ever told me I gonna die, I'd tell him 'You gonna die too.' In the end, everyone gonna die, whether they be high and mighty or the lowest of the low."

Doug had told us Doonie smoked Camel cigarettes. Ed pulled out a few and offered them. Doonie reached out. There were nubs on both hands where all his fingers, except for his thumbs, had been amputated. Still, he was able to cradle the cigarettes with dexterity. As he put them in his pocket, he asked Mrs. Bryan for a dollar.

"You come over here to meet these boys or ask me for money?" she said as she handed him a bill. "Don't tell me what you gonna spend this on now."

When Doonie left, Ed and I walked out with him. Ed was eager to know where Doonie got his "medicine." Doonie said he and a few other local men used to make moonshine themselves, but no more. "Revenuers come and took the pot," said Doonie. We later figured out they were agents of the Internal Revenue Service's Bureau of Alcohol, Tobacco, and Firearms.

As we walked, Ed pumped Doonie for information on how to make moonshine. Mrs. Bryan was not going to provide him with alcohol, Ed realized, and there was no store on the island where he could buy it, so he was fishing for another way to feed his addiction of choice. Doonie's explanation was complicated, and the process required equipment we didn't have. I tuned out, but Ed listened intently. He really wanted to make his own booze.

At a quiet, gated area, Doonie stopped and pointed. "White buryin' ground," he said. Ed and I opened the gate to the Mary Dunn Cemetery and entered. Worn tombstones of generations of white settlers and slave-owners dated back to 1790. The privately-run graveyard, neat and well-kept, had been reserved for white families for nearly 180 years. We didn't see any signs spelling it out, but no Blacks were allowed.

Doonie waited outside the gate. We asked him where Black people were buried. Several cemeteries, he said, including one at Bloody Point, where European settlers massacred local Yemassee Indians in 1715. Slaves were buried there during the plantation era, but many of the graves had long since washed away. Most Black people now were buried at Mary Field Cemetery, Doonie said. Ed asked if he'd show it to us. "Nah, I ain't goin' there, they gonna have to drag me feet first," said Doonie.

When we returned home at dusk, Mrs. Bryan was in the kitchen, talking to the wood stove as she stirred skillets and pots and pans. "C'mon, Prince, do your stuff." That night we followed a routine that we repeated every night for the next ten weeks. Mrs. Bryan served the meal and said grace. While we ate, Ed entertained us with stories and jokes. After dinner, I cleared the table, put away the leftovers, and washed the dishes, heating water and pouring it into buckets and wash basins. Ed went outside to feed the dogs, secure the chicken coop, and close the shutters. Weary from the work of the day, Mrs. Bryan dragged her gimpy leg into the living room and plopped down on the couch in front of the black-and-white television. Ed brought her "eyeball juice" for her glaucoma and sprinkled a couple of drops into her eyes. Then he and I sat in over-stuffed chairs while we talked, laughed, and watched whatever was on the two Savannah channels the TV's rabbit-ear antenna could pick up.

That night Mrs. Bryan told us Doonie's story. Years ago, as a smart young man with an itch to make a life away from Daufuskie, he'd taken a bus to New York City, where he lived for six years. But it was hard to find work. He'd started drinking, and one bitter-cold winter night he passed out on a Manhattan street blanketed in snow. Without gloves, his hands became frostbitten. When he was discovered and taken to the hospital, all his fingers, except his thumbs, had to be amputated. With no other options, he returned to Daufuskie. Living on his own in a tiny shack with no wife or kids, he survived on a small disability check from the government and the odd jobs he could do for Mrs. Bryan and a few others. He was a kind, warm-hearted young man from a good family, she said, but alcohol had ruined any chance he might have had to fulfill his dreams.

6.

The ceiling in the semi-attic where we slept sloped down at a sharp angle, so I had to hunch over every time I stood up. Ed and I had twin beds, each warmed by several patchwork quilts that Mrs. Bryan had hand-stitched out of rags. That first night neither of us could sleep, and Ed started talking. He'd decided that moonshine was too hard to make, but he had a recipe for homemade hard cider that required only apple juice, yeast, sugar, and a gallon bottle air-locked by a balloon. Mrs. Bryan had several gallon jugs in her pantry and he could get the other ingredients the next time we went to Bluffton. This project bored me, and I had no idea he was serious, so I turned away and began writing a diary.

The next morning, the sweet scent of a crackling fire in the wood stove wakened us at dawn. "All right, boys, git on down here," yelled Mrs. Bryan. "All right. Ed. Zach. All right." Benny with the Penny's Gospel

Hour drifted up from the radio, music so rich and beautiful and warm that we didn't mind getting up in the morning chill to put on our clothes. In the cramped pink-and-green kitchen, Mrs. Bryan had already prepared a delicious breakfast of juice, fresh eggs from her chickens, sausages, toast with butter and her own strawberry jam, corn grits—the first time I'd ever tasted grits—and steaming hot tea.

It was a cold day, frost on the road, the ponds ice-caked, but we were eager to explore the island. The Nethertons had promised to take us around, so we headed for their place. Within a couple of minutes, Doonie joined us, a lit cigarette balanced in his hands. Off in the distance, we could see a young man running on the dusty road. He had a snake draped around his shoulders and was making loud, whooping cries. "That Willie," said Doonie. "Snake daid, don't pay him no mind. Boy fool as a coot, his bread is soak."

Doonie was our unofficial guide. When we heard loud gun shots nearby, I stopped in my tracks, alarmed. I'd never heard a gun fired before. But Doonie pointed out a few young boys waving at us from the woods, rifles in hand, and said they were just shooting at pine cones. They couldn't have been more than 11 or 12 years old. All the boys had guns, Doonie explained. They hunted, and that was their main recreation.

When we arrived at the Nethertons' trailer, Henry was filling out federal forms for Stella and Donkey Hamilton, an elderly couple who had brought him a live chicken to show their appreciation. Helping Daufuskie residents navigate government bureaucracies seemed to be mostly what Henry did as a VISTA volunteer. Rhea ran the VISTA school and library from a building on their property, but no one came in winter. She was packing boxes with used clothing for a couple of kids to take home. Henry gave us a map of the island and said if we got the OEO car the next day, they'd come with us and introduce us to Daufuskie's residents.

As we headed for the dock with Doonie, a few little kids followed us. One of the boys was riding a bike, and Ed ran beside him in a friendly race. A couple of girls were trailing me. I stopped, and this turned into a game of tag.

The fun ended when a rusting pickup truck passed us on the road and the driver, a grizzled older man named Plummey Simmons, leaned out and said someone had been shot. We followed him to the dock. Several people were gathered around an 11-year-old boy. "My nephew," said Doonie.

Ervin "Rickey" Simmons, son of Doonie's younger sister Janie and the boat captain Willis Simmons, was one of the boys we'd seen in the woods earlier. A friend's rifle had gone off accidentally and a bullet had hit him in the arm. Rickey seemed stoic as Lance Burn, a chunky, square-jawed 50-something white man with an impressive head of white hair and ruddy cheeks, cleaned up the wound and taped a splint on his arm.

This was the first time we'd seen Lance, who headed Daufuskie's OEO program and its emergency/disaster relief program. He was also the magistrate in charge of handling local disputes. The handful of white people on the island had been appointed to all the best-paying government positions. Lance's wife, Billie Burn, was the post mistress and school bus driver. Hinson White was the constable.

As Lance took charge and got his speed boat ready to rush Rickey to Bluffton, I looked over at the others comforting the gangly young boy. His mother Janie held him tight, reassuring him. His uncle, Doonie's youngest brother Franklin Wiley, helped Rickey into the boat. Franklin would accompany the injured boy to Dr. Gatch's office for treatment. I watched as Plummey Simmons, in his late 60s on a minimum-wage OEO job, reached over the boat railing and quietly, almost unnoticed, slipped some bills into Franklin's hands. A few days later, Rickey returned to the island with his arm in a sling. He recovered fully not long after.

7.

The next morning we walked to Lance Burn's house to borrow the OEO car, as the Nethertons had suggested. A surly, distrustful man, Lance did not welcome "the California college boys." He was content with the way things had always been on Daufuskie. He had a beautiful water-front house, a car, a boat, a short-wave radio to the mainland, and a decent income from his various jobs. He and his wife Billie enjoyed their quiet country way of life.

They'd married in 1935 and moved to Daufuskie. After Lance returned from World War II, where he'd served as an infantry sergeant at the Battle of the Bulge, they lived in Florida. In 1959, they returned to Daufuskie for good and raised their son Gene there. The boy attended school by himself, as the only white kid, rather than share a classroom with the Black kids on the island. Gene was a young man now, but we didn't meet him because he was away fighting in Vietnam.

"You boys can't drive this car by yourselves," grunted Lance. "OEO regulations state you must be accompanied by a federal worker at all times." In his most innocent Eddie Haskell voice, Ed explained that we had valid licenses, we would drive cautiously, and the Nethertons would be with us.

Lance tolerated the Nethertons. He considered them do-gooders, like all the VISTA volunteers, but they were white and old and posed no threat. Ed and I and all the California boys, on the other hand, represented something Lance feared most—change. He resented our rude intrusion into his comfortable, private fiefdom. His wife Billie, sociable and friendly, was more open to new people and ideas. She liked the previous California boys—one of them was planning to be a minister—and as a devout Christian woman, she genuinely cared, in her own way, about the Black people of the island.

Billie convinced Lance there was minimal risk in our driving the car from their house to the Nethertons' trailer unaccompanied, and Lance grudgingly handed over the keys. We picked up the Nethertons, who brought along a large bag of used clothing to distribute, and set out to meet the people of Daufuskie.

And what an astounding array of characters they were. Sarah Grant, 81, still sharp and spry, the island's midwife and undertaker since 1932—"I bring 'em into this world, and I bring 'em out,"—showed us the plain pine coffins she kept in a shed in her backyard. They cost $200 apiece, and one was for herself. As we were leaving, she took us out to a shed filled with jars of her home-made wine, and jam, pumpkin, and ochre preserves she'd put up herself. She gave us a jar of pears.

Next we paused outside the home of the well-liked, live-and-let-live constable, Hinson White, a tall, jolly white collector of 1936 jalopies who was born and raised on the island and spoke a pure sing-song Gullah. Nearby, three Black men were hacking weeds at the shoulder of the dirt road—Josephus Robinson, a short, gray-haired older man; James Williams, who didn't look happy to see us and had a distinct limp; and Doonie's handsome younger brother Franklin Wiley, whose skin was smooth as porcelain. Operation Mainstream, a rural beautification project funded by the federal OEO and overseen by Lance Burn, hired older men at minimum wage, but funds had been cut and two of their co-workers had recently been let go.

Sarah Grant, midwife and undertaker. Photo by
David Morrison

Josephus was married to Blossom Robinson, the powerful matriarch of the large Robinson family, who had a grating voice as loud as a foghorn. We visited her next. Blossom was outside, wielding a hoe, preparing her garden for planting while looking out for her many grandchildren playing in the yard. Next door, Blossom's daughter Bertha was drinking with her best friend, Doonie, who seemed to be everywhere we went.

Bertha, a warm, deeply thoughtful woman, launched into an unsolicited speech. "We're all one," she said. "Color of your skin don't matter. I cut your veins, your blood red. I cut my veins, my blood red. You eat eggs and bacon for breakfast, you get a full stomach. I eat eggs and bacon, I get a full stomach." Bertha knew nothing of Shakespeare, but I couldn't help thinking this was her Daufuskie version of Shylock's famous speech from *Merchant of Venice*–"hath not a Jew eyes…if you prick us, do we not bleed?"

The Cooper River neighborhood, where most of the drinking and partying took place, was located toward the northern end of the island. We stopped at a couple of adjoining houses to drop off clothes for the Washington and Smith kids. Flossie Washington, a beautiful woman with jet-black eyes and high chiseled cheekbones, had 11 children with her husband Jake, who was recovering from tuberculosis, taking 28 pills a day. The kids arrived home from school and were excited to meet the new California boys. The young ones, spotting a zany, fun-loving playmate, immediately latched on to Ed. One of the older girls, Margarite, 11, lingered by the door. Tall for her age, all skinny arms and spaghetti-thin long legs, she had the same high cheekbones as her mother. She gave me a big white-toothed shy smile, her eyes lively, innocent, and curious. And though we didn't say two words to each other, I knew then that of all the Daufuskie kids, she was the one who would eventually steal my heart.

Daniel "Fast Man" Mitchell, one of the recently laid-off Mainstream workers, was outside, drinking a beer with Jake. Fast Man got his name because he did everything—work, walk, talk—at a rapid clip. He listened constantly to the radio and loved imitating the weather forecasters. When we felt a couple of rain drops, he launched into his own weather report, which I had trouble following because he talked so fast and I was still getting used to hearing Gullah: "Partly cloudy skies today, sunny, non-sunny, partly wet, partly dry, 50 to 60 degrees temperature in the shade, 60 to 65 in the sun, non-sun, 35 percent chance afternoon showers, 50 percent evening showers, winds five to fifteen, north to northwest, south

Albertha Robinson. Photo by Edward Flaherty

by southeast, small craft warnings for small boats, big craft warnings for big boats, pause for station identification, thanks to the highest."

On our way back home, we met the island's master carpenter, 79-year-old Sam Holmes, a World War I veteran who had built many of the homes on Daufuskie, and Johnny Hamilton, a widower in his late 60s, who lived off the beaten path by himself. Johnny had no radio, no TV, no electricity, had never learned to read. He told us he sat at night with a kerosene lamp and a fire, trying to stay warm. "It's just me and the Lord," he said, "but I'd like to see someone else once in a while too."

It had been an exhilarating day. With good memories of the previous California boys, everyone we met was welcoming and friendly. Though obviously poor, at least on the surface Daufuskie's residents seemed happy, decently housed, and well fed—not what I had expected.

But then we made one last stop to drop off a blanket. The two-room shack—kitchen and bedroom—was in terrible condition. Outside, the boards were falling apart, exposing gaping holes in the roof and walls. Inside, an old woman, Agnes Graves, sat alone in her kitchen, her wrinkled skin sagging off her bones, her frail body toothpick-thin. It was dark—she had no electricity, not even a kerosene lamp—and it was freezing. She had a wood stove, but there was no fire in it. She had no wood, she said. Newspapers covered the walls, a failed attempt at insulation. Dirty pots and pans were piled in a corner, giving off a foul stench. Agnes's watery eyes looked up at us, pleading, her voice cracking. She was sick with cancer, she told us, coughing up phlegm. Her nephew had been living with her, but now he was gone and she had no one. She was hungry and weak. She sat there, crying once in a while, waiting for death to come.

While Henry stayed with Agnes, we drove to the Nethertons' trailer and Rhea brought back a couple of sweaters and a bag of food. Ed and I gathered wood in Agnes's yard and started a fire in her stove. And then we drove home in silence.

I was in shock, feeling sad and scared and helpless. I'd never seen anyone living like this. I kept thinking about testimony Dr. Gatch had given to a congressional committee. "I had a patient this morning," he said. "Sixty-two years old. She said, 'Please, doctor, I hope you haven't forgotten me.' She said she didn't sleep good at night, she had no wood for her stove, she didn't own any blankets. She was hungry, cold, friendless, Black, God forgive her. There's a lot of work to do. We aren't doing it. There aren't enough hands."

Johnny Hamilton on Office of Economic Opportunity's boat to Savannah.
Photo by David Morrison

I wondered if Agnes Graves was the patient he had described, and I wondered how many others there were like Agnes Graves in the United States of America in 1969.

8.

"A friend ain't a friend unless he there when you sick," said Mrs. Bryan that night. Agnes Graves was in that situation, she felt, because the Daufuskie community she'd once known was disappearing. People no longer just gave of themselves. They took what they could get and they hung on to it. With the older folks, it was different. Plummey Simmons, Sarah Grant, a few others—they had a sense of community. But somehow that never got communicated down to the young.

As we talked, a tiny, young white woman with a foot-high beehive of blond hair and a pure, sweet voice came on the television and started singing a sacred Christian song. A skinny middle-aged white man with gray hair coiffed in a duck tail joined her in a duet. He was wearing a white cowboy suit covered with sparkling rhinestone wagon wheels. Mrs. Bryan listened for a moment, then said, "That little girl can sing." That was our introduction to a little-known 22-year-old country singer called "Miss Dolly"—Dolly Parton—and the show's slightly smarmy but jovial host Porter Wagoner. The country music was actually good and the hokey banter wonderfully camp. Ed and I were smitten, and for the rest of our time on the island we watched Miss Dolly and Porter every week without fail.

The sacred song touched something in Mrs. Bryan. She was a religious woman, she said. Like Miss Dolly, she sang soprano, and for many years she had been the choir director of Daufuskie's church. Every Sunday she attended services, and three nights a week she prayed in the praise house with Sarah Grant, Plummey Simmons, and a few other elders. But since the pastor died a year ago, she explained, there were no longer church services or a choir on Daufuskie. The young people weren't interested, she said. If she wanted to go to church, she had to travel to Bluffton. Sarah Grant, who sang alto in the choir, made the trip every week, but it was too much for Mrs. Bryan. As she spoke, tears welled up in her eyes. Wiping them away quickly so perhaps we wouldn't notice, she turned her attention to Porter and Dolly cutting up on the TV.

Plummey Simmons on OEO tractor. Photo by David Morrison

Crossroads on Daufuskie. Photo by David Morrison

9.

Each day Ed and I walked the island's dusty roads. Often Doonie accompanied us. Wherever we went, people would be outside, making fires, cutting wood, fixing, cooking, washing, feeding animals, building, gardening, walking, hauling supplies. Daufuskie life, we started to understand, was very different from the relatively soft life that so many people in modern America enjoyed. Life here required hard physical labor just to eat, to transport necessities, to keep the house warm, to put clothes on your back. All the comforts and conveniences we took for granted—cars, indoor plumbing, showers, flush toilets, kitchen appliances, supermarkets, air conditioning, washing machines, dryers, phones—simply didn't exist here.

By the end of our first week, we'd met nearly all of the hundred or so residents and a few of the high school kids who came back from the mainland on weekends. Interesting as this was, we still had no idea what we'd be doing for the next 10 weeks. The first California boys taught typing to the older kids. The second pair did odd jobs and carpentry. But there was no ongoing program we could slip into.

Our informal community steering committee, which was supposed to decide what we'd be doing, had scheduled a meeting for the next day. To clear our heads, Ed and I took a walk on a seldom-used footpath to the beach on the Atlantic side of the island. The rough path was pocked with ruts and holes and surrounded by dense jungle-like foliage. We passed an abandoned shack with a rusting, vine-strangled pickup truck parked in front. On the dilapidated porch, a three-by-five-foot faded Confederate flag sagged. At the end, the pathway emerged into a breathtaking, pristine white-sand beach. Most of the island residents had not learned to swim. In summer, a few might trek to the beach for a picnic. But in winter, on a chilly day, not a single soul was anywhere in sight. It was peaceful and silent, except for the sound of waves lapping the shore.

"This place needs big changes," said Ed, "and we're just walking around making small talk."

To be of use, as the poet Marge Piercy had written. That was what both of us wanted. And we agreed that where we could be most of use was with the kids, the future of the island. I thought of Nate Goodman, the after-school coach at my elementary school. He'd been more important to me as a kid than any teacher. His example, his spirit, his way of teaching us about life through sports had changed my life. I suggested to Ed that perhaps we could set up an after-school program that would include tutoring and sports.

"I'm into it," said Ed. "And if it works, the next California boys can keep it going."

We decided we would present our plan to the steering committee.

When we got home, Mrs. Bryan was sitting outside shucking oysters that Lance Burn had harvested from the brackish estuaries surrounding Daufuskie. From the 1880s to the early 1960s the island's oyster industry had thrived and provided employment for most of the Black residents. Harvested, shucked, and canned in a factory on the island, Daufuskie oysters were considered a delicacy around the world. Legend had it that the only oysters one of the czars of Russia would eat were smoked Daufuskie oysters. But by the mid-1960s, the Union Camp paper and bag company had polluted the Savannah River, decimating most of Daufuskie's oyster beds. The local industry collapsed, and the island's main source of employment disappeared. Most of the young able-bodied men sought work on the mainland, leaving behind the current residents—women, children, and the elderly. All that remained of the oyster industry were piles of shucked shells and the crumbling factory building near the public dock.

For his own use, Lance still harvested some of the surviving oysters, and he always paid Mrs. Bryan to shuck them. With years of experience at the factory, Mrs. Bryan shucked the shells with amazing dexterity, like a magician doing sleight of hand. She greeted us, but Lance just glared.

"You boys didn't bring the car back the other night," Lance finally said, his voice dripping with controlled rage.

"We brought it first thing in the morning," said Ed. "It was late, and..."

"Rule is, you borrow it, you bring it back that same day, not the next day. I don't know how you boys are raised out there in California, but here a rule is a rule. And we respect rules." He was getting worked up, his face turning a deep red. "People start disrespecting rules, you get chaos, anarchy. End up like you folks out in California—prostitution, drugs, pornography, free love, hippies, draft dodgers and fairies running wild in the streets, destroying property, stealing and looting. Oh yeah, I see the whole stinkin' mess on the TV."

Through this rant Mrs. Bryan just kept shucking. I was speechless, and feared that Ed would get into it with him. But Ed knew the drill.

"Sorry, sir," he said. "We respect the rule, sir. From now on we'll be sure to return the car on time, sir." Ed was, after all, the son of an Air Force colonel.

10.

On Monday, January 20, 1969, Richard Nixon was inaugurated as President. Mrs. Bryan barely noticed. "He's just President," she said. "He ain't God." That same day, all over the South, offices and businesses closed in honor of Confederate General Robert E. Lee's birthday. On Daufuskie, life went on as usual. Our steering committee consisting of Mrs. Bryan, Sarah Grant, and Lance Burn gathered in Mrs. Bryan's living room. Joining us as "observers" were the Nethertons and a special guest, Mr. Earl Cherry, Southeast region director of OEO, who happened to be on the island.

Trying to appear as harmless as possible, Ed and I sat silently through most of the meeting, as did Mrs. Bryan and Sarah Grant. Earl Cherry, a wiry white man in his late 40s, dominated the conversation, touting all the programs he'd developed at OEO. Even Lance shut his mouth in the presence of his confident, take-charge OEO boss. Only Henry Netherton dared bring Cherry back to the purpose of the meeting—what to do with the California boys. Ed began to explain our proposal, but Lance cut him off. We had too many fancy ideas, he said, and we were moving too fast.

In the end, Cherry decided, and the others nodded in agreement, that the best use of our time would be to help Daufuskie's residents put up fences around their gardens with materials generously provided by Earl Cherry's OEO. As for after-school recreation, we'd have to get permission from Mrs. Julia Johnson, the school principal, and approval from the community club/PTA, which wouldn't be meeting for another two weeks.

Ed and I were frustrated. We had limited time on the island, we saw problems, and we were eager to help solve them. And here were these older white men—Lance, Cherry, and Netherton—all standing in our way, telling us what we could and could not do. That night Mrs. Bryan counseled us to calm down, watch Porter Wagoner and Miss Dolly on TV, do chores around the house, and wait. Her entire life she'd been told by white men and women what she could and could not do. She understood patience.

But this approach was new to us. Ed had been president of his high school, star football player and wrestler, a charismatic and popular leader of his peers everywhere he'd ever lived. Though I was less outgoing, I'd been editor of my high school newspaper, number one on the tennis team, most valuable player on the basketball team. We were both high achievers, used to getting things done, leading, persuading others to follow us, and being rewarded for it. It was clear to us that Cherry and Lance were throwing up roadblocks, robbing us of precious time. The impatience of youth—we had a nasty case.

The next day we walked over to the two-room schoolhouse to talk to Mrs. Julia Johnson. School had let out and the kids were gone. Tall and burly with straightened black hair, Mrs. Johnson was an imposing presence. She'd graduated from college on the mainland and boasted that she was "the best teacher ever on Daufuskie," though we later learned that opinion wasn't shared by too many others. In her late 30s, she'd been on the island only a couple of years, serving as principal and teacher of the upper grades.

We introduced ourselves and Ed turned on all his charm to ask for her blessing of an after-school program. Ingratiating, respectful, deferential, he even cracked a joke or two. But Mrs. Johnson, stern and serious, just stared at him, unblinking. Her cold eyes said it all: this was her turf, and she wasn't about to yield an inch of it to a couple of smart-ass white boys from California. I asked what equipment the school had for sports, and Mrs. Johnson opened a cobwebbed closet that stored a flat basketball, a lumpy volleyball, and a couple of baseball bats. That was it.

"These kids don't need sports," she said. "They need reading, writing, and arithmetic." Ed volunteered that we would be more than happy to tutor the kids too. Mrs. Johnson peered at him through her thick glasses. She didn't reject the idea outright, but because it would be an after-school program, she said, it wasn't up to her. Approval would have to come from the parents at the PTA meeting.

We spent the next morning doing house chores for Mrs. Bryan while she took the boat to Savannah to shop for groceries. Doonie came over to chop wood for Prince, the wood stove. With no fingers and a cigarette dangling from his lips, he somehow was able to handle the axe. While Doonie added to the woodpile, pausing occasionally to take a swig of his "medicine," Ed and I washed our clothes outdoors with water we heated over a fire and then poured into a metal basin. Scrubbing the clothes on a washboard was tedious but effective. The clothes smelled so fresh that we couldn't wear them without first washing up the only way available— taking a sitz bath. Ed sat in the basin first, sponging himself down with hot water and soap. After he finished, I poured fresh hot water into the basin and followed the same routine. It was the first time I felt clean since we left Santa Cruz.

It was always fun to hang out with Doonie, but he didn't have any kids. We needed to talk to parents who were in the PTA and could help us get the recreation program going. So Doonie took us over to see Bertha Robinson, who had two kids in school. She was outside feeding her cow, Bobby.

Ed described the recreation program to her and then asked directly, "Would that be okay with you?" She said, "Yes sir, that's right," and I realized instantly that we'd asked her to rubber-stamp plans that we'd made without any input from her or anyone else. This wasn't her idea or her program or her kids' program. It was ours. If she had questions about how her kids would be transported home after the recreation program was over, how many days a week or how many hours it would be, who would be in charge, who would be responsible if there was an accident, or why her kids needed this, she didn't ask them. Bertha was a very smart woman, and she understood what we were proposing. But one thing was obvious: she didn't trust us. Why should she? She simply nodded and replied, "Yes, that's right," to whatever Ed said.

It was an important lesson that Ed and I talked about as we walked home. A yes answer didn't mean a thing. It all depended on your question and how you approached people. The truth was, cocky as we were, with all that college book learning, we were young and inexperienced. We'd landed in a very different world from any we'd known before, and we didn't know what the hell we were doing. We decided to catch the next boat to Bluffton. Maybe Dr. Gatch could give us some advice.

Mrs. Bryan returned from Savannah in late afternoon. As we helped her put away the groceries, she told us that Lance wanted us down at the dock at 7:30 the next morning to load boxes of books onto the OEO boat. The Nethertons had tried to start a library on the island, but nobody ever used it. So the unread books were going back to the mainland.

"Perfect," said Ed. "We're going to Bluffton tomorrow anyway."

Mrs. Bryan shook her head. "Lancey say it's a oil and gas run. No passengers."

"Another Lance rule?" said Ed, irritated. "I'm going over to talk to him right now."

"Careful," warned Mrs. Bryan. "You boys already on Lancey's bad side, he callin' you Flannery and the Russian Jew."

"What?" I said. "How does he even know I'm a Russian Jew?"

Ed reminded me that the first day Netherton had asked what kind of name Sklar was and I'd told him. "Netherton must have told Lance. But Flannery? How dare he drag my fine Irish name through the mud!" said Ed in mock indignation. "Generations of Flahertys are rolling over in their graves!"

Ed walked over to Lance's by himself. "Chin music gonna be the death of that boy," Mrs. Bryan told me. Maybe, I thought, but Ed had the guts to confront Lance, which was more than I was doing. Was I afraid? My own passivity in this situation bothered me. Mrs. Bryan might be right about Ed. Still, I envied his willingness to stick out his neck and speak up. And I was learning just how effective Ed's silver tongue could be. Somehow he persuaded Lance that since we were going to load the books on the Daufuskie side, we should also be there to unload the books on the Bluffton side.

11.

The next morning we stood on deck with the sun and wind in our faces, the only passengers on the boat to Bluffton. After unloading the books, we walked two blocks past the church and Goodman's Store to Gatch's clinic in the center of town. Gatch was busy seeing patients who, as usual, packed the waiting room. Terry, a doctor's daughter, had been enlisted to do EKG's. Carol and Fredi were about to drive to Savannah to pick up medical supplies. They invited us to join them.

We hopped in Carol's back seat. Excited and speedy, Fredi turned around.

"You're not going to believe all the far-out shit we're into here," Fredi said, her words tumbling out in rapid-fire clusters. "Gatch sees poverty and hunger and health care as international issues. He says the conditions he's treating here are the same conditions that most of the world is living with. He wants to hook up with guerrillas in Mexico and Ho Chi Minh and Biafra, and everywhere, don't you see, they're all connected. And he wants us to put him in contact with the Panthers in California. It's mind-blowing! And by the way, we heard some really freaky gossip about Daufuskie…"

"Whoa, slow down, Fredi, take a breath," said Ed. "Okay now, what about Daufuskie?"

"Well, there are these really militant Black guys from Penn Center in Frogmore—y'know the place where Dr. King used to go for retreats—and they told Gatch that this rich developer, Charles Frazier, who owns most of the resort on Hilton Head Island, and Earl Cherry of the OEO, and possibly along with the Nethertons and Lance Burn, are in a conspiracy to buy up land on Daufuskie and develop it into another Hilton Head. And Gatch told Carol."

Considerably calmer than Fredi, Carol confirmed that Gatch told her all this and added that a contract to build a bridge to Daufuskie may have already been signed. "But it's all just rumors, there's no evidence," said Carol.

This was the first I'd heard of Charles Frazier. Based on my brief interaction with Earl Cherry, I didn't trust him. Anything was possible in this strange world we'd entered, but it seemed highly unlikely that either the Nethertons or Lance Burn could be involved in such a plan. The Nethertons were a retired, well-intentioned couple who freely admitted that they'd bought a small piece of Daufuskie land when it appeared they would lose the rented trailer they were currently occupying. As for Lance, he already had his Daufuskie dream house and railed against any development that might threaten his bucolic way of life.

"I'm not sure Dr. Gatch is always reliable," said Carol.

"What do you mean?" said Fredi, rushing to his defense. "He's brilliant, a visionary."

"Yes," said Carol, "but he talks a lot when I'm driving him places, and sometimes he seems a little paranoid to me, that's all."

Later that night, back at Gatch's compound, we caught up with the doctor. As usual, he was leafing through files and articles in the second house. He looked weary, painfully skinny and frail. But when we told him about our situation on Daufuskie and asked his advice, he listened carefully and then spoke in a calm, quiet voice. The best way to figure out what the people of Daufuskie wanted us to do, he said, was simply to ask them. He suggested we take an extensive survey of everyone, including kids old enough to understand, and ask them about their views of Daufuskie, what its future should be, what changes would make them happy, if they wanted to stay on the island, if they wanted a bridge, and how the California boys could be of service. "We got a grant to do this kind of survey in the Bluffton area. I'll be testifying to the Senate Hunger Committee, and I'll report the results. You could do the survey on Daufuskie, and I think it would help you too. Talk to Terry."

With that, he wandered off, leaving Ed and me to consider his suggestion. A few minutes later he returned from the bathroom looking lost, his eyes glazed. It was as if Ed and I weren't there. A syringe dripping with blood fell from his hand to the floor. He didn't bother to pick it up, and neither did we.

We retreated to the women's cabin. Ed made a beeline for Terry to talk about the survey, and they disappeared into her bedroom. Nearly every night Ed had been bending my ear about the woman of his dreams back in Santa Cruz, an innocent-looking, freckled waif he called little Annie. Though he wrote long letters to her, she never wrote back. But Ed didn't let rejection, faithfulness, or loyalty discourage him from pursuing other women, particularly when a pretty, dimpled Irish blond like Terry was right in front of him. It was hard for any woman to resist Ed's boyish Irish charm, but according to Ed, after a little fooling around, resist him she did. She wanted to remain faithful to her longtime boyfriend in Santa Cruz.

I was far too freaked out by Gatch's disturbing behavior to think about romance. I cornered Carol, Gatch's closest confidant, and asked what was going on with the good doctor.

"Let's just say he isn't exactly Dr. Schweitzer," she said.

"Fredi and Terry and Tree all talk about him like he's a saint."

"He's incredibly dedicated, does great work, saves lives. I've seen it myself. One night at three in the morning I drove him to this remote place where he had to wade through a swamp to get to this one-room shack to deliver a baby. But he's also into drugs—uppers, downers, I don't even know what he and Anita are shooting up."

Carol put a leash on Phoebe and motioned for me to join them on a walk. It was a moon-lit night, spooky, silent. Spanish moss hung from the oak trees, casting eerie shadows that felt like harbingers of doom. Phoebe sniffed and scratched in the scrub brush and proudly dropped at my feet what she'd uncovered——a used syringe.

"Look, Gatch is a seeker, an experimenter," said Carol. "An atheist, very down on Judeo-Christian suffering on earth for a place in heaven. And his personal life is just nuts. When he lived in Savannah after he interned there, he managed a racially integrated, gay nightclub. Characters from those days still come out here at all hours of the day and night, looking for drugs and I don't know what else. The scary part is he's fascinated by violence, sees it as some kind of weird cleansing."

"Does he have guns?"

She shook her head. "He's not violent, he's actually shy. But he romanticizes revolution, wants to be part of it. When I told him how I went with my boyfriend Jaime to bring food to the students in prison in Mexico City after the '68 strike, he pushed me to put him in touch with the guerrillas in Mexico. He wanted to fly down there. So I called Jaime, and reality check, he said, 'Don't you realize the danger you'd be putting everyone in if he came here? It's crazy.'"

Carol's despairing voice was almost a whisper now as she led Phoebe back inside. "I don't know what to think any more."

I lay down on the living room couch, confused thoughts racing through my mind. What had happened to the heroic Dr. Gatch, the courageous, selfless physician? Who was this spaced-out junkie, wanna-be revolutionary that Carol described?

I couldn't sleep at all that night. The next morning, my head still spinning, Carol drove us to Savannah to catch the boat back to Daufuskie. On the way, Ed asked her to stop at a supermarket. He was too young to buy alcohol legally, but he emerged from the store smiling and carrying a big bag. It contained all the supplies he needed to make his own brew.

12.

The atmosphere at Daufuskie's public landing was convivial, the usual characters gathered to meet the boat. As we landed, I overheard Lance Burn's conversation with Henry Netherton.

"Fella came out here today," Lance was saying. "Wants permission to drill for minerals. I said not on my land. They find somethin', next thing you know, they be developin' and then buildin' a bridge, and then we gonna have the same mess they got out in California. Longhairs trained in Moscow and Cuba, protesters in the streets, I'd hang 'em all..."

"I used to carry a flask around on my head to protest prohibition," interrupted Henry.

"Ever get knocked on the head?"

"Not while I was sober," Henry replied.

Doonie, smoking a Camel, greeted us. He was sharing a bottle with Bertha Robinson, who offered us a ride in her oxcart. We helped her carry a few boxes from the boat onto the cart and then the four of us headed out, pulled by Bobby the cow.

"My medicine," said Doonie. He took a swig and passed the bottle to Bertha. She looked upset, her face lined with worry. "Oh Lord," she wailed, "I gotta move tomorrow and then I s'posed to get a operation next week, Lord I scared."

Ed offered our services to help her move. Bertha thanked him, and I could see tears forming in her eyes. She took a long drink. "Religion don't mean to take away all your pleasure," she said.

Ed drank with them the rest of the way to Mrs. Bryan's. I passed. I didn't know what was in the bottle or who made it. But back home after dinner, Mrs. Bryan brought out a carafe of her home-made wine—a thick, sweet combination of grapes, pears, and peaches—and I joined her and Ed in the living room for a few drinks. Ed acted as DJ, and we listened to Mrs. Bryan's old-time blues records—Bessie Smith, Blind Lemon Jefferson, Big Bill Broonzy. Rags, she called them, as opposed to the sacred church music she listened to on the radio.

Flashing a big grin that made her eyes sparkle, Mrs. Bryan got up from her couch and shimmied on skinny legs, her heavy body moving with an easy grace —"kicking up," as she put it. The music and wine reminded her of fun times in her youth when she worked as a maid in Savannah for 50 cents a day, dancing and drinking all night, then getting up at 6:30 in the morning to make breakfast for the white family she served. Though she had no children of her own, she was married, and in the beginning she was faithful, she said. But after her jealous husband Robert started accusing her of infidelity, she decided to get herself a boy-friend for real. It was only fair—he had a girlfriend on the side. For 14 years she kept her affair secret from her husband. "Wild times," she said. "I did my share of sinning, but all that concerns me now is the Good

Marster. I just want to do right, not lie, be a good girl, and hope the Good Marster will treat me kind. It's His world."

Ed asked her if she had a boyfriend now. We suspected it was Plummey Simmons, who dropped by to see her now and then. But she didn't answer.

The next day, Lance picked us up in the OEO truck that would carry Bertha's belongings to her new home. "Y'know, these colored folk don't help each other out," Lance confided in a voice just above a whisper. Even though he didn't like us, I guess he still considered us part of the whites-only club. "Bertha's been staying for free in a house owned by Sarah Grant's sister up in New York. Now the sister decided to charge $20 a month rent. She knows nobody pays rent on Fuskie, and Bertha doesn't have it anyway. Sister just wants Bertha out. See what I mean, colored folk just don't help each other out."

But as soon as we arrived at Bertha's house, all we saw were Daufuskie folks helping Bertha move. Willis, Thomas Stafford, Joe Bryan, and Willie Miller lifted boxes and furniture out of the house and into the truck in a daisy chain. We piled it all up in the truck bed and then jumped in ourselves, hanging on as Lance drove the bumpy dirt road up to Bertha's new home, an abandoned shack at the Cooper River end of the island. It felt like a short version of the Joad family's trip to California in *The Grapes of Wrath*.

Just as we arrived at the shack and started unloading, we spotted the Cooper River crowd walking toward us on the road—Fast Man and Jake Washington, then the women, Flossie and Susie Smith and several others, carrying brooms, buckets, mops, and cleaning supplies. They all pitched in and cleaned out the old shack and arranged the furniture, drinking and talking and laughing the whole time, making what could have been a sad day into a party. Lance just watched, didn't lift a finger. As soon as the truck was empty, he drove off.

In the two weeks we had to wait before the PTA could consider our proposed recreation program, we did odd jobs. With the Operation Mainstream crew, we unloaded posts and rolls of fencing wire from the boat. We dug postholes and put up garden fences with anyone who asked us to help. Mostly we walked from one end of the island to the other, interviewing people for the survey that Gatch had suggested.

Mrs. Bryan thought the survey was a good idea. Most families on Daufuskie owned land and homes they'd inherited from ancestors, but she warned that if we asked questions about current income, "some of these peoples gonna drop dead." We stuck to broader, less personal questions, with predictable results. Nobody wanted a bridge or extensive development or mining for minerals on the island. Everyone wanted daily free boat trips to the mainland, access to affordable health care, better housing, and more jobs. Everyone liked the California boys and wanted us to help with carpentry, odd jobs, putting up fences, and tutoring the kids.

The survey allowed us to spend time with the people of Daufuskie in their own homes and hear their stories. But I always wondered how much we could really get to know them—or they us. How could we overcome the inevitable distrust that a 60-year-old Black man in the South felt for white people? What could we say to a 55-year-old Black woman who'd seen dozens of white liberals come and go with their smiles and promises and high talk of better times, only to disappear, oftentimes taking a little cash with them? Part of me asked, "What the hell are we doing here? All these people want is to be left alone to live out their days in peace. What right do we have to come to this island and force them, by our very presence, to put on just one more act for a couple of white college guys?"

For some, like James Williams, a 39-year-old man with a bad leg, unmarried, living alone, working on Operation Mainstream, our questions were clearly unwelcome. When we tried to start conversations with him, we hit a brick wall. He seemed hostile, which made me feel like a rude intruder, so we stayed away.

But most people were friendly and open, even if they were acting out a role, putting on a well-worn mask that they had all learned to use to disguise their true feelings every time a white face confronted them. Mrs. Bryan had told us that Isaiah Graves, a tall, thin, 70-year-old church deacon, didn't like white people. Yet he greeted us with warmth and invited us into his home. He told us about his struggles during Hoover times—everyone on Daufuskie called the 1930s Depression "Hoover times." He traveled to Philadelphia and Rhode Island in search of work, but had no luck. He could find no job anywhere.

At Lemon Grant's house, Fast Man was outside cutting wood for her stove. We went inside and tried to ask questions, but soon gave up because

Lemon's daughter Ella Mae and her five kids were running around and shouting, making it impossible to hear. So we just sat with Lemon and watched *Edge of Night* on her black-and-white TV, as she filled us in on the plot. "That evil one, Pamela, was Adam's wife," she explained. "Now Adam's in love with Nicole. I think Pamela put some poison in Nicole's drink to get rid of her and get Adam back." I was amazed that Lemon was so engrossed in the soap opera—and that we got hooked as well.

Watching television, I realized, was not just fantasy escape from the hard reality of life on Daufuskie, but wish fulfillment. You could immerse yourself in a world where Matt Dillon always got the bad guys, where the good guys triumph and live happily ever after. Where even doctors and lawyers had juicy love affairs and heartache that everyone could gossip about. Where if you'd been kicked around all your life, you could watch the people's theater of professional wrestling and vent your cumulative anger and frustration by shouting at the screen, "Kick his ass, c'mon boy, kill him."

We were eager to interview Doonie's parents, Richmond and Geneva Wiley. After we helped Richmond build a shed, we sat with Geneva in their living room. Family was most important to her, and she told Ed and me that we both were very lucky that our parents were still alive. She had 13 kids herself, she boasted with great pride, 10 of them still living. Midway in the interview, she showed us a photo of Doonie as a handsome young man in his early 20s in New York City. Wearing a suit and tie and smiling, he looked alert and smart, ready to take on the world. I focused on his hands. His fingers were all there, thin and long and graceful.

The day before the PTA meeting, we had our longest and most thought-provoking interview with Miss Frances Jones, who for 30 years had taught the younger kids at the Mary Fields School. Born and raised on the island, Miss Jones lived across the dirt road from the schoolhouse and was well-liked by everyone. When she was three, she was crippled in an accident and needed crutches to walk. She knew that in all probability she couldn't get a man, so she decided to get an education instead. Her grandparents scraped together enough funds to send her to high school in Savannah. After graduating, she returned to Daufuskie to teach, and got her college degree by taking summer classes. Because of her disability, she explained, she'd been passed over for the principal's job. There was no love lost between her and the current principal, Mrs. Julia Johnson.

Though she didn't have any solid evidence, Frances repeated the suspicions of the Penn Center militants that Earl Cherry and Charles Frazier were trying to buy up land and develop Daufuskie. "I'm on the OEO board, I hear Cherry talk. He says there'll be a bridge in five years," she said. Frances didn't trust the man who'd recently come over to drill for minerals. "Why doesn't he drill on the rich man's land? Bostwick owns half the island, up to Haig Point. [George Bostwick, an heir to the Standard Oil fortune and an accomplished steeplechase jockey, had bought more than 1,000 acres in 1961 but never lived on Daufuskie.] But no, this fella had a map with people's names and houses. Where'd he get that? He bought Coolie a battery for his truck to drive him around, and he offered $20 to anyone who'd let him drill on their land. It smelled rotten, and everyone said no—except one fool gumps. And he'll go to hell for a dollar," said Frances.

When we got back home, there was a small crowd of Black people jammed into Mrs. Bryan's living room. Judging by their hair, Angela Davis-style naturals, they weren't Daufuskie residents. We waited outside until Mrs. Bryan called us in. The leader of the group was Thomas Barnwell, who'd worked for OEO a few years back, but now was organizing fishing and shrimp co-ops on neighboring Hilton Head Island. Surrounded by his family, the regional co-op director, and several co-workers from the shrimp co-op, Barnwell introduced everyone and then, like Groucho Marx muttering "Hello, I must be going," added that they were just on their way out. Clearly, he didn't want to discuss his business in our presence.

After they left, Mrs. Bryan was very agitated. Barnwell's organization wanted to help determine Daufuskie's future, she explained. Barnwell told Mrs. Bryan that he'd talked to South Carolina's governor, Robert McNair, who said that all the residents of Daufuskie should be moved to the mainland so the island could be developed into a resort. Mrs. Bryan was talking so fast that it was unclear to me whether Barnwell was on board with this plan—which didn't seem likely—or was raising it only as a means to mobilize Daufuskie residents against it.

Whatever his intentions, Barnwell had scared the hell out of Mrs. Bryan. She didn't know what or whom to believe. Neighboring Hilton Head had a bridge and was already being developed as a paradise for the rich. Daufuskie was prime real estate. Cherry and the white-run OEO had plans for the island. The Black Penn Center militants had their own plans. Barnwell and his co-op friends had other plans. Charles Frazier's plans remained a mystery. And someone was drilling for minerals—but no one knew exactly who or why. Mrs. Bryan felt that everyone who claimed to be helping Daufuskie, white and Black, was lying, concealing, and jockeying for power. She was so angry and confused she wanted to tell them all to leave her alone and go to hell.

For Ed and me, the young white outsiders, it was impossible to know what was really going on. That night, we decided we couldn't allow ourselves to be sucked in or get discouraged. All we could do was plug on and try to get the PTA to approve the after-school recreation program for the kids.

The PTA meeting took place in the schoolhouse with Ed and me present as guests. About a dozen people, almost all women, sat uncomfortably in kids' chairs as PTA secretary Bertha Robinson took roll call.

After Mrs. Bryan and Sarah Grant led everyone in a song and a prayer, the meeting rambled on with no discernible structure. The usual leaders—the white folks who liked to talk—were noticeably absent. The Nethertons were away on vacation, and Lance and Cherry hadn't shown up. Hamp Bryan, the chair, tried to stick to an agenda, but he spoke quietly and didn't want to offend anyone, so he let anyone jump in any time on any subject. There was a lot of loud bickering about who would sell what food at the PTA's upcoming Valentine's Day fundraising party. Billie Burn wanted to discuss when the cows should be taken in. Geneva Wiley talked about spring in the air. Frances Jones reported on her trip to Charleston for a PTA convention that she arrived at only after it had finished because she got lost. Bertha kept interrupting, trying to get straight for the minutes who was going to sell what at the party.

The temptation for middle-class, formally educated white guys like Ed and me was to take over and run the meeting in the efficient, organized way we were accustomed to. But we'd learned enough by then to be patient and wait quietly.

Finally, when there was a lull, Ed handed a quarter to Bertha, said we were joining the PTA on behalf of the Cowell College Extra-Mural Project, and asked that they consider the proposed after-school recreation program. He then described how it would work. The kids would stay after school, and we would tutor and supervise them in sports for an hour. Then we would drive them home in the OEO truck.

"Lancey tell me you can't use the truck," said Mrs. Bryan. "Cherry say you gotta pay OEO $3,000 insurance."

Blindsided, I froze. But Ed, unflappable, was quick on his feet. "We'll talk to Cherry and straighten it out," he replied. "We're going to Bluffton anyway to talk to the superintendent about getting more equipment. In the meantime, we'll pay Plummey Simmons to take the kids home in his truck. We can start next Tuesday."

The meeting had run on for more than an hour and a half by then, and everyone was ready to go home. So with no further discussion, the PTA voted unanimously to approve the recreation program. Ed and I both breathed a sigh of relief.

"I motion that this fool-as-a-coot meeting be over and done with," said Mrs. Bryan, who had reached the end of her patience. "Good riddance to bad linens."

13.

Fredi and Terry picked us up at the dock in Bluffton. I asked where Carol was.

"Gone," said Terry. "Suddenly. Just packed up, threw Phoebe in the car, and left. Two weeks ago, the day she took you guys to Savannah."

"What?" said Ed, stunned.

"She left a note saying her fiancé in Mexico had been shot and she had to go help him," said Fredi. "But it's really mysterious. She'd withdrawn completely from us and spent all her time with Gatch. My guess is he freaked her out with all the weird shit going down here."

It had become obvious, they explained, that Gatch and Anita were addicted to drugs, shooting uppers and downers, dropping acid, rarely sleeping or eating. A male friend from Gatch's bisexual club-hopping days in Savannah now seemed to be involved in a threesome with Gatch and Anita. Fredi and Tree had discovered explicit Polaroid photos of them that had been left out in the living room after they passed out. Gatch had already been charged with sodomy once and expected to be again. In addition, sheriff's deputies were going through Gatch's prescription records and checking them against his in-office pharmacy supplies.

Since Gatch, Anita, and his Savannah friends were using a considerable amount, it was only a matter of time until discrepancies were found and charges brought.

Reporters were constantly calling and poking around, wanting to interview the latest incarnation of Albert Schweitzer—a press-invented version of Dr. Gatch who didn't exist in reality. Armed Black political activists were frequently meeting in secret with Gatch—about what, nobody knew. And the local Ku Klux Klan, according to Terry and Fredi, regularly parked their cars outside Gatch's compound and monitored everything that went on. Gatch had received several anonymous bomb threats—one so serious that Tom Barnwell had banged on the women's door in the middle of the night and rushed them to a safe house in Savannah where they stayed until morning. On top of all this, there was the usual medical practice to keep up, including emergencies at all hours of the night.

Far from being frightened, Terry and Fredi seemed excited, on an adrenaline high. But the madness of Dr. Gatch's turbulent world left Ed and me overwhelmed. We'd grown used to the slow pace of Daufuskie.

Back at Gatch's compound, we tried to focus on Daufuskie business. Our phone calls to Earl Cherry about insurance for the OEO truck and to Beaufort County's school superintendent about recreation equipment went unanswered. So we decided to drive to Beaufort to research recent Daufuskie land transactions to confirm or refute the rumors we'd heard. At the county courthouse we leafed through the Register of Deeds, which looked like something out of *Bartleby the Scrivener*, but the records proved inconclusive.

We headed back to Bluffton in the funky brown jalopy we'd borrowed from Anita Gatch. An aging gas-guzzler, it was cluttered with papers and garbage, had cigarette burns on the upholstery, and stunk of tobacco. We rolled down the windows, turned up the radio, and sped along the rural two-lane highway surrounded by forests and lowland scrub brush. We were on the open road again, feeling free, listening to Creedence Clearwater Revival singing "Proud Mary"—rollin', rollin', rollin' on the river—when the engine made a loud clunking sound and a geyser of steam spewed from the hood.

The car rolled to a halt in front of a small, weather-beaten house— one of the few we'd passed for miles around.

"Overheated," said a young white woman who appeared from the house. A toddler of three or four wobbled by her side, clutching one of her hands, and she cradled a baby with the other. "Nothin' to do, just wait till it cools down. I used to work at a service station. Pour water on it, you gonna crack the block. But you better get this car outta here before dark 'cause niggers come by here and they gonna steal it or kill ya, you hear me?"

"Ma'am, please, do you have a phone we could use?" asked Ed.

"Nope." With that, she turned and headed back into the house.

Ed and I waited in silence. After a few minutes, a car approached, and we stood in the road, waving until it stopped. A Black man in his 20s got out. Two more Black men and two Black women stayed in the car, drinking beer.

"This Dr. Gatch car, ain't it?" said the man. "You friends of his?"

We said we were and that the car had overheated.

"Pour water on it, it'll start right up," said the man.

We explained that the white woman in the house had told us that would crack the block.

"Well, I fix cars, and she wrong, but I ain't gonna argue with no white lady. She probably got a shotgun in that house, aiming at us right now."

"If you could give one of us a ride to Dr. Gatch's house, we could get help," Ed said.

"Sure enough. Hop in."

I slid into the back seat, and Ed stayed behind to keep an eye on the car.

"Good thing we came along," said the man as we drove off. "You get stuck out there in that car after dark, crackers gonna mess with ya or even kill ya. They hate Dr. Gatch."

On the 30-minute drive to the compound, I found out that everyone in that car and their families had been treated by Dr. Gatch. He was their friend and hero. When they dropped me off, I offered some money for the ride. They wouldn't accept it.

Fredi and I borrowed another car and picked up Ed. Anita's rusting heap would have to be towed and repaired by a mechanic. But that was the least of Dr. Gatch's problems.

That night we met Gatch in the cluttered middle house, as he shuffled through piles of magazines and papers. When I tried to hand him the summarized results of our survey, he waved me off and told me to give them to Terry.

"So what happened with Carol?" Ed asked.

Gatch looked up. "I've never seen a person change so fast," he said. "I asked her to put me in touch with her boyfriend in Mexico, and then she vanished. I don't know why that would panic her. She was aware of my work with revolutionaries all over the world.

"A day of reckoning is coming very, very soon," he continued. "Blacks everywhere are organized and armed to an extent that whites just cannot understand. All this talk about Black Power and threats to burn down cities—that's all well-calculated distraction. But the real revolutionary activity will come in a form that most white people would never guess. And it's all starting on February 10."

Ed's jaw dropped. "That's two days from now," he said.

"Most people won't realize anything is happening," said Gatch. "You won't see it reported on the evening news."

"So what is it?" asked Ed. "What should we be looking out for?"

Gatch, ever cryptic, didn't reply. He turned back to thumbing through his piles of papers.

14.

The next morning, Terry took Ed and me to Savannah to catch the boat back to Daufuskie. Immediately I felt calmer, happy to leave behind the ambiguity, tension, and chaos of Dr. Gatch's world. We'd been living with Mrs. Bryan on Daufuskie for only a few weeks. But when we arrived at the island's public dock, it felt like we were coming home. Old Sam Holmes was there with his ox and cart to help carry supplies. Plummey and Jake Washington were sharing a beer, talking about the most pressing issue on their minds—how Fast Man could get away with seeing two women at the same time. The sun was bright, the air clear. It was a simpler, more grounded world, and I felt more comfortable in it.

We spent the next couple of days washing our clothes, working on fences, arranging with Plummey to drive the kids home from recreation. On February 10, Ed got up early, eager to turn on the TV. A believer at heart, Ed was disappointed to find that, as Gatch predicted, the morning news shows reported nothing out of the ordinary, just the usual local crimes, corruption, weather. Mrs. Bryan didn't understand what all the fuss was about. Never for a moment did she think there would be a revolution.

I remained skeptical. For me, this was just another reason to think that Dr. Gatch was a very complicated mixed bag, a brilliant and serious person you could never dismiss, but couldn't really trust either.

Later, Fredi told us that on the night of February 10 she and the other Cowell women had been rushed to Gatch's office where they joined Gatch, Anita, and the kids. They all spent the entire night there, huddled together, not sleeping a wink. Dozens of Black militants armed with rifles surrounded the office, protecting them. From what exactly, they were never told. What, if anything, happened that night? Was there some kind of planned insurrection? Was it all a paranoid fantasy emanating from Gatch's drug-addled imagination? There was no way to know, and 50 years later, I still don't know.

February 12 was a national holiday, Abraham Lincoln's birthday. Though Confederate General Robert E. Lee's birthday was celebrated throughout the South, Lincoln's passed unnoticed. The next morning, Doonie helped us tear down the dilapidated fences around Mrs. Bryan's property. When we stopped for lunch—Mrs. Bryan's fried chicken and potatoes—Ed brought out the gallon jug of hard cider he'd been brewing. It was finally ready, he announced proudly. He poured each of us a small glass, and we all toasted and drank. Doonie chugged his glass in one gulp, set it down, and smiled. "Make you feel good," he said. Ed refilled it, and Doonie knocked it back again in one gulp. While Mrs. Bryan and I had one glass each, Ed and Doonie had three or four. It tasted okay, and it didn't seem to affect any of us. It was only 3 to 4% alcohol, like a weak beer.

After lunch, we finished tearing out the old fence posts, and Doonie left to go on about his business. That night, after dinner, we settled in the living room, as usual. Ed gave Mrs. Bryan her eyeball juice and turned on the TV. I'd been looking forward to this moment for a week. Somehow, sandwiched between Porter Wagoner and Dolly and Goldie Hawn on *Laugh-In*, the Royal Shakespeare's production of *A Midsummer Night's Dream* was being aired. A few minutes into it, I was already drunk on the exalted language and the magnificent production. It had been a long time since I'd heard English spoken like that.

"Talk, talk, talk," said Mrs. Bryan. She couldn't understand what they were saying. "That's natural trash."

I told her it was a story about romantic love, the misunderstandings between men and women, but she would have none of it. "You wanna know about mens and womens," she said. "I tell you, when I was a young girl about same age as this one cuttin' the fool on the TV, Johnny Hamilton used to brag about his manliness. Like he the only pebble on the beach. So one day out in the schoolyard, all the girls done git together and sat on him. And one girl open up his zipper and look in there to see where all this manliness was. And it just shrivel up to where you couldn't even find it." She laughed at the memory.

But I was irritated. I didn't care that she thought Shakespeare was natural trash. I was amazed that such wildly diverse realities could co-exist and we could jockey back and forth between them—Shakespeare, Benny with the Penny's morning Gospel Hour, Porter Wagoner, Santa Cruz hippies, Gatch's revolutionaries, and on and on. But it bothered me that Mrs. Bryan kept interrupting and wouldn't just let us watch Shakespeare, something from our world that mattered to us. In retrospect, I know, of course, that countless times we unwittingly trampled on her beliefs about manners and religion, bedrocks of her world that mattered most to her.

This was the only time I recall ever getting angry at Mrs. Bryan. But we were guests in her home, and I said nothing. Soon enough, she mumbled, "Another day's journey," and dozed off. In peace, Ed and I watched the ending of *A Midsummer Night's Dream,* then climbed up the narrow stairs to the attic and went to sleep.

15.

"Y'know, Doonie dead." A voice pierced the stillness of a freezing dawn, Valentine's Day, February 14, 1969. I was curled up in the attic, warm under patchwork quilts, in the nether world between sleep and wakefulness. Was I dreaming?

Ed rolled over in his bed. "Did you hear something?" he asked.

I nodded, and then Mrs. Bryan's voice came again, this time clear and unmistakable. "Y'know, Doonie dead."

Stunned, I buried myself under the covers, hoping sleep would wash away this awful nightmare. Sleep did not come. The scent of smoke from the wood stove wafted up as usual, but this morning it did not sooth my restless mind. I felt an emptiness, an indescribable vacuum, a helplessness and a senselessness, overwhelming me. My body went limp, and I felt myself groping in vain for something bigger, stronger, wiser, flashing for the first time in my life on what the need for a god might be about.

Downstairs at breakfast, Mrs. Bryan said Billie Burn had come by in the school bus bearing the sad news that Lawrence Wiley, called Doonie, was dead. Old Josephus Robinson had gone out just before dawn to look for his cow and had found Doonie lying in a field. Mrs. Bryan knew no more details, except that out of respect the PTA's Valentine's party was canceled.

"I can't believe it," said Ed. "He was here yesterday tearing down fences with us, he was going to work with us again today."

A terrifying thought haunted me. "He drank our hard cider," I said. Could Doonie's death have been caused by the cider? Was it poisonous?

Mrs. Bryan read my mind. "Don't you fret, wasn't that cider," she said. "We all drank it, we all fine this morning. Dis ain't the first time Doonie pass out on the Marster's good earth. Everyone know Doonie jedgment day was comin'. You boys better get on over there now, they gonna need help."

Ed and I walked in silence to Josephus Robinson's home. The air was bitter cold, well below freezing. I spotted Plummey's red pickup truck and a group of men—Josephus, Plummey, Thomas Stafford, Lawrence Jenkins, Hamp Bryan—gathered in a loose circle in a nearby field. Ed and I stayed back, not sure if a couple of white boys from California would be welcome in this situation.

From a short distance, I stared at Doonie's body in fascination and horror. He lay inside the circle of men in an awkward position, face up, one arm across his stomach, head back, eyes open, knees together and bent up. His body was charred, the coal-black blistering reaching all the way up to his nostrils, peeling the skin on his torso and face. His clothes, the same as when we'd last seen him, were burned from the waist up, front and back. His jacket lay scorched about 20 feet from the body.

I looked away. I'd never seen a dead person before. I'd been to one memorial service, but there was no body or even a casket. I felt numb.

Janie Bentley and Agnes Simmons arrived on foot, saw the body, and started whooping and hollering, waving their handkerchiefs. "Oh Lord, oh Lord, Doonie, Doonie, oh Lord." I had no experience with this kind of raw emotion and had no idea how to respond.

Lance Burn skidded to a halt in his OEO car. As the magistrate, he'd already been to the scene earlier and had gone back to his house to radio

Josephus Robinson in his yard. Photo by David Morrison

the coroner. "Well, from what I told him, coroner seems to agree what happened," said Lance. "Doonie was over to Lawrence Jenkins' place last night, got drunk. Started to walk home, it was cold, probably saw this fire still smolderin' in Josephus's field, tried to light a cigarette in it, warm up a bit, leaned in, clothes caught fire. Maybe he stumbled, fell in the fire. Rolled over, couldn't get the flames out, tore off his burnin' jacket, threw it over there. But couldn't get up, kept burnin', passed out, burned to death or froze. Either way, coroner said we could move the body now."

As several of the men lifted the body into the flatbed of Plummey's pickup, Sam Holmes's horse and cart pulled up, carrying Bertha, Flossie, Susie, and a couple of others from Cooper River. Bertha had to be helped out of the cart. Bowing and shaking, she started screaming, "Oh Lord, Doonie gone, Doonie all I got, oh Doonie, oh, oh, Lord, Lord."

Sam Holmes held her as Plummey's truck rumbled off, carrying Doonie's body back to his house. Then Sam took a few people in his cart, and the others followed along the narrow trail on foot. Bertha lingered behind, stumbling and wailing, overcome with grief. Ed and I stayed with her, not speaking. As we slowly made our way to Doonie's house, she walked a few steps, stopped, then grabbed her stomach and fell to her knees, crying, "You know Doonie and me was best of friends, no one miss Doonie like me." And then she grabbed her stomach again. She'd told me earlier that Dr. Gatch wanted her to have an operation, but she hadn't gone through with it. Was her anguish now from physical pain or grief—or some of each? She grabbed on to our arms. We lifted her up and took a few more steps. It was a long walk.

Outside Doonie's two-room shack, an empty plain wooden casket had been placed under a tree. Normally, we were told, the body would lie in the casket on the front porch. But Doonie didn't have a porch.

Inside in the small living room, a few women had gathered around Doonie's mother, Geneva. Richmond, his father, had been working in Savannah and was on his way home, sailing in his open dinghy. Franklin, Doonie's brother, asked Ed and me to help him chop firewood for the wake to be held that night. I was glad we could be of some use, and it was a relief to be outdoors, away from the grieving people. But as we finished and brought the wood to the back of the house, Jake Washington leaned out a window and beckoned us to come inside.

Doonie's naked body lay on a bed in a cramped, dark room that couldn't have been bigger than 8 x 10 feet. There was no embalming on

Daufuskie, no mortician to sterilize the process and shield you from the stench and rot and ugliness of death. A man dies. You bury him, and fast, before his body decays and putrefies. As undertaker for decades, Sarah Grant had done this many times, but at 81, she had recently retired.

Jake Washington, who'd had a little experience, was in charge. He'd managed to strip off Doonie's clothes, pour turpentine into orifices, and wash and clean up the body. But he was having trouble dressing Doonie, the final step in preparation for burial. Though Fast Man was there to help, he knew as little about this process as we did.

At first, we followed Jake's directions—lift here, lift there. The nauseating death-stench—a noxious combination of burned flesh and hair, unidentifiable bodily fluids, and turpentine—made me cringe. Touching the body gave me the willies. Doonie was as rigid and cold as a concrete block, frozen in such an awkward position that it was almost impossible to get clothes on.

Trying to maneuver Doonie's right arm inside a shirt sleeve, we were getting nowhere fast. Lemon Grant elbowed her way into the room and looked at Jake.

"What's the matter, you scared?" she said.

"No, no, I ain't scared," said Jake. But he was scared, like all of us.

Unafraid, Lemon took over. She pulled on Doonie's arm and talked to him. "Doonie, Doonie, Doonie, c'mon, Doonie, move your arm. That's it, Doonie." And gradually, little by little, Doonie's arm moved just enough. Then the same with his leg.

Ed and I realized that to accomplish this task and not fall apart, we had to turn off our emotions. As outsiders we were the least personally connected to Doonie, so we were in the best position to act like detached morticians. Working with Lemon and Jake, we decided to cut the clothes in back and slip them on Doonie's body in two sections. He would face up in the casket. No one would see his back.

Finally, we got Doonie dressed in a white shirt, dark suit, and tie, as his family had requested. Together with Jake and Fast Man, we placed the body in the casket, which had been brought inside because it was starting to drizzle. That's when the stench got to me. I had to get out of there fast, or I'd throw up.

Ed excused us, and we headed for the closest place with clean water, the schoolhouse. We spent a long time scrubbing our hands, trying to rid ourselves of the sickening smell. We hadn't known about it, but an emergency community club meeting was being held in one of the classrooms. We stood in back and listened, grateful for a distraction from the intense emotions stirred up by Doonie's death. Earl Cherry and Lance Burn were doing most of the talking, and they were hopping mad.

According to Lance, a couple of days before, Captain Willis Simmons had been drinking when he piloted the OEO boat back to Daufuskie on its regular run from Savannah. He made a couple of failed attempts at landing and eventually crashed the boat into the dock, endangering passengers and crew and causing minor damage to the boat's bow. The next morning Willis was drinking again, and Lance told him not to run the boat. But Willis went ahead anyway. Lance radioed Cherry, who met the boat in Bluffton, and they all returned to Daufuskie for this emergency meeting.

Actually, it felt more like a trial or an interrogation. Lance charged. Willis defended himself. Cherry asked questions. Was Willis drunk? Had the other crew members, Thomas Stafford and Joe Bryan, been drinking? Had any alcohol been found on the boat? Was it Lance's word against Willis's?

You could feel the tension hanging over the room like a dense fog. The jobs of three men with wives and young children were on the line. The fate of the island's lifeline, the OEO boat, was at stake. Ed and I were relieved that we hadn't witnessed the events and couldn't weigh in.

The only eyewitness who'd been on the boat during the docking incident was Emily Miller, the mother of Joe Bryan's five children. The drama escalated as Cherry repeatedly asked her what she'd seen and whether the crew had been drinking. Fearful of both Cherry and Joe, Emily didn't answer. Cherry's frustration mounted. You could hear a pin drop.

Finally, Thomas Stafford, himself on trial, broke the silence. "Mr. Cherry, excuse me, she stutter, sir."

Emily was so nervous and suffered from such a severe stammer that the interrogation had paralyzed her. She couldn't even get out a yes or a no.

Cherry backed off, and everyone began talking at once. The transportation committee was to make a recommendation in the matter. After a few minutes of deliberation, old Sam Holmes announced the committee's decision. It found the entire crew guilty of being drunk on the job. But the committee suggested that they be shown mercy.

Cherry reluctantly agreed. "But this is your last chance," warned the OEO director. "If I hear a single report that any of you have been drinking on that boat, the whole crew will be fired and the boat will be shut down."

Captain Willis smiled and embraced his mates. Lance fumed in silence. Ed and I walked back to Mrs. Bryan's to change out of our stinking clothes and eat.

Mrs. Bryan had supper waiting—pig's feet, which we'd been eager to try. She wanted to hear everything that had happened. As we tried to tell her, I felt myself getting more and more nauseous. I ate nothing. Pig's feet would wait for another day.

After the sun set, it got colder and the pouring rain turned to sleet. But foul weather wasn't going to stop Ed and me from paying our respects at Doonie's wake. We took our flashlights and braved the mean night, the inky sky illuminated by occasional brilliant bolts of forked lightning. Dogs yelped as we approached Doonie's house.

Inside, we passed the open casket in the tiny front room. In the back room, Doonie's family were sitting on boards balanced between chairs to serve as benches. It was cramped and dark. Doonie's house had no electricity or indoor plumbing. The only heat came from a fire in the wood stove. Kerosene lanterns cast dim light on the drab green walls. And there was no escaping that awful stench from the body in the next room.

I had no clue about what happens at a wake or how to act. Franklin had hidden his axe behind the stove. He told us that some wakes ended up in drunken brawls and he didn't want anyone to get hurt. But on this night no one was drinking alcohol.

I felt out of place and terribly uncomfortable. At first I stood and let some of the ladies sit down. But Geneva Wiley, Doonie's mother, asked me and Ed to sit, so we did. It was such a small room that there was no place to hide, no way to seek refuge as an observer or to help with tasks because there were none. The only thing we had all gathered here to do was to mourn the dead.

The evening was somber and quiet. The subdued conversation turned to how the waterways around Daufuskie were built. Sarah Grant and Doonie's father, Richmond Wiley, did most of the talking. I wondered what was going on in Richmond's head. Franklin had told us earlier that Doonie once tried to kill his father. But no one talked about that. No one talked about Doonie at all, except in brief references. During

Richmond Wiley on doorstep of his home. Photo by David
Morrison

lulls in the conversation the only sounds were the constant rain and the pinging of sleet as it beat a tattoo on the tin roof. "Doonie trying to cover his tracks," said Sarah.

After awhile, Thomas Stafford suggested we sing for Doonie. Sarah started off, "Some glad morning when this life is over, I'll fly away…" but no one joined in. She tried again, and again no one joined her. She stopped and said, "If no one's gonna sing, I ain't gonna sing by myself."

The awkward moment passed when some of the women brought out plates of fried chicken from the kitchen. We hadn't eaten anything all day. Even though I knew it might be insulting to the family, I couldn't eat. Whatever might still be on my hands and the pervasive death-stench had killed my appetite.

I spoke very little that night. The conversation seemed like dull meaningless talk. Perhaps that was the idea. To forget. But I couldn't forget Doonie's body lying in the other room. And I doubt that any of the others could either. The one who seemed most upset was Doonie's sister, Janie Simmons. All through the night, she wept and whispered to her young children, making sure they were respectful and behaved themselves.

At about one in the morning, Ed and I decided to say our goodbyes. We offered our services if the family needed anything. Geneva asked if we could help dig the grave the next morning. Burial was scheduled for three in the afternoon so relatives from the mainland would have time to get there. We said "Of course," and then headed home in the sleet. The others, we learned later, stayed until sunrise.

In the morning, after breakfast, we met Franklin at his house and walked together to Sarah Grant's to pick up shovels and find out which plot in the Mary Field Cemetery was for Doonie. It had warmed up enough that the sleet had turned into a light rain.

Plummey met us at the graveyard. In contrast to the pristine white cemetery, this "colored" cemetery that Doonie had not wanted to show us was in the middle of the woods and covered by scraggly bushes. A few worn headstones poked through the brush at cockeyed angles. Muddy artificial flowers were scattered here and there in plots arranged in no particular order that I could discern.

Plummey read the directions Sarah had written out, then measured and marked the borders of Doonie's final resting place. Ed and Franklin started digging while Plummey and I lit a giant bonfire to keep us warm.

It was freezing and the rain beat down steadily. For two and a half hours, we alternated digging in silence, first Franklin and Ed, then Plummey and I. It was back-breaking work, and the heavy quagmire of mud made it harder. When Franklin and Ed dug, Plummey and I stood warming our hands in the fire. He told me stories of the old days on Daufuskie when everyone—300 or 400 people—would come out for a funeral. The singing was so loud you could hear it everywhere on the island. "Not like now," he said, resignation and sadness in his voice.

It was nearly three o'clock when we finished. Franklin threw a stick over the grave before we headed over to Doonie's house. "Old folks told me to do that," said Franklin. "If you leave a grave open like this and someone falls in, it's bad luck."

About 25 people in rain coats and boots had somehow jammed into Doonie's house for a short service. Doonie's body lay in the open casket in the next room. When his mother, Geneva, went in to have a last look, she started jumping up and down, screaming and crying, shaking with fear and anguish and sorrow. As Richmond tried to comfort her, Plummey began to read haltingly from the Bible. The island's preacher had died the year before, so Plummey, as senior deacon, led the service. He was a short, thin man, but he spoke in a clear, strong voice. He had barely read a sentence when Bertha, dressed all in black with a black scarf on her head, broke down crying and screaming, "Oh Lord, Doonie gone, Doonie gone."

"Bertha, stop crying," her husband Thomas Stafford scolded. "Not supposed to cry now."

Bertha kept crying. "I ain't got nobody left," she wailed.

"Bertha, you got...."

Plummey stopped reading and turned to Thomas. "Stafford, if you want to talk," he said, "I'll give you the Book."

Thomas apologized and Plummey finished reading the Bible passage, with Bertha, Geneva, and Janie all sobbing in the background. Then Plummey asked if anyone had anything to say. Coolie Grant and Thomas Stafford both urged people to "get down on their knees and pray."

"If nobody has anything to say about Brother Wiley, I do," said Plummey. "All men have their faults, but Brother Wiley never done no harm to no one. The only harm Brother Wiley done was to himself. I knowed him all his life. He growed up and went away and had an accident that took his fingers, but the Good Marster allowed him to go on and he made it back here. He was outside when the Lord stopped him, said he could go no farther. And he was stopped by the wayside. Some say Brother Wiley go to heaven, others say he go to hell. No man know. That between Brother Wiley and his Lord. And that is a lesson for us all. We all gonna stop by the wayside, no one know night or day. We all better prepare to meet the Lord. That's all I got to say."

A few of Doonie's relatives moved the casket into Plummey's truck, and the mourners crowded into the school bus for the short ride to the cemetery. As Lance Burn drove the bus on the rain-slick road, his puffy red face showed no emotion. He'd once had troubles with alcohol himself, he'd told us, but he'd found Jesus and had been sober for years now.

Shivering in the cold, we gathered around the empty grave. The rain had tailed off to a drizzle. Six men, including Ed and me, picked up the casket from the truck and placed it on boards above the grave. Thomas Stafford and Joe Bryan looped ropes under it, and Plummey removed the boards. Using the ropes, we began to lower the casket into the pit. I was holding one corner. Across from me, Thomas held another corner.

Suddenly, Thomas stumbled and lost his grip on his end. I felt a tug on the rope, and the casket tumbled loose, landing with a thud on the muddy floor of the grave. Unable to balance on his club foot, Thomas fell into the pit, sprawled on top of the casket. The women standing a few feet back gasped in disbelief.

Swearing to himself, Thomas crawled out of the grave. For a few moments, everyone was stunned, not knowing whether to laugh or cry. Then, breaking the awkward silence, Willis Simmons and Joe Bryan picked up shovels and began filling in the grave. As mud splattered on the casket, Sarah Grant's lone voice rang out, echoing through the woods. "If you miss Brother Lawrence, you won't find him nowhere…" Stella Hamilton joined in. "C'mon up to God's glory, he'll be waitin' up there…" Plummey and a few others added their voices. I knew the song from a Pete Seeger album, but with different words written for the civil rights movement. "If you miss me at the back of the bus…" I joined the small chorus, but our voices sounded lonely and mournful, the steady drizzle dampening everyone's spirits.

As we sang, an older relative of Doonie's from Savannah asked Willis for his shovel and pitched more dirt into the grave. Franklin, Richmond, and a few others took their turns as Geneva sobbed. When the casket was completely covered, Franklin and his wife, Ethel Mae, placed a bouquet of fresh flowers on the grave.

Before everyone went home, Isaiah Graves, the deacon, said a final short prayer, but I couldn't take it in. The last two days had shaken me to my bones. I was beyond exhausted.

16.

In the days that followed, Ed and I took long walks to the beach and talked endlessly, trying to sort out what we had just experienced. Introspection and self-doubt came naturally to me. But Ed, who as far as I could tell had never previously spent a moment questioning his own actions, had also turned inward, asking himself what we were doing and to what end.

This was the first time either of us had seen death up close, and it hit us hard. Healthy young men like Ed and me too often feel immortal and dismiss or laugh off fears and doubts that plague elders. That is one reason older men are able to recruit young men to fight their wars. So many of our peers, our classmates from high school, were now soldiers in far-off Vietnam, risking their lives, seeing their buddies die, killing unknown "enemies." In Vietnam, no matter how much weed a soldier smoked, there was no avoiding death. Although Ed and I had escaped Vietnam and the draft with college deferments, there was no escaping the sobering truth we'd learned from Doonie: we are all going to die.

The two days from Doonie's death to his burial were a turning point for Ed and me. We'd experienced the island on a deeper level, and we'd come to view the community in a way that hadn't been apparent to us before. Daufuskie was dying. Its population had fallen steadily as jobs disappeared, as transportation to the mainland grew more difficult, as the temptations of a modern, wealthier world on the mainland beckoned. Long gone were the days when 300 or 400 people would turn out for a funeral and the singing could be heard for miles. The church was empty, the last preacher had died a year before. There was no choir. Mrs. Bryan had tried to teach some of the younger children music and how to sing in a choir, but interest waned. The sense of a shared community was vanishing as the island split into cliques and rivalries.

Most of all, the powerful faith that had sustained the island through so many trials was fading. The older people—Mrs. Bryan, Sarah Grant,

Geneva Wiley, Virginia Washington, Coolie, Plummey, Isaiah—lived for God, even without a church or a preacher on the island. But many younger people, especially the able-bodied young men, had moved to the mainland for work and a more exciting life, leaving behind the elderly, women, and children. Those younger men who'd stayed had turned to alcohol to help ease the pain of living. Five young men in the last two years had died as a result of alcohol. Doonie was the latest. Who would be next?

Inevitably, the elders were going to die. It was just a matter of time until everyone else would be forced to sell their land and leave their homes. The tide of history seemed obvious to us now. The island was going to be turned into a resort. The immaculate beach where we took our walks was as magical a place as there was on planet Earth. Daufuskie residents might organize and resist, but the idea that they could hold out against wealthy developers was wishful thinking. One side had power, money, high-priced lawyers, and political connections. The other had nothing but themselves—a hundred poor Black folks struggling to get by as best they could. The game was rigged.

When we'd arrived on Daufuskie, we were eager to "help"—foolish white saviors, though we never thought of ourselves that way. In our heads, we had lots of plans and programs for the island. Revive the church, start a fishing co-op or a farming co-op, transplant healthy oysters to revive the oyster industry, incorporate the town, help Dr. Gatch start a comprehensive health clinic to wipe out parasites and malnutrition. In the shadow of Doonie's death, all these ideas now seemed impossible fantasies.

The strange paradox was that in the weeks before Doonie's death, Ed and I had fallen in love with Daufuskie, its people, its way of life. At the same time, we'd grown increasingly alienated from the society we'd left behind. But now it seemed to us that the Daufuskie we'd fallen in love with probably had no viable future. What to do?

"We're in way over our heads," I said.

"Look, we can still help the kids," Ed replied. "Prepare them for our world, give them tools they'll need to make it on the mainland. Reading and writing so they don't flunk out of high school. Just get them used to dealing with white guys like us. I mean, we have skills, we know how to succeed in our world. That's what we have to help them learn."

"Really?" I asked. "Help them join a society we don't even want to go back to ourselves? Okay kids, welcome to war, racism, and capitalism.

Welcome to plastic and gas-guzzling cars and pesticides in your food. Let's fuck up the planet together! Really?"

"Hey, they can reject our world if they want, they can fight to change it, or they can try to make it out there," said Ed. "They deserve the same options we've got. And to have those options, they need our skills."

"But I wouldn't want these kids to lose what's so special about Daufuskie."

"I wouldn't either," said Ed. "Look, amigo, all we can do is be ourselves."

"Be ourselves?" I said, incredulous. "Ed, we don't know what the fuck we're doing."

"Sure, we're gonna screw up, everybody does," he replied. "So what? We're not bad dudes, we don't have a hidden agenda. Hey, remember, we're pure of heart."

17.

Just when we needed it most, we found an unexpected advocate for the after-school recreation program—Billie Burn. Her husband Lance continued to block our efforts, insisting we needed insurance before we could use the OEO truck to transport the kids. But as school bus driver, Billie knew the kids and she was smart enough to understand that they were starved for outside stimulation. Billie radioed her boss on the mainland and found out that all the kids were automatically insured for one hour after the school day ended, whether they took the school bus or went home by other means.

That meant we could have a recreation program for 45 minutes and still have time to drive the kids home in the OEO truck. On the first day, we picked up the truck from Lance and covered the holes in the cargo bed with boards to make it safe. Arriving well before the end of the school day, Ed asked Mrs. Johnson if she might release the kids a few minutes early so we could have a full hour of recreation. She glared at Ed as if he were proposing to burn down the building, but it was the end of a long hard day, so she agreed.

If ever there was an antidote to our bleak, hopeless mood after Doonie's death, the excited energy of these kids was it. They burst out the door, glee in their eyes, joy in their chattering voices, eagerness and curiosity in their questions. Twenty-three of them stayed that day, gathering around us in a circle on the sandy playground in front of the schoolhouse. They looked to us to find out what was going to happen. Believing in the democratic approach of Herbert Kohl in *36 Children,* we threw the question back at them.

"What do you want to do?" I asked.

There was a short silence, followed by a cacophony of loud voices all drowning each other out. Ed calmed everyone, and we decided to separate into two groups. I took the older kids, boys and girls 10 to 14 years old, who said they wanted to play basketball, and Ed took the younger kids who had no idea what they wanted to do.

I was a jock. I had played on basketball teams from elementary school all the way through high school and had learned the game from some fairly sophisticated coaches. But I quickly realized that none of that mattered on Daufuskie. The first order of business was to find a pump and inflate the one flat ball that might pass for a basketball. Next we had to secure the old hoop that was hanging precariously from a post in the ground. When I turned the kids loose and let them play on their own, I saw there was no organization to the game at all. The playground had no paved area, just sandy dirt, so there was no court defined by boundaries or lines, and the uneven terrain and deflated ball also meant that no one bothered to dribble. Whoever had the ball just hurled it at the hoop. Someone else grabbed it, then ran around and heaved it up again. There were no teams, no passing, no plays, no defense. This was Daufuskie basketball—an individual sport with no rules.

With the little kids, who ranged from five to nine years old, Ed was equally lost. They were out of control, running around like whirling dervishes, thrilled just to feel free. Though Ed tried to round them up and organize them, he had little luck.

Before we knew it, the hour was over. We piled the kids into the truck's cargo bed. Ed drove with a couple of the older kids in the front seat next to him. I sat in back, squeezed in with all the rest of the kids, jostling and pushing each other with every bump in the road, everyone laughing and shouting and waving goodbye as we dropped each kid home. It was chaos, but the kids were happy. It was a good start.

For the next month, we led after-school recreation three times a week. The kids were always eager to run outside and we had to get them home within an hour, so we never got around to reading or writing or arithmetic. Ed began channeling the wild energy of the little ones into exercises and acting out animals and making sounds of instruments and trains and boats. I played sports with the older kids. Because of the unusual physical facilities this required a lot of improvisation. With baseball, which the kids called bat ball, there was no playing field, so trees stood in for bases. Of course the trees grew all over the place, making our playing surface a weird shape that had no resemblance to a diamond.

In their version of football, the kids didn't have plays or positions or teams, and they had never heard of a huddle. Someone would grab the ball and run and all the others would try to tackle him or her or strip the ball away. I tried to organize the kids and teach them the fundamentals that my older brother and my coaches had taught me. As we played, I introduced them to some of the principles and language of sport—teamwork, offense, defense, in bounds and out of bounds, ball, strike, time outs, innings, huddles, pinch hitters, touchdowns, plays, and strategy. I wanted the kids to have fun, but also to learn the rules of all the games as they were played on the mainland. Eventually, when they went to high school, they would have to play under those rules. Though soccer was not yet popular in the U.S., one day I even showed them how to dribble with their feet and attempt a goal with a header—an exercise that ended when Edvina Washington shook her bruised forehead and said, "What kind of fool game is this?"

There were the predictable frustrations. When we went to pick up the OEO truck, we'd have to listen to Lance rant about pornography in the mail or drug-crazed hippies. Kids would stay for recreation some days and not others. A few silly fights, minor scrapes and bruises. And the truck, which Lance was supposed to have fixed, would break down now and then, leaving us stranded with 20 or more kids. On these days we'd pass the time by singing and playing tic-tac-toe with the kids as we walked them home.

At first it was hard to see much progress. But one day when I divided the older kids into teams—boys vs. girls—all the kids got very excited and everything seemed to click. They chose names for their teams—the girls Hawks, the boys Crows. I asked them to elect captains to lead their teams and assign their players to positions. Most important, in football, there had to be a quarterback to organize the huddle, call the plays, and tell everyone what to do.

Whether it was basketball, football, baseball, relay races, or kickball, the games became spirited and competitive. But it worried me that the girls—Edvina and Margarite Washington, Janice and Cynthia Stevens, and Sallie Ann Robinson— were bigger and stronger and more aggressive than the boys. They dominated the games, just as their mothers and grandmothers dominated Daufuskie life. The older boys, Jackie Robinson, Al Smith, and Ervin Simmons, tried hard and occasionally got close, but the girls always seemed to win. As soon as a game started, Margarite, tall, thin and a natural athlete, would cast off her shyness and become a fierce, passionate, and vocal leader of the girls. She reminded me of myself when I was her age. I would come home from a day at the park with a hoarse voice, having screamed so much during a game.

I tried to stay neutral in these epic contests between Hawks and Crows, usually serving as referee to settle disputes. But one day the boys and girls were almost tied in a basketball game and I decided to call a questionable foul on one of the girls. I wanted to give the boys a chance to win for once.

"What? Zach, why you always helpin' these pitiful boys?" Margarite shouted at me.

I didn't have a chance to answer. Everyone started yelling and calling each other names. It looked like there might be an old-fashioned brawl, in which case I didn't give the boys even a remote chance of coming out on top.

But Ed and the little kids saved the day. Hearing all the fuss, they came running over to separate the two sides with their tiny bodies. Waving their hands in the "V" of the peace sign, which Ed had taught them, they screamed, "Peace, peace, peace!"

I waved my peace sign at Margarite and silently mouthed, "Peace." Our eyes made contact, and she softened. Flashing her lovely smile, she waved her hand in the peace sign too. "Peace," she shouted, and the other girls picked up on it. Soon the boys followed, and every kid on the schoolyard was holding up both hands in the peace sign and laughing and shouting as loud as they could, "Peace, peace, peace."

18.

In the mornings before recreation started, Ed and I helped some of the older men put up fences around their vegetable gardens. Digging post holes, stretching wire, and nailing fencing to posts proved satisfying, even when I was banging my fingers with a hammer or wrestling with wire in the rain. It was hands-on and tangible, and unlike everything else we'd tried to do on Daufuskie, we could see the immediate fruits of our labor.

More important, working together brought us closer to these older men. When we'd dug Doonie's grave with Plummey and Franklin and dressed the body with Jake, we'd shared an intense experience and earned respect. Now as we built fences, we found that we'd reached a new level of trust and friendship with some of Daufuskie's men.

After we'd spent a few hours digging post holes with Coolie Grant, he invited us in for a lunch of fire-roasted scrunched squirrel prepared by his wife Alice. Coolie had always been reserved around us, never revealing much about himself. But this time, while we were talking with Alice, Coolie left the room briefly and returned with a plaque.

"Retired after 37 years working on the dredge in Savannah harbor, rain or shine, freezing or sweltering," he said. "Liked it for a while, but the last 20 years, no." He shook his head and held up the plaque. He wanted us to see it, to know he was proud of his work, but also bitter at how he'd been treated. "Thirty-seven years. This is all they gave me."

Trust worked both ways. Though shy at first, I became more willing to reveal who I was and what I really thought to the people of the island. One day I was talking to Fast Man. He said he was genuinely puzzled about the Vietnam War, which he'd been hearing a lot about on the radio. "What you think?" he said. "All these rockets, hundreds, thousand, millions troops? Jet planes, bombs, napalm. Why we can't win over there in that jungle place? Westmoreland, North Vietnam, Viet Cong, Cambodia, Russian-made tanks, Tet offensive—what it all mean?"

I'd read a lot about Vietnam, and I had spent the previous summer on a peace caravan with the American Friends Service Committee, speaking against the war and doing draft counseling. After all we'd been through, I was able to let go of fears from my childhood and no longer even cared if Fast Man or anyone else on Daufuskie thought I was a Communist or a hippie. I explained my view that the people of Vietnam were against U.S., French, or any other foreign intervention, that the government did not represent the people, that the Vietnamese never showed their true feelings when they spoke to the U.S. media or government officials, hiding their rage the way Black slaves in the U.S. did when they talked to white slaveowners.

Samuel Holmes (left) gets a palm reading from Ed Flaherty

Kickball, Crows vs. Hawks, schoolyard. Photo by Edward
Flaherty

Rather than being offended, Fast Man was fascinated. He said he'd never heard that before and wanted to talk more. But in other situations where I didn't feel as confident or comfortable, I wasn't so forthcoming. One day Ed and I visited Doonie's bereaved parents, Geneva and Richmond Wiley, to see how they were doing. Geneva was still grieving. She told us she could feel Doonie's spirit following her around, haunting her. Her facial muscles would tense when his spirit hovered over her, tormenting her. When she went to someone else's house, his spirit would follow her and knock on the door and say, "I know my mama's in there, I saw her tracks."

We excused ourselves to help Richmond with his fence. After we finished, we sat in the house with him and Geneva. Richmond, a deadpan storyteller, got onto the subject of Jews. Geneva asked if either of us was Jewish. "What's your people?" I chose not to answer. I wasn't hiding or afraid. I wanted to know what Richmond would say about Jews if none were around. He told a story I'd heard many times about a Jew, an Irishman, an Italian, and a Pole who get up a fund to pay the fare over the River Jordan for the first one to die. The Pole died first, so the Italian and the Irishman put 15 dollars each in the Pole's coffin. Then the Jew goes up to the coffin and drops in a check for 15 dollars. No one reacted, so Richmond then launched into his theory that Jews were clever at business and owned all of Savannah.

Geneva interrupted him and said, "I worked in service for Jews in Savannah, and they were very nice people, treated me real good."

I didn't say a word. And neither did Ed.

19.

The kids had lifted our spirits and renewed our sense of purpose. We took the boat to the mainland so we could meet with the school superintendent in person, explain the after-school program, and appeal for much-needed supplies and a few new balls for the kids.

After landing at Bluffton, we walked up to Gatch's office to use the phone. Normally on a weekday it was crowded with patients, but this day the waiting room was empty. We found Fredi, who hugged us and said, "There's trouble, big trouble."

There was always trouble at Gatch's, I thought. That's why we didn't want to go there.

"Last Thursday at the office Gatch was acting strange," said Fredi. "He was seeing patients, but he was obsessing on worms. He kept imagining them crawling out of patients' feet, like he was hallucinating worms everywhere."

"Sounds like a drug freakout," said Ed.

"Maybe," said Fredi. "But he'd been exhausted for weeks, sick, hadn't been eating, and the pressure on him was just too much with the sheriff's investigation and all the media coming around after his testimony to Congress. Somehow he got through the day, but that night, around one in the morning, he cracked. A complete physical and mental breakdown. Fits and spasms, total loss of control. And he was coughing up worms. They'd infested his whole body."

Over his protests, they'd rushed Gatch to the hospital in Savannah. "He told Terry the doctors wouldn't help him there," said Fredi. "We thought he was being paranoid, but he was right." For the first 12 hours, no doctor would even see him. Finally, Terry located the one doctor in the area Gatch trusted. Gatch convinced him to sign release papers from the hospital, so he could get treatment up north instead.

The Cowell women had chartered a private plane and arranged for a doctor and a bed to be waiting for him in a Washington D.C. hospital. Terry had flown up with him and was at his bedside. Gatch was feeling better, but it was unclear when or if he would return to Bluffton or practice medicine ever again.

Meanwhile, Anita, a mental and physical wreck herself, and their two young boys had flown back to England to stay with her family. The clinic was closed until further notice. And Fredi and Tree were left alone in Bluffton to deal with all the reporters who'd traveled from as far away as Australia to interview the noble Dr. Gatch, the new Albert Schweitzer.

Dr. Gatch was eventually stripped of his license to practice in South Carolina. He cleaned up his life and moved to Arizona, where he continued to treat poor patients on a Navajo Indian reservation. A few years later, he volunteered as a doctor for Catholic Relief Services, treating refugees in war-torn Cambodia. That's where he died in a car accident at the age of 49.

Overwhelmed by what had happened to Dr. Gatch, I didn't know what to say or do. But Ed remembered why we were there and phoned the Beaufort County school superintendent's office. Miraculously, he wangled an appointment for us to see the superintendent himself, H.E. "Emmett" McCracken, that afternoon.

We borrowed Gatch's car and drove to McCracken's office in Beaufort. As we waited in the hallway, I was feeling weak and a bit woozy. I told myself I was just shaken up by the news about Dr. Gatch. But by the time McCracken ushered us into his office, I was feeling increasingly nauseous.

A gray-haired man in his early 60s, McCracken loomed large from behind his desk. His skin was lined with deep wrinkles, and he wore wire glasses and a suit and tie. He talked slowly with a thick South Carolina drawl, as if his voice was coated with honey. "What can I do for you California boys?" he asked.

Ed explained our recreation program and told him that Daufuskie kids needed new balls and bats and gloves, a volleyball net, a tetherball. He added that we'd also appreciate a projector so we could show movies.

McCracken listened like a good father indulging his children, then said, "I know Daufuskie. I know the problems. I was born and raised here, lived here my whole life. But there just aren't any answers."

"Daufuskie doesn't have the most basic equipment that schools on the mainland have," said Ed. "We're not asking for much, just the same as everyone else."

"Y'know," answered the superintendent, "I can sum up the problems with the Mary Fields School in two words—Frances Jones. She's been there 39 years."

I didn't say anything. I was feeling feverish, trembling.

"Why don't we fire her?" McCracken droned on. "Well, it isn't that easy. We're trying. Got Mrs. Johnson out there now, a good principal, educated, but can't always find a good teacher to go out there to replace Frances." (Miss Jones retired a few months later in June 1969. Her replacement was Pat Conroy. His book *The Water Is Wide* recounted his experiences teaching on Daufuskie and was later made into the movie *Conrack* starring Jon Voight.)

Ed tried to steer him back to our simple request, but McCracken was a cagey, tough politician who knew how to give a couple of California hippies the run-around. "You boys got no idea how much I've done for Daufuskie over the years," he drawled. "Stealing from other schools' budgets to get turkey dinners out there on Christmas…."

I couldn't listen to another word. My throbbing head felt like it was going to burst. Feeling faint, I broke into a cold sweat. I tried to stand.

"Excuse me," I groaned, covering my mouth as I vomited, narrowly missing McCracken's desk and spewing noxious debris all over the floor of his office.

McCracken watched, speechless. As I staggered out the door, desperate to find a bathroom or trash can to throw up in again, I heard Ed laughing and saying to the old superintendent, "My friend's not feeling too good."

20.

After my brief illness, it had taken me a few days back on Daufuskie to recover. By the day of the PTA's rescheduled fundraising party I felt fine. When Doonie died, on the gloomiest, coldest night in February, the Valentine's party had been canceled. It was now several weeks later, early March, and the first whiff of spring wafted in the air. That morning we'd borrowed Frances Jones's churn and spent the afternoon helping Mrs. Bryan make ice cream. At dusk Billie Burn picked us up in the school bus, the same vehicle that had carried us in stunned silence to Doonie's rain-soaked burial a few weeks before.

Now Daufuskie was ready to leave behind the sadness and grieving of winter and let loose—at least for one night. The Cooper River community center, a vacant one-room wooden building, vibrated with excited anticipation. It had gone unused since the previous California boys taught typing there. Kids were running around, chattering, laughing, greeting each other. Older folks were setting up tables displaying the food they would be selling. Younger men cleared out the center of the room, moving chairs toward the perimeter walls. And several teenage girls were decorating the dim lights with colorful tissue paper and choosing which 45s to play on a portable phonograph.

The mood was joyous, and the evening's festivities began with a wild rush to sample the tasty delights the women had made. Virginia offered hardboiled eggs, Frances hot dogs, Bertha pig's feet, Flossie fried chicken, Sarah peanuts and candy, Billie cupcakes, Susie soft drinks, and Mrs. Bryan ice cream. Everything sold for a dollar or less, all proceeds going to the PTA. No alcohol on sale, so no one was drunk.

As everyone ate, Mrs. Bryan's high-pitched voice could be heard across the room: "Ice cream, ice cream, made in the shade, sell in the sun, if you ain't got no money you can't get none." Tinny music blasted from the record player and little kids dashed from one end of the room to the other. Ed and one of the older girls, Janice Stevens, were taking photos. Some of the men—Plummey, Franklin, and Fast Man—talked as they hauled in wood to keep the fire in the stove going. Johnny Hamilton, dressed in spiffy turquoise shirt, dark tie, white vest, and bowler hat, strutted back and forth in time to the music. Eating a bowl of ice cream, Willie Miller stepped outdoors and threw a spoonful into the night air. VISTA worker Rhea Netherton grabbed my elbow and explained, "It's just what Willie does when he's happy." Meanwhile, Rhea's husband Henry was chatting with Lance Burn and a white weekender we'd never met before. A big smile on his face, happier than I'd ever seen him, Lance walked up to me and said, "I haven't had so much fun in years."

Still wary after my stomach trouble in Beaufort, I was reluctant to eat much. But Johnny Hamilton insisted that since we'd helped him put up his garden fence, he wanted to buy me a pig's foot. I took it in my hand, but it seemed to be mostly bone. Trying to get at the meat, I succeeded only in smearing the greasy sauce all over my face. Margarite, Edvina, Janice, Sallie Ann, and several of the little kids watched this sorry spectacle and couldn't stop laughing. Finally, Margarite intervened and showed me how to eat the damn thing, a feat I've never attempted since.

And then the dancing began. Jenewese Smith turned up the volume on the record player. Aretha Franklin and Otis Redding reverberated through the room. No one waited to be asked or danced in boy-girl couples. Instead, all the kids moved to the middle of the floor, swaying and shaking, everyone dancing together, boys with boys, girls with girls, girls with boys, all mixed up in a group, or alone. I watched as the older girls and little Nora, Plummey's six-year-old granddaughter, took over the spotlight, dancing with spontaneous joy and grace.

I felt intimidated. Though my mother was a Martha Graham dancer, she'd never danced in my presence, and I'd always felt uncomfortable dancing myself. Here I was with these wonderful dancers showing off their flashy moves, and rather than joining them, I sat on the sidelines, an uptight white guy. Upset, I went outside to think. What was I afraid of? Would I embarrass myself? Would they laugh at me? They'd already done that, and it was all in good fun. Would I lose their respect? Nobody cared whether I was a good or bad dancer, or not a dancer at all. But even if they did, what did it matter? If Ed and I had learned anything on Daufuskie, it was to be ourselves and not be ashamed or afraid, no matter the situation.

I went back inside and jumped into the middle of the dancing, losing myself in the music and basking in the welcoming smiles of the kids all around me. Jenewese kept spinning disks, and we all danced until there was a break for children's games. Suddenly, from the record player came the familiar voice of Pete Seeger. Pete had been my guiding spirit since I was a young child, but I'd thought he was known only to red-diaper babies like me. To my surprise, here was his friendly recorded voice on remote Daufuskie Island, singing children's game songs, which all the kids knew. Somehow in this moment, the Communist ideal of brotherhood that I'd been raised with, of people all over the world getting together through music, became a beautiful reality. All the kids, big and small, formed a circle and followed Pete's prompts, jumping and singing and tapping their feet and nodding their heads and pointing at the moon. The older ones helping the little ones, and no one afraid or reluctant or embarrassed to play.

"All right," Sarah Grant shouted, whisking the kids off the floor. "Now the old folks are gonna dance." Eighty-one years old, spry and spunky, Sarah could still walk the road with her walking stick, and she could still dance. But none of the other old folks joined her, so she danced the Charleston all by herself.

And then Thomas Stafford dragged a chair to the center of the room and sat. He started clapping his hands and stomping his feet in a slow rhythm, moaning out a bluesy chant, and soon everyone was clapping and stomping with him. Two young boys, Alfred and Sherman, bounced out on the floor and danced solos, twisting their bodies like pretzels to the spellbinding rhythm, everyone standing in a circle around them watching and clapping.

And then the chant morphed. Everyone started singing the happy birthday song to Virginia Washington, who had just turned 76 that day. Singing, the whole crowd asked, "How old are you? How old are you?" And Virginia sang back, "I ain't sayin', I ain't sayin'," as she hopped to her feet and did a little dance by herself, everyone cheering her on and clapping.

After that, the tireless older girls—Margarite, Edvina, Janice, Cynthia, Sallie Ann, Lasceny—took over the floor and danced for the rest of the night by themselves. No one else could keep up. Around 10:30, Mrs. Bryan yelled, "All right, I fixin' to leave, get your ice cream now."

Within a half hour, the community center was cleaned up, leftover food packed, and partygoers loaded on to the school bus. It was raining, and I'm sure I wasn't the only one who thought about the last time we'd ridden in that bus in the rain for Doonie's burial. But I didn't dwell on it. Like everyone else, I felt exhausted and happy. Another Daufuskie lesson for a California boy: life goes on.

21.

The end of our time on the island was in sight. In a couple of weeks we'd be going back to California. I wasn't looking forward to it, and neither was Ed.

"Everybody's going to ask how it was, and I won't know what to say," I said.

"Just tell them it was great," he replied.

"Well, I'm sure you'll spin some wonderful stories. But how can we communicate what it's like here or what we feel about it?"

"We've been whipsawed. Every time we feel good, something happens to bring us down. Every time we feel down, something lifts us up. I don't even know how I feel any more, so how could I explain it to someone else?"

I dreaded going back to the Santa Cruz I'd left behind—all that college angst, the sophomoric philosophical discussions, the theoretical righteous politics, the academic ivory tower on a hill removed from anything real. I knew I'd changed, though I couldn't articulate exactly how. Before I'd left for Daufuskie, my father had urged me to take notes and perhaps write an article about my experiences. But that was the last thing on my mind now. That was something the old California, achievement-oriented Zach would do, not the post-Daufuskie Zach. And I knew, as Thomas Wolfe had written, you can't go home again. I couldn't envision fitting in back at Santa Cruz or in L.A. with my parents. But I couldn't imagine staying on Daufuskie either. Where was home now? Was there any place where I felt I belonged?

"I tried to write to little Annie what it was like here," said Ed. "I poured my heart out. She never answered. I guess that was just a sweet fantasy." He stopped and for a rare moment Ed seemed to allow himself to feel sadness. But then he snapped out of it. "Hey, maybe somebody back there will relate to building fences and playing sports with kids. But what we went through with Doonie or Gatch? How can anybody back in zap California begin to understand that?"

"The day after we get back, I'm supposed to go to the wedding of one of my housemates," I said. "He's marrying an Orthodox rabbi's daughter, and it's going to be an old-fashioned Hassidic wedding with seven rabbis chanting Hebrew prayers, the *huppah*, the whole bit. What would Fast Man make of that?"

"Culture shock, amigo," Ed laughed. "Brace yourself for some big-time culture shock."

Like war buddies, Ed and I, as different as we were in so many ways, had shared experiences that we were sure no one else could ever understand. But we both knew how much Daufuskie had changed us.

Over the next five decades, Ed and I lived far apart. After graduating from UCSC, Ed went to film school in London, lived for a while in Libya and Iran, ended up starting his own film production company based in Paris, where he lived with his Russian wife and two children. Alienated from American society, he never again called the U.S. home. As a freelance cinematographer and director, he traveled all over the world, a wanderer's way of life he'd been born into as an Air Force brat.

But no matter how far our lives diverged over the years, our Daufuskie experience bound us together as dear friends for the rest of our lives.

22.

For a few weeks, Ed had been gently reminding Mrs. Bryan that a good way to make sure the sacred music that meant so much to her would be passed along to the younger generation was to record the songs. She loved this idea, but with her soprano voice not what it used to be, she was reluctant to sing on tape by herself. She wanted Lillian Stafford, her favorite young alto from the church choir she'd directed, to sing with her. Lillian had been away at high school on the mainland, but finally, a week before we were to leave, she came home for the weekend. We scheduled a recording session for a Saturday afternoon, and Mrs. Bryan invited a few others from the old choir to join us in her living room.

It was a windy March day. Preparing that morning, Mrs. Bryan was nervous as she always was in anticipation of guests. About two in the afternoon, Sarah Grant arrived and hung her walking stick on a chair. A little while later Lillian showed up, accompanied by Susie Smith and Flossie Washington. They'd walked all the way from Cooper River.

Everyone crowded into the living room, and Ed pulled out his cassette tape recorder. For an hour and a half, Mrs. Bryan, Lillian, and Sarah, backed up by Susie and Flossie, sang their most cherished spirituals, including "Amazing Grace," "New Burying Ground," and "I'll Fly Away," which Sarah had started to sing at Doonie's wake. The recording ended with Lillian's pure voice soaring above everyone else's in an inspired version of "Nobody But You, Lord" that seemed to come straight from her heart: "You put shoes on my feet, Lord, nobody but you. When I was in trouble, you pulled me through, nobody but you, Lord, nobody but you."

Afterwards, we all dug in to Mrs. Bryan's fried chicken backs, Willie Miller wandered in to share a piece of cake and homemade ice cream, Susie put some records on, and everyone was having a good old time, cuttin' the fool. Mrs. Bryan was so jolly she got up and started dancing on her bum legs, chattering about her dream of going to California. Ed was taking photos. As he leaned back to get a shot of the whole group, he bumped into the window curtains and they came tumbling down on his head, rod and all. Everyone burst into uproarious laughter, a fitting conclusion to a special afternoon.

But unnoticed in the confusion, Mrs. Bryan's laughter had turned into a hacking coughing fit. That night at dinner, after the others had left, Mrs. Bryan was exhausted and irritable. I said the prayer we began each meal with. And then Ed began to talk, recalling the highlights of the day.

Suddenly, Mrs. Bryan cut him off. "None of your stories now, Ed. You gonna make me laugh, and then I gonna start to coughin' and then I can't eat, can't swallow nothin'."

Ed started to answer, but Mrs. Bryan stopped him. "No, Ed, no more stories. You a lyin' child, professor liar, and you stubborn as a mule. Ed, you got to learn to be still and listen."

Taken aback, Ed said nothing. But Mrs. Bryan wasn't finished. She turned to me. "And you, Zach, you always got your hands in your pockets. You got to take your hands outta them pockets and do something. You like a snake in the grass. Hiding, sly, sneaky, holding back. Nobody know what you thinking or who you are."

I was stunned, and so was Ed. We both felt confused and guilty that somehow we'd caused Mrs. Bryan to suffer. Mrs. Bryan said she wasn't

Viola Bryan (right) and Sarah Grant singing in Mrs. Bryan's living room. Photo by Edward Flaherty

feeling right, excused herself, and retired to her room. Ed and I finished our dinner and cleaned up in silence.

Mrs. Bryan was perceptive and wise, and she understood people. It wasn't until many years later when I was in therapy that I realized just how insightful she'd been about both Ed and me. Ed had grown up a military brat, always moving from place to place, making new friends among strangers with his charm and his gift of gab, never pausing to really listen to those around him or even to his own innermost voice. I had grown up during the blacklist and had unconsciously adjusted to the fear all around me by hiding my true self, never fully committing to action or relationships outside of my safe family, metaphorically standing alone in silence on the sidelines with my hands in my pockets.

But Mrs. Bryan was wrong about one thing. She said a doctor in Savannah had told her she couldn't eat or swallow because she had a bad case of nerves. And she believed her nervousness was caused by Ed's stories and our bad manners at meals. No doubt we did aggravate her sometimes in ways we weren't aware of. But she learned later, months after we'd left the island, that her inability to eat or swallow was caused not by us, but by cancer, a tumor on her esophagus that was diagnosed too late to be treated. She died later that summer, age 62, and was buried in a Black cemetery in Savannah.

The next morning Mrs. Bryan was feeling better. We joked and laughed at breakfast as if nothing had happened, and she seemed back to her old self. If anything, our nightly conversations became deeper and more personal. Mostly, Mrs. Bryan talked and we just listened as her voice was so much older, wiser, and more experienced.

Dr. Gatch had told us that we'd know people trusted us when they started talking about sex. One night Mrs. Bryan told us that marriage didn't mean a thing if you wanted someone. Passion, she said, causes people to get angry enough to kill. She admitted that she had once pulled a gun on her husband Robert and was ready to kill him, but her conscience stopped her. Now as a widow, she was content to have occasional visits from an admirer. She confided that Plummey had been her boyfriend for years, but that they had occasional tiffs because she felt he was too stingy. Slipping a woman some money now and then, she said, was a sign of affection.

One night she told us how she got religion. After a particularly difficult time, she was seeking God through prayer, but for many months her prayers went unanswered. And then, when she least expected it, Jesus appeared to her in a dream. And kept appearing in dream after dream. "Once you find Jesus, He doesn't leave you," she explained. She was sure that despite her sins, Jesus had forgiven her and after she died, she would go to heaven. "As I see it, it'll be clean and bright, have lots of lights," she said.

I thought it might be risky, but I felt close enough to her to admit honestly that I didn't believe in God. I had nothing against faith, in fact I'd love to have it, I told her, but I just didn't have it. That upset her.

"I'm worried about you, Zach. If you don't believe, you could be condemned to hell," she told me. "But inside you're a good fella, and I believe one day you're gonna find faith."

23.

Our last couple of weeks on the island it felt like we were coasting in to the finish. We'd worked hard to earn the trust of Daufuskie's people, both adults and kids, and now we were relaxing and enjoying each other.

Two days before we were to leave, we helped publish Daufuskie's very own newspaper. For weeks we'd talked to Mrs. Johnson and Miss Jones about starting a newspaper with the kids, and finally they'd agreed to try it. We asked the kids to write whatever they wanted—a poem, a scary story, a dream, a joke. When they turned in what they'd written, guided by their teachers, it wasn't what we'd expected.

One of the articles, written by eighth-grader Janice Stevens, welcomed readers and provided a brief description of Daufuskie's geography. Another simply copied section one of the 15th Amendment, the right of suffrage—the result of Mrs. Johnson's assignment to eighth-graders to copy parts of the Constitution and memorize the Preamble in order to graduate. To lighten things up, Margarite Washington added a joke about her older sister, headlined "Edvina Washington Discovers George Washington." It read: "Edvina: George Washington was President in 1492. Margarite: No, Edvina, Columbus discovered America in 1492. George became President in 1789. Edvina: Oh! Am I 297 years late?"

A few of the older girls stayed after school to help us edit, design, and type up the articles. Ed doodled silly illustrations of animals that we inserted on the pages. As we began to duplicate the paper on a ditto machine, it became clear that the girls had something else on their minds. One of the older high school students, Lasceny Stafford, had just returned from Florida and had been telling them about life as a teenager on the mainland. All the girls were bursting with excitement, yearning to tell us what they'd learned from Lasceny, and yet too embarrassed and shy to come out with their newfound knowledge in front of the California boys.

Finally, Edvina said, "She told us all about la-la," and all the girls screamed. "La-la," continued Edvina, "is another word for love." At the word "love," they all started chattering among themselves, excited and innocent and eager.

"And love is another word for sex," said Ed, as they all shouted and pushed and pulled on each other.

"Stop now, Ed, you not supposed to say that," said Janice.

"Why not?" said Ed as we ran off copies of the paper. "It's natural."

The loud screams and laughter drowned out the clickety-clack of the ditto machine. The kids hadn't had this much fun since the Valentine's party.

"Lasceny said it's the most popular thing in the world," said Margarite. "Everybody does it."

"Well, not everybody," said Ed. "But it's true, a lot of people do it."

And with that, Ed held up the finished pages of Daufuskie Island's very own newspaper. "Voila!" he said. "That's French for la-la." They all screamed and laughed, and he added, "Not really. C'mon, let's staple this baby so we can hand it out to everyone tomorrow."

We'd hoped the paper would be a project that the next California boys would keep going. But it turned out to be the first and only edition.

On March 19, our last full day on Daufuskie, the sun sparkled in a clear deep blue sky, offering a warm welcome to spring. Blossoms popped out on the trees, bright pink and white and yellow. We drove around the island in the OEO car with the Nethertons to say our goodbyes. Though we'd been there only 10 weeks, everyone seemed genuinely sorry to see us go. We thanked them for their generosity and hospitality, for taking such good care of us. They hugged us, thanked us, and wished us well.

In early afternoon, a tether ball and a movie projector from the school superintendent arrived on the boat from Bluffton. Apparently the messy scene I'd created at McCracken's office had made an impression. After school, we set up the tether ball and taught the kids how to play. And for the culmination of the recreation program, we had one final kickball game between the Hawks and the Crows. For the first time, without any help from Ed or me, the boys' team won, 10 to 6. The boys celebrated their victory with high-fives. The girls were furious.

"Now, c'mon, girls," I said. "This is our last day here, and we don't want to leave with you mad at us."

"We ain't mad at you, Zach," said Margarite, flashing the peace sign. She looked over at her team, and the rest of the girls followed her lead, flashing the peace sign too.

For the last time, we drove the kids home in the OEO truck, dropping them off one by one. When we stopped at Margarite's house, she gave me a quick hug. "Thanks for all you done for us," she said. "Write me a letter from California?"

"If you promise to write me back."

"Promise," she said as she jumped off the flatbed of the truck.

It wasn't until we hugged the last child goodbye, little Nora Simmons, Plummey's granddaughter, that I felt overwhelmed by sadness. My eyes moistened, but I was too drained to cry.

We brought the truck back to Lance's house and then took a final walk out to the empty beach on the Atlantic side. We watched the pink-and-orange sunset in silence.

The last morning Mrs. Bryan, Ed, and I were all quiet at breakfast, trying to appear cheerful. Lance, looking chipper, arrived early to drive us to the boat. He couldn't wait to get us off that island. He'd told Mrs. Bryan we were the worst California boys yet—which we considered a compliment.

We loaded our bags on to the truck. Then we turned to Mrs. Bryan, standing alone in front of the house. For 10 weeks she'd been everything to us—mother, caretaker, confidant, counselor, therapist, friend. I hugged her, and I understood what Dr. Gatch had meant when he talked about the importance of arms around. All the feelings welling up in me were in that warm embrace of Mrs. Bryan's—the strength and the love and the sadness of parting.

From the truck, we waved one final goodbye, and Mrs. Bryan waved back, a big radiant grin spreading across her face. As the truck rumbled off, Ed and I laughed, a Daufuskie laugh of joy and sorrow. I was exhausted, but my heart was full of love for this island and its people. I had never felt so alive.

Me picking coffee, San José coffee farm, 1984. Photo by Janet Essley

REPORT FROM NICARAGUA'S COFFEE FIELDS

In 1984, the Reagan Administration's *contra* war against Nicaragua's Sandinista government had reached its peak. Most of Nicaragua's able-bodied men had been mobilized in the army, leaving a shortage of hands to pick the coffee and cotton crops. When the Sandinistas put out a call for support, I volunteered for an international harvest brigade and picked coffee for a month in the mountains near Matagalpa. This report was originally published in *The Nation* magazine on February 9, 1985.

IN THE EARLY MORNING THE COFFEE FIELDS of northern Nicaragua are a picture of tranquility. Dark green trees, three to eight feet high, stretch in endless rows up steep rocky mountains, down ravines, through dense foliage. Clusters of bright red coffee beans hang from the branches, merry as holly in the pale sunlight. All is still and quiet.

The calm is illusory. The coffee fields are a battleground, one of the primary targets of the U.S.-backed *contras* in their three-year terrorist war against the Sandinista government. Coffee, which brought in $150 million in export revenues last year, is Nicaragua's principal source of foreign exchange. A small harvest would have disastrous consequences for the country's economy. It is no coincidence, therefore, that in 1984 the *contras* destroyed 80 state-owned and a dozen private coffee farms in the provinces of Matagalpa and Jinotega, where 75 percent of the crop is grown. They also killed 400 peasant leaders in that region, kidnapped an equal number and threatened many others in an effort to scare *campesinos* away from the fields.

The realities of the war have not been reported in this country. Most American journalists are based in Managua, away from the fighting, and have focused on other issues—opposition leader Arturo Cruz's role in the elections, press censorship, draft resistance, shortages, grumblings about Sandinista inefficiency. What they have failed to convey to American readers is the single most important fact about Nicaragua today: it is engaged in a full-scale war.

In 1981 there were fewer than 1,500 *contras*. Now, with the help of $73 million in authorized U.S. aid (and much more in covert and private aid) they have grown into a well-equipped force of 10,000 to 15,000 guerrillas. In the last three years, nearly 8,000 Nicaraguans have died in the war against the *contras*. At least as many more have been wounded or kidnapped or are missing, and an estimated 120,000 have been displaced from their homes. For a tiny country of 3 million, those figures are staggering. If the United States had had the same proportion of its population killed in the Vietnam War, the number of dead would have been about 400,000. And although Congress cut off official funds for the *contras* in June, unofficial funding has increased and Nicaragua's casualties continue to mount—3,000 dead in the last year, more than 300 of whom were children under 12.

Because the war is being fought mostly in the northern part of the country and consists largely of scattered acts of terrorism by the *contras*, reporters and visitors rarely witness the violence. But in Matagalpa province, where I worked in the coffee harvest last December with 16 other North Americans, its scars are everywhere. At a party welcoming us to one farm, a *campesino* broke down and wept as he described how the *contras* had killed his brother 15 days earlier, while he was planting trees in a reforestation program. Such stories are not uncommon. More often, though, the effects of the war are revealed in less dramatic ways. There are severe shortages of many basic items—medicine, water, shoes, toothpaste, toilet paper, school supplies, batteries, gasoline, spare parts. There is wreckage too. Altogether, the *contras* have caused $250 million in damage, destroying health- and day-care centers, schools, farms and other property.

To deal with the urgency of the war, in January 1984 the Sandinistas began conscripting men age 16 through 22, depleting the labor force available for the coffee harvest. In November, following the U.S.-manufactured MIG scare, the government decided that the 20,000 students in Managua who were to have picked the crop would remain in the capital in case of an American invasion. It then issued a call for volunteers, and 60 men and women from 17 countries in Western Europe, Latin America and North America responded by joining the Maurice Bishop international harvest brigade. Ranging in age from 12 to 74, we were the first of thousands of *"brigadistas,"* including 500 more from the United States, who have gone to Nicaragua to pick coffee and cotton this winter. Our brigade, sponsored by UNAG, the national union of farmers and ranchers, worked at two farms, San José and La Lima, located in a relatively secure area of the war zone, just north of the city of Matagalpa.

Nestled in a verdant, sprawling valley surrounded by rugged mountains rising to 3,000 feet, San José was taken over by the state in 1979, after its owner, a general in Somoza's National Guard, fled to Miami. Before the *contra* war, 75 permanent residents lived in the tiny wooden shacks scattered along winding dirt roads. By December, however, 23 young men from the farm were serving in the army, and the 300 migrant laborers who usually help with the harvest had been transferred farther north to pick in the more dangerous border areas. The only people available to harvest San José's crop were women, schoolchildren on winter break, our brigade and a skeleton crew of experienced men. Because of the shortage of pickers, the farm's production quota had been greatly reduced to 1,000 quintals (about 10,000 pounds) of export-grade coffee beans. Three years ago, San José's workers harvested 1,700 quintals.

Aware that their efforts were directly linked to the economic survival of the country, the *campesinos* worked exceedingly hard—and so did the *brigadistas.* We rose before dawn and were in the fields by 6 a.m. On clear days the work was slow and tedious but not difficult. Passing over the young green beans, we plucked the ripe red *"rojitos"* from the branches one by one. The reds, the highest quality beans, are processed and exported, bringing in $140 per quintal. We also picked the dead or diseased black beans, charitably described to me by one *campesino* as "very aromatic." They are separated out and used locally.

We wore baskets tied around our waists, filling them with beans, then emptying them into white 100-pound sacks. Again and again we went through this process, carrying the sacks from row to row. Our backs ached, our hands grew raw from insect bites and when it rained, which it often did, the steep hillsides were turned to mud and we frequently slipped and fell. The monotony of the day's work was broken only by a

The Harriet Tubman Brigade, with our Nicaraguan leader, front row, third from left.

Nicaraguan coffee pickers and *brigadistas* on a break, guarded by soldier with rifle, San José farm. Photo by Janet Essley

lunch of rice, beans and tortillas and by the songs and chants of many lands that echoed through the valley. At 3 or 4 o'clock, the toot of a cow's horn sounded in the distance, telling us it was time to quit and weigh in. The results were invariably and laughably the same: the Nicaraguans would each fill about a sack a day; the inexperienced international volunteers, less than half that.

Because the *contras* were an omnipresent threat, we always returned to our quarters before dark. Wherever we went, we were accompanied by armed militia. One who guarded us in the fields was a 64-year-old man with dark, leathery skin and a stubble of gray beard. Every day he sat at the end of a row, hunched in concentration over a notebook, his AK-47 automatic rifle slung on his shoulder. Sometimes he would join me and talk. He said that when Somoza was in power, two of his children had died before the age of five from diarrhea and malnutrition. Since the revolution, he had learned to read and write in the adult education program at San José. With a proud grin, he showed me his careful, elegant signature: "Tomás Rugama Zelaya, Nicaraguense."

At night, we occasionally heard gunfire and saw red tracers arching like fireworks through the black sky. Still, the protected setting made us feel remote from physical danger, until one day the news crackled over the shortwave radio that a volunteer brigade of 21 Telcor (telephone and postal) workers on their way to pick coffee had been ambushed north of Estelí. The *contras* had blown up their bus with mortar fire, hacked the few survivors to death with machetes and set their bodies on fire.

That night our brigade joined hands with the people of San José and sang a hymn for the murdered workers. The memorial service was held in San José's wooden one-room schoolhouse, which is named for a local hero, Salvador González, a teacher whose framed photograph hangs on the wall. In three years, he taught all but five of the previously illiterate residents of San José to read and write. Like the Telcor workers, Salvador González was killed by the *contras*. When he died, on January 19, 1984, he was 22 years old. He left two small daughters, who are now counted among the approximately 500 war orphans in the region.

San José is a productive and well-run farm, but it is underdeveloped and its people are struggling to survive. Most homes have neither electricity nor running water, many children go without shoes, and the basic diet consists of rice, beans, and tortillas. Despite those hardships, the *campesinos* I talked to were proud of what they had achieved since the revolution and were ready to defend it.

"Under Somoza we were slaves," said Isabel Espinoza, 44, an intense man with bushy sideburns and long brown hair bristling out from under his Lee work cap. "The bosses used hunger to force us to continue working. All we had to eat was beans, no rice. If you cut an orange off a tree, you were beaten and fined. We worked from dawn till dusk every day, no vacations, for six cordobas a day [about 60 cents at the 1978 exchange rate], and that was for the best picker. If you picked less, you were paid less. Women were paid three cordobas. Our children died of starvation and disease; we were all illiterate and we lived in terror of the National Guard. If you thought of complaining to Somoza, well, you might as well have thought about the gallows first."

Today, according to Espinoza, everyone at San José eats three full meals a day and all the fruit they can pick. Malnutrition, once so prevalent, has been wiped out, as have polio and diphtheria. The government provides the farm with free medicine and a full-time nurse; all who wanted to, have learned to read and write; and the workers, organized in their own union, participate in decision-making about production. As a result of their protests last spring, base pay was raised to 42 cordobas a day (about $1.50 at the present exchange rate) for men, women and children and will go up to 62 cordobas after this harvest. They work eight hours a day, six days a week, with Sundays off. Each worker gets 15 days' paid vacation every six months. Pregnant women receive three months' paid maternity leave, and old workers retire with full pay and benefits. Next year a free day-care center will open, and there are plans to give every family materials to build their own houses and a plot of land and seeds so they can plant their own vegetable gardens.

"Why shouldn't we love our revolution?" Espinoza asked me after reciting this litany. "We have a great amount. This is what we are fighting for. We want peace, but tell Reagan that he'll have to kill us all before we'll give up what we've won."

Because the Sandinistas consider the coffee harvest an integral part of the war effort, it extends beyond the individual farm. When the workers of San José had finished the first picking of their fields, they moved to La Lima, about 19 miles north, and our brigade went with them. Unlike San José, La Lima is disorganized and poor, even by Nicaraguan standards.

Local farmers drying coffee beans, San José farm. Photo by
Janet Essley

The state purchased the farm less than a year ago from a private owner who had neglected it. Our housing facilities were in bad repair. We slept two to a hard wooden bunk in quarters that did not have lights, running water or, for the first four days, latrines.

At a meeting of the local union, which we attended, La Lima's production secretary reported that the farm's harvest situation was critical. About 75 percent of the beans had ripened, and the farm didn't have enough hands to pick them. This was not La Lima's problem alone, he explained. Nearly 35,000 young men from the region were in the army, and all the farms of Matagalpa and Jinotega faced a serious labor shortage. Unless La Lima increased its production immediately, he stressed, a large portion of the valuable red beans would be lost. The workers talked among themselves and then voted unanimously to adopt two measures proposed by the union leaders: to work on Sundays and to begin picking at the first light of dawn. Their sacrifice would not go unrewarded. Pay would increase proportionately for the longer hours, and everyone would get double time for Sundays.

As our skills improved and good weather provided more time for picking, our sacks grew heavier. Workers from neighboring farms joined us, and the days passed quickly. But one afternoon near the end of our stay I looked out at the endless rows of red spreading before me, and I understood for the first time just how shorthanded the war has left Nicaragua. Work as hard as we might, we would never come close to doing it all. About half of those juicy red beans were destined to turn black on the branches or shrivel and fall to the ground.

The Sandinista government had hoped to export 1.4 million quintals of coffee beans this winter, but by late December it was apparent that the harvest would fall far short of that. Until the final figures are in, nobody will know the full economic impact, but the loss of foreign exchange will undoubtedly cause more shortages. The government, already forced to spend 40 percent of the national budget on defense, will have to postpone or abandon worthwhile projects—new schools, health clinics, housing, day-care centers. The transportation system will continue to deteriorate.

Americans easily forget that many of those problems, big and small, are the direct result of the *contra* war. Just how easily, I realized on the day we left La Lima for home. The farm's truck dropped us in the city of Matagalpa, where another truck was to have met us. But it was nowhere

Kids in living quarters, San José farm. Photo by Janet Essley

to be found. For eight hours we waited as UNAG officials searched for some means of transportation to get us back to Managua. Bored and irritated, some of us complained, just as Nicaraguans do, about the bumbling Sandinista bureaucracy.

When a truck finally arrived, we heard the explanation for the delay. That morning the *contras* had burned down seven private haciendas and one coffee storage plant to the north, near Yalí. As a last reminder of the pervasiveness of the war conceived and financed by our own government, the truck scheduled for us had been commandeered to help transport the eight dead and seven wounded.

Photo collage by Simi Nallaseth

Nyoko

This is a meditation on my 25-year friendship with Nyoko, a beautiful, brilliant, complex Japanese-American woman whose parents had been imprisoned in an internment camp during World War II. That shameful episode in United States history had a tragic ripple effect on Nyoko and her entire family. Ann Nyoko Osaki is not her actual name. I have used this pseudonym and changed other names to protect the privacy of her family.

EVERY JULY 22ND FOR THE LAST 29 YEARS, I've taken a drive west on Peekamoose Road in New York State's Catskill Mountains toward Buttermilk Falls. The road climbs through pine-covered mountains past an icy crystalline pool called the Blue Hole. Just beyond a one-lane bridge it levels out and runs alongside a finger-shaped pond toward an old house with slate roof, gables, and stained-glass windows.

I always look forward to this drive, but I don't pause at any of these picture-postcard spots. I go straight to the caretaker's quarters behind the storybook house and sit down in front of a fenced-off area with an abandoned shelter for a dozen or so dogs.

In the late 1980s and early 1990s, the caretakers here bred springer spaniels. And it was here, with the springers, that I remember Nyoko at her happiest. Ann Nyoko Osaki and I were friends for 27 years, but it wasn't till the last five that I really started to know her. From 1988 to 1993, on nearly every Memorial Day, July 4, and Labor Day weekend, she left behind her job as a Federal Communications Commission lawyer in Washington D.C. and stayed with me and my life partner Sarah in our home in Olivebridge, not far from the aging-hippie refuge of Woodstock.

On each of Nyoko's visits the highlight was our ritualistic drive up Peekamoose to see the newborn springer spaniels. Nyoko would get down on her knees and a dozen yelping puppies would rush to her, jumping all over each other in a mad scramble, licking her face, cuddling her, their joyous excitement tingling in the air. Nyoko would gather as many of them in her arms as she could, laughing, her face beaming, her long black hair shining in the sun.

She never wanted to leave. And when it was time to go home, we always lingered as Nyoko weighed the pros and cons of adopting one or two puppies. She loved them. But it was hard transporting a puppy on the train to Washington. And she didn't want to cause more problems for Felix, an abused stray black cat she'd taken in, who didn't get along with dogs. She came very close, but in the end she always went home alone.

Every July 22 since 1993, I drive to that fenced-in area behind the caretaker's quarters. I contemplate the empty, lifeless shelter, and I feel a sadness descend over me. And every year I wonder the same thing: if she had just taken one of those puppies, might things have turned out differently?

One of a handful of Asian-Americans in an all-Jewish high school, Nyoko was 15, nearly two years younger than I, when we met in 1965. The counterculture, Black Power, Haight-Ashbury, anti-Vietnam War protests, and the women's liberation movement were all in their infancy. Relations between men and women were entering unknown, confusing territory.

I was a senior in high school in Los Angeles. Nyoko had skipped a year and was only a semester behind me. Her scrawny, undeveloped body and flawless skin made her look pre-adolescent. I had no idea then that she would later mature into a breathtakingly beautiful woman.

At the time, I was going out with a tall, thin, dark-haired poet named Kathy whose favorite outfit was olive army fatigues and combat boots. Unlike generations of high school seniors before us, we didn't date. We hung out, often with groups of friends. Annie Osaki—everyone called her Annie in those days—was Kathy's best friend, one of five girls who palled around together. Kathy and Annie were straight-A students, but they cut school a lot. They'd go over to Melrose Avenue, smoke dope, and eat Abba Zabbas and navel oranges.

When I saw Kathy, Annie always seemed to be there. I remember her sitting cross-legged on Kathy's bedroom floor, chain-smoking cigarettes, her back straight as a tree trunk, her oval face impassive. Kathy chattered and moved around a lot, punctuating her words with animated gestures, but Annie almost never spoke. She sat. She observed. And I had no idea what was going on in her head. Even on expeditions to the Santa Monica pier or the Griffith Park observatory, even when Kathy and I were groping each other, Annie sat in the back seat and smoked, her face blank.

I didn't have a separate friendship with her then, but I learned a few facts. She was born in L.A.'s Boyle Heights to Japanese-American parents who migrated to a Jewish neighborhood when she and her older brother were still very young. They lived in a large two-story Spanish-style house not far from our high school. Her father wanted his children to grow up with Jews, who valued education as much as he did. We jokingly referred to Annie as an honorary Jew.

A cinderblock wall surrounded the Osaki house, and a palm tree shielded it from the sun. Inside, I remember a living room cluttered with antique furniture—her father's obsession—and a piano on which Annie played classical pieces with her elegant bird-boned fingers. In the kitchen, her elderly grandmother, who lived with them and spoke only Japanese, always seemed to be cooking fragrant pots of rice or vegetables.

Annie's room was upstairs. It had a padlock on the door that she opened with her own key—another of Annie's eccentricities. Like the little-girl outfits she'd wear—tights, Boy Scout shirt, roller skates and pigtails. Like her use of the powerful stimulant Benzedrine. Her father was a doctor, we reasoned, and she took samples from his office to help her study late into the night. Yes, we were aware she often fell asleep in class and wore heavy eyeliner to cover the circles under her eyes, but somehow we didn't connect the dots.

In high school, I thought I knew my friends and that they knew me. But we all put up façades. I kept secret from my friends the most important factors shaping my life—that my parents had been Communists and my father, a writer, had been blacklisted from the movie industry during the McCarthy era. I knew that one of my best friends, Alan, was a child of Holocaust survivors. But I had no clue what this meant to Alan because we never discussed it. And I remember a brief mention in history class of the Japanese internment camps in California during

World War II, but Annie never talked about them. I didn't know then that her grandparents and parents had spent much of the war in those camps.

Annie rarely expressed emotion. I don't recall her crying or even laughing. I can still see her face staring into space, devoid of feeling. This was not a cultivated look of sophistication, like a supermodel. She was numb, and I didn't realize it.

I did know that Annie spent two or three nights a week sleeping over at Kathy's. On the nights she wasn't at Kathy's, she spent much of her time hanging out at an all-night hot dog stand or the nearby 24-hour laundromat. I found that amusing and wrote it off as more Annie weirdness. I never asked why.

In the late 1960s, the University of California at Santa Cruz was, as Max Rafferty, California's Superintendent of Public Instruction, called it, "a cross between a hippie pad and a brothel." From my point of view, as a freshman, it was a thrilling place—a rigorous academic environment set amid redwood trees, a place where authority was questioned by smart people, a center of countercultural experimentation, all accompanied by new albums from the Beatles, Otis Redding, and Jefferson Airplane.

I often took long walks on campus in meadows where cattle roamed. One April afternoon in 1967 I came up on a bluff overlooking Monterey Bay and suddenly, heading toward me, there she was. "Little Nyo," I shouted. Annie smiled at the term of endearment that only Kathy used, ran towards me, and gave me a big hug. I was stunned.

"What are you doing here?" I asked.

"New student. Just enrolled today."

"But it's spring quarter, how could you …?"

"Graduated in February, couldn't wait to get out of L.A. They said they had a bed open in the trailers. Cool, eh?"

I hadn't seen her in nearly a year. She'd grown up. Her hair spilled down almost to her waist. She wore sunglasses and a tie-dyed shift that couldn't hide the curves her body had developed. Most striking was how happy, open, and expressive she seemed.

I'd changed, too, in Santa Cruz. My hair was long, and I had a full beard. I'd overcome some of the fear I'd grown up with during the blacklist years and, despite my parents' reservations, had gotten involved with the anti-war movement. I'd taken readily to the campus's communal lifestyle, which I saw as a modern-day evolution of my parents' Marxist dreams. But one thing I'd steered clear of was drugs. I considered them an apolitical hippie indulgence. And they scared me. I might get busted. Worse yet, I might lose control of my mind and my rational western view of reality.

Annie, an experienced drug user, pushed me to try marijuana. I resisted. So one night she baked me weed-laced brownies and shamed me into eating them. I lay down on a couch. "I don't feel anything," I said, settling back to listen to a recording of a little-known blues singer named Champion Jack Dupree.

When I stumbled into the kitchen and dug into a carton of melting chocolate ice cream with my bare hands, Annie laughed––something she was doing more and more of since she'd left L.A. "Z-man, you're stoned," she said. "Have another brownie."

I never got into the drug culture. Annie used more than I did, but she'd given up speed in favor of psychedelics and was flourishing at school. It was a small campus, and here again, she was one of a handful of Asians in white-bread land. She wore quirky colorful outfits and floppy hats and radiated a confident vitality that was impossible to ignore. When occasionally she wore a silk kimono to dinner, no one could take their eyes off her. She had her pick of all the men swarming around, and she went through her share of them, never sticking with anyone in particular. Those making unwanted advances got the silent impassive face she'd perfected in high school.

I felt the same attraction everyone else did, and at one point in my sophomore year I tried flirting with her. Kathy wasn't an issue—she'd gone to another college and had written me letters about her sexual adventures with her new boyfriend. So one night Annie and I got stoned, and I sat down next to her on the floor. I put my arms around her shoulders and awkwardly tried to kiss her, but she turned away. She sat in silence, cross-legged, and smoked. I wondered why she didn't respond, but I was shy, inexperienced, and too proud to push it.

In the tumultuous year 1968––Vietnam War protests, King and Bobby Kennedy assassinations, Chicago Democratic convention––Annie decided to take time off from school. With two of her high school friends she went to Paris, which was in revolt, and lived in a commune with some exiled American draft resisters and French hippies.

I had been on a field study on Daufuskie Island, South Carolina—a rural community of dirt-poor, Gullah-speaking Black people cut off from mainstream 20th century America. For the first time I'd left my sheltered bubble and found a world of struggle and suffering. I'd had my first experience with death—helped bury a man, dressed his putrefying body, dug his grave. I'd begun growing up.

Upon returning to Santa Cruz, I felt alienated, unable to fit into the college life that had been so exciting before. I spent the summer hitchhiking alone cross country with a backpack and a sleeping bag. In the fall, I moved into a sprawling communal ranch house on Branciforte Drive with Ed, the friend who'd been on Daufuskie with me, and six other students. Gradually, as I entered my senior year, I reintegrated into the strange student society that was Santa Cruz in 1969.

Annie returned from France that winter and moved into a vacant room at the Branciforte house. I slept in a small cabin in back. During this year, I got to know Annie better. She was delightful, bubbling with life, hip, part Annie Hall dressing in crazy outfits, part traditional Japanese, part L.A. flash, part scholar, part artist, part mystic—an exquisite enigma. She spent a lot of time reading, drawing, throwing the I Ching, interpreting Tarot cards, and dropping acid. On her nights to cook, she spent hours shopping and crafting sashimi dinners. One night when Ed ordered in pizza on his night to cook, a furious Annie roller-skated up to him in her tights and Boy Scout shirt and threw the whole pie in his face.

Around this time I heard about a book called *Farewell to Manzanar* being written by Jeanne Wakatsuki Houston and her husband James Houston, a professor at the university. It was about the experience of one family in a Japanese internment camp. For the first time I asked Annie what had happened to her family in World War II. She told me that although they were American citizens, they were treated like the enemy. Her grandfather, a prominent columnist for a Japanese-American newspaper and an outspoken supporter of the U.S. war effort against Japan, was among the first to be sent to an internment camp at Tule Lake, California. The rest of his family, including Annie's father, then a 29-year-old doctor, went with him. They were forced to sell their house in Boyle Heights and all their possessions at a fraction of their value. Her uncle lost his farm the same way. Annie's mother, then 20 years old, and her entire family were sent to the camp at Manzanar. They also lost their home and possessions.

After nearly three years in confinement, with the war over, they returned to Los Angeles to try to rebuild their shattered lives. Annie's father and mother met there and soon got married. Her father began a medical practice from nothing, and her mother worked in his office, while raising their children.

To an outsider, the Osaki family appeared to be an American success story. But one night over a bottle of wine, Annie finally revealed at least part of what she'd been escaping when she slept at Kathy's or the laundromat during our high school years. Her parents never talked about what had happened at the camps. But she was convinced that the humiliation and degradation they suffered had damaged them and taken a terrible toll on the whole family. When she was still young, her parents' marriage disintegrated. They couldn't afford to separate. So they continued to live under the same roof, occupying different parts of the house, not speaking to each other.

Her mother was distracted and remote. She'd grown up in poverty during the Depression and, constantly worried about money, pushed her children to professional careers to assure their security. Her father, highly respected in the Japanese-American community, was a perfectionist. He demanded a level of achievement that he hoped would help his children overcome the racism they were bound to encounter in America. For the children, the equation was simple. If they got straight A's, they were loved. If they got anything less, love was withheld.

Her father's expectations were highest for Michael, Annie's brilliant older brother. Michael wanted to follow his father into medicine, but the emotional stress of living in a divided family caused his school grades to drop. A sensitive teenager, Michael seemed unable to defend himself against his father.

Annie had always adored and looked up to Michael. "I couldn't bear to see him hurt," she said. A sexual and cultural radical, she had already stood up to her father many times. Now she further defied him, protecting and hiding Michael in a closet to distract her father, taking the brunt of his anger upon herself.

Michael never made it to medical school. He became a biochemistry researcher and escaped into competitive badminton, becoming a nationally ranked master-class player. The one Annie spoke of with special affection was her grandmother. Though Annie knew only a few words of Japanese, she became the primary caregiver for her bed-ridden grandmother during the last months of her life. When her grandmother died, Annie felt more alone than ever. That's when she left for Santa Cruz.

I didn't know how to react to Annie's story. I muttered something innocuous about all families having problems. And then it hit me. Although not nearly as traumatic or violent as what the Osakis had suffered, the stigma my own family had endured as "dirty reds" during the blacklist had some similarities.

"Did I ever tell you about the time when I was nine and these two guys in suits and hats came to the front door of our house?" I asked. Annie shook her head. "FBI agents. My father told me not to answer, and then I watched him take his shoes off and sneak out the back door. I was terrified. After they left, I went out to the backyard and found my father cowering in some bamboo behind my little playhouse."

"Why would he leave you like that?" she asked.

"He was afraid he'd be subpoenaed."

I explained that in the early 1950s the House Un-American Activities Committee had conducted a witch hunt, calling witnesses and compiling a list of subversives in the movie industry. My father, along with hundreds of others, was named. Those blacklisted could not find work. Some of my father's closest friends had turned informer, naming others so they could clear their own names. But my father and many others refused. Some had moved to Mexico or Europe to find work. My parents chose to stay in L.A. My father wrote novels. My mother taught modern dance. And we got by. All of us, my older sister and brother and I, learned to do with less.

But the blacklist, like the internment camps, had taken a psychic toll on the family. My father had lost his nerve. He retreated, rarely leaving the house, avoiding the possibility he might run into an informer, not answering the door. My mother was worn down by both running the household and working to pay the bills. An atmosphere of fear and distrust pervaded the house, affecting our relationships outside the family, our decisions, and our actions.

That night I tried to explain all this to Annie. It came out in a jumble, but she nodded and said, "I see." On some level, we were kindred spirits, sharing the mindset of the stigmatized, isolated outsider.

But there was a fundamental difference between us. My family had pulled together during the blacklist, embracing a circle-the-wagons mentality, us against the world. Annie's family, living out their own legacy of internment, had imploded and fragmented. "Everyone on their own," Annie seethed, slicing the air with a karate chop.

That ended the conversation. We each went back to our own room alone.

Though she brought home a number of lovers that year, there was something different about Kenneth. A philosophy student/carpenter, he was regaling all of us at the Branciforte house with stories one night, and Annie said, "I dig your numbers."

"Numbers are infinite and universal," he replied.

That did it. He became Annie's first serious long-term lover.

Annie was temperamental and elusive. Kenneth spent many nights with me trying to sort out what was going on. I just listened. I'd had little experience with women. I'd built a wall of distrust and fear around myself that prevented me from getting involved in a lasting relationship with anyone. Not unlike my father, I'd retreated to my little cabin.

I didn't know if I'd ever find a soul mate. But part of me felt Annie might be the closest I would ever come. Some day, after she'd run through all the others, I would still be there, and two lonely souls, offspring of stigmatized families, would find refuge in each other. This fantasy, which occasionally recurred in later years, was all in my head. Annie was content with our friendship as it was. In me she'd found someone safe, who knew where she'd come from, who would be there for her, unencumbered by messy sexual or emotional involvement.

Kenneth went to Europe for a couple of months early in 1970, and Annie couldn't bear being alone. She held out for a couple of weeks, but then got involved with Kenneth's best friend, a political organizer with intense dark eyes. When Kenneth returned in the spring, the soap opera reached a climax. The friend was banished, and Kenneth and Annie tried to patch things up.

Annie was unsure about the relationship and wanted some clue about what the future might bring. At a Renaissance Faire on campus in late April, a white-haired art history professor who claimed to be a witch was reading palms in a tent. I had no use for such hocus-pocus, but Annie persuaded me to go along with her. The witch read my palm and declared, "You will have an exalted emotional life—in middle age." Not exactly what a lonely 20-year-old wanted to hear. Annie asked for a Tarot card reading. She turned over several cards and then drew one depicting a prostrate figure lying under a black sky with several swords piercing his body. The witch stared at the card, looked up at Annie with a worried expression, and refused to go on with the reading. Annie emerged from the tent shaken and terrified.

The next day, on April 30, 1970, Richard Nixon announced that United States forces had crossed over from Vietnam and invaded Cambodia. We had scheduled an open-house party for May Day, and it was too late to call it off. Hundreds of students and hippies showed up at the Branciforte house, and the partying extended late into the night.

A long-haired mountain man said he wanted to thank me for hosting the party and handed me a capsule. I showed it to Ed, who assured me it was mescaline and would last only a few hours. I took it, and my private nightmare began. I saw a tall skinny guy waving a big knife and another smaller guy rushing away with blood dripping from his hands. Panicky, I went to a bathroom to calm down. There in the shower I discovered Annie, face down and passed out. Her fully clothed body was blocking the drain, the water was running, and the pool on the floor was rising toward her breathing passages. Convinced that she was trying to kill herself, I dragged her onto a bed.

She slept through the night and was okay the next day. She insisted she'd just felt sick and, trying to revive herself with a shower, had simply passed out from too much booze and dope.

I believed her, but I was a freaked-out mess. Whatever else that capsule had in it, there must have been a lot of speed. I hallucinated for only one night, but I didn't sleep for three. Hyped up and scared, I ran miles and miles in a vain attempt to knock myself out, and clung to Annie and Ed, neither of whom could help much.

I was seeking some semblance of normalcy, but everything was in turmoil. Six friends, evicted from their house, were crashing on the floor at the Branciforte house, bringing our already chaotic mini-commune to 13 people. The Cambodian invasion had ignited protests across the nation. On May 4, the National Guard killed four student protesters at Kent State in Ohio. Ten days later two student demonstrators were killed and several wounded at Jackson State in Mississippi. Our campus, along with many others, went on strike, and I spent most of the month trying to regain my equilibrium.

In mid-June, I graduated. Annie and another housemate, Dave, helped me load up a car with my belongings, and we drove down to L.A. I dumped my stuff in my parents' house, and that night Annie and Dave and I went over to a favorite local folk music club, the Ash Grove.

A multi-racial band was playing timeless, swinging rhythm and blues to a packed house. Eddie "Cleanhead" Vinson let loose on a soaring alto sax solo, and the music seeped into my soul. Dave was pounding out the rhythm on the table with his hands. Annie turned to me, placed her hand on my arm, and gave me a big smile. I didn't have any idea what I was going to do with my life, but for the first time in many weeks I was able to relax.

Over the next couple of years I traveled and worked various jobs, from teaching junior high English in South Carolina to salmon fishing in Alaska. In 1972 I came back to Santa Cruz. With a couple of friends, I rented an apartment a short walk from where Annie lived.

Annie had never left. She'd graduated, spent a miserable summer as a skee-ball barker on the boardwalk, then got a job as a secretary at the university. Kenneth and she lived in the rear half of a vine-covered duplex near the center of town. This may have been the calmest, most stable period of her life. She was drug-free. They got an Airedale puppy she named Momo—"peach" in Japanese. She was taking art classes at the university and joined a group of Asian-American students who met regularly to discuss racial and ethnic issues. More and more she was identifying with her Japanese heritage. She kept a photo of her grandmother in a special place by her bedside. And she made it clear that she no longer wanted to be called Annie. She preferred her middle name, Nyoko. It was not only an assertion of identity but also a political statement set against the backdrop of the deepening horror of the Vietnam War.

When Kenneth got into architecture school, they went to Berkeley to rent an apartment together. The real estate agent stared at Nyoko, then turned to Kenneth and said, "Going to move in with a little Suzuki, eh?" Nyoko bolted from the office, swearing like a sailor at the agent and Kenneth too. Not long after that, they split up.

Nyoko stayed in the same house in Santa Cruz, and soon fell in love with Daw, a gifted art student from Thailand, who moved in. They grew a lush garden in the backyard and painted and drew together every day. They both painted oils, mostly abstract, but Nyoko also did meticulous still-lifes, portraits, pencil drawings, and tie-dyes on silk fabric. I remember her standing out in her backyard in a white paint-spattered smock, dabbing left-handed at a canvas on an easel, her eyes focused in concentration.

She became a regular with the old Italian fishermen down at the pier, baiting her hook and casting out her line into the chilly waters of Monterey Bay. If she got lucky and reeled in a red snapper, my roommates and I would join her and Daw for dinner. We'd pick blackberries from the garden, and together bake a pie for dessert.

The early '70s were a golden age in Santa Cruz. The university had brought people with energy and ideas to the fading resort town. A viable counterculture had flourished, and development had not yet ruined the natural environment. It was a community with an idealistic vision fired by liberated sexual energy, expanded by drugged consciousness, driven by rage at the way things were, inspired by the generous bounty of nature. It was process over product—co-ops, communal houses, organic food, alternative schools and media, grassroots politics, hitching and bicycling, rainbow colors, dancing in the streets.

The culmination of all this came in January 1973, when the community mounted a counter-inaugural parade as an antidote to the beginning of Nixon's second term as President. Sitting around, depressed by the prospect of more Nixon and more war, a few friends and I dreamed up a scripted scenario for a street-theater parade down the town's main street, Pacific Avenue, on January 20. We put out a call, and hundreds of people from the community spontaneously joined in to make it happen. There were masked Nixon and Kissinger impersonators on stilts, live bands, coffins and mock burials, papier-maché floats. Nyoko and Daw worked hard building a float called "Death Rides a Pig," featuring a scythe-wielding grim reaper on the back of a pink pig holding an American flag. Thousands of people lined Pacific Avenue to cheer and join in the parade, our statement that rather than accepting Nixonian America's reality, we would create our own. It was a heady day, and Nyoko, like all the rest of us, seemed genuinely thrilled.

But in the months that followed, as Watergate broke wide open and the nation plunged into crisis, Santa Cruz also headed into a period of disillusionment. That winter two mass murderers operating separately, both local boys, began bloody rampages. Among the victims was a tiny Nisei woman friend of Nyoko's who had helped assemble Death Rides a Pig. When her beheaded remains were discovered on the beach near Natural Bridges one foggy morning, Nyoko broke into tears.

We all huddled behind locked doors as rain pounded the empty streets and the body count mounted. In six months there were 21 murders and 10 rapes. This was a dark side of America that Santa Cruz's counterculture could not escape—drug addiction, suicides, black-magic cults, violence in the streets, the destructive pall of the war that had hung like a curse over everyone for ten brutal years.

Later that year, inspired by Woodward and Bernstein, I left Santa Cruz for graduate school in journalism at New York's Columbia University. I was never again to live in the same place as Nyoko. She and Daw spent a year in Thailand with his family. Unable to speak or understand Thai, she spent a lot of time reading. Her letters to me reflected her loneliness.

By the time they returned from Thailand, Nyoko had suffered through several bouts of depression, and her relationship with Daw had become an emotional roller coaster. In Santa Cruz, they lived as poor artists, painting large oil canvases that didn't sell. Daw found work in a local cannery, but Nyoko, feeling pressure from her high-achieving family, was ashamed to go back to secretarial work or even to pursue studies in art, which wasn't considered a serious profession. Her brother had eventually gone back to graduate school and completed his Ph.D. in biochemistry. Nyoko, the rebel of the family, felt she had deeply disappointed her parents. She was also frightened by the insecurity and lack of structure inherent in an artist's life. So she decided to apply to law school. Though her beauty and eccentricity often made people overlook it, she had a brilliant analytical mind. The elite Boalt Law School at UC Berkeley accepted her, and she left Santa Cruz, the counterculture, the artist's life, and Daw for good.

In the late 1970s, after graduating from law school, Nyoko moved to Washington D.C. It was near the end of the Carter presidency. She took a job as a staff attorney at the Federal Communications Commission, writing complex briefs, regulations, and policy papers. The new media—cable, fiber optics, internet—were in their infancy and the big media conglomerates were pushing for deregulation. But it wasn't the challenge of the job that had brought her there. She'd come to Washington for love.

She'd followed a classmate from Boalt, a younger man who worked as a Justice Department lawyer during the day and played electric guitar at night. They made the move from Berkeley to D.C. and lived together for a few years in a small apartment. They weren't going to get rich as government lawyers, but it was the kind of stable, comfortable life she'd yearned for. Nearing 30, Nyoko hoped for marriage and children, a life that would at last earn her parents' approval. In the past, she had always been the one to end her relationships with men. This time, he ended it, claiming he wasn't ready to settle down.

So there she was, heartsick and alone again, this time in Reagan-Bush-era Washington. For a beautiful young Japanese-American woman with an artist's soul and a communal past that she held dear, it was not a nurturing place to call home. She lapsed into a deep depression and sought help from a psychiatrist who prescribed a cocktail of anti-depressant and tranquilizing drugs. The effect, numbness reminiscent of her high school years, enabled her to work and get through the days. She bought a lovely co-op apartment across the street from the National Zoo, and she rescued a fierce black kitten from the streets. She named him Felix.

During these years I didn't see Nyoko much. I was busy in New York, editing *The Nation* magazine and then books about the CIA for a small publisher, Sheridan Square Press. I'd fallen in love with a Cuban exile named María. With a personality that resembled her favorite flower, the *flamboyan*, María managed to break through the walls of distrust I'd built around myself. But the relationship ended shortly after my mother died of a brain tumor.

I went to therapy and dated various women, but I kept thinking about Nyoko, about that time she'd visited me at my parents' house in L.A. after my mother's brain surgery. I was helping to care for my mother as she underwent radiation treatments. Unlike many of my friends, Nyoko had seen illness up-close when she'd nursed her dying grandmother. It didn't faze her that my mother had lost all her hair. Nyoko fashioned a stylish turban from one of her own textile prints and gently placed it on my mother's head. The turban covered her baldness and restored both her beauty and her dignity. The sensitivity and selflessness of Nyoko's gesture had stuck with me. And once again I fantasized that some day she and I would get together for good.

In reality, all through the '80s, I saw her only a few times in Washington when we'd meet to march for peace in Central America or for a nuclear freeze. More often she'd come to New York for a weekend of museum and gallery-hopping.

She talked about changing her life, selling her apartment and moving to New York where there were lots of artists and Asians, or back to California where it was sunny and she blended in better. But she felt trapped. Her job provided steady income and health insurance that paid her psychiatrist's bills. She'd become dependent on the anti-depressant drugs he prescribed, and she was afraid to stop taking them. Several times I tried to persuade her that there were plenty of jobs for lawyers in New York and plenty of shrinks too. She always perked up for a moment, imagining what a new life might be like. But then her face would go blank, and the possibility vanished.

One autumn an admirer gave her tickets to the finals of the U.S. Open tennis championships. I'd played competitive tennis in high school, so she invited me to go with her. We sat together in box seats and watched a masterful performance by 19-year-old Pete Sampras, winning his first U.S. Open over Andre Agassi.

Nyoko's spirits were high as we left Flushing Meadow. But her mood darkened when we got to Penn Station at the end of that weekend. Amid all the people coming and going, we couldn't find the right platform for the Metroliner back to Washington. Nyoko looked over at a line of straight, conservative men in expensive suits and ties. "That's it," she said sadly. "That's Washington."

She was going back to a city where she felt alienated and starved for love. No matter where she went, there were always men in her life. But she looked at that line about to board the Washington bullet train, and she sensed at some profound level exactly how most of those successful young men saw her. To them, she was an exotic Asian, possibly the most exquisite woman they'd ever laid eyes on, maybe a toy for a night, maybe a mistress for a while longer. But she was convinced that she was not the one they would marry, not the one they wanted as the mother of their children. She knew that wasn't how an ambitious young white man got ahead in Washington in the 1980s.

At the end of 1984, when I was 36, I volunteered to pick coffee with an international harvest brigade in war-torn Nicaragua. When I returned home, I got involved with Nicaragua Exchange, the committee that organized the brigades. One of the main organizers was a dark-haired flutist named Sarah, who lived a block and a half from me on the Upper West Side of New York. One night I saw her playing with her Andean-classical music group. Her lovely face radiated openness and warmth. Her playing and the music she'd composed had an elegant simplicity. I knew immediately that the witch's prophecy——that I would have an exalted emotional life in middle age——was going to come true. Sarah was the one. It took some coaxing and patience, but eventually Sarah came around.

Over the next few years, my life underwent major changes. I moved into Sarah's apartment, and we began a life together that has now lasted 37 years. I got sick with a lingering, mysterious illness called Chronic Fatigue Immune Dysfunction Syndrome. I was incapacitated, forced to leave my editing and proofreading jobs. To her credit, Sarah stuck with me as I gave up on western doctors and turned to alternative healers who changed my diet, my habits, and my view of the world. Realizing that I needed nature, fresh air, and quiet to get healthy, Sarah and I bought a house in Olivebridge, 100 miles north of New York City.

My father wasn't as lucky when he got sick. He was alone, my mother having died nine years earlier. In May 1988, he died of heart failure. Sarah and I spent a good portion of that summer in L.A. with my brother and sister, cleaning out the old cluttered house on Fuller Avenue we'd grown up in.

One day, after hours of sorting through books and papers, we went over to the neighborhood public pool for a swim. And there she was, in a black tank bathing suit—Nyoko! She'd come to L.A. to visit her parents and was going back to D.C. the next day. We went over to Canter's on Fairfax and had blintzes and potato pancakes for dinner. She was gracious and fun, as striking as ever. When she pulled me aside to tell me how beautiful she thought Sarah was, I knew she was genuinely happy that I'd finally found love. My romantic fantasies about Nyoko ended at that moment. And our friendship became closer than it had ever been.

"We'll be back in Olivebridge in a couple of weeks," I said. "Why don't you come up and spend Labor Day weekend with us?"

Nyoko laughed and wiggled like an excited little girl.

That Labor Day 1988 was the first of many such holiday weekends we shared over the next five years. Often we were joined by Jeff, our mutual friend from high school, and by other friends from Santa Cruz. We swam, we hiked, and we always made our ritual journey to see the springer spaniel puppies.

We cooked all our meals together and ate them at our big round dining room table with the lazy Susan, my favorite heirloom from my parents' house. After dinner, we'd sit on the front porch. I'd pull out my guitar and we'd sing folk songs Jeff's mother had taught me when I was a kid. Bessie, our cocker spaniel, usually sat cuddling with Nyoko. They'd adored each other ever since Bessie found Nyoko's lacy white bra one day and brought it downstairs to nuzzle. Before going to bed, we'd lie in the backyard, gazing up at the Milky Way and hoping for a fireball to streak across the sky.

Those lazy summer days were a refuge for Nyoko, a reminder of the communal life we'd shared in Santa Cruz. She didn't have to carry around a big bag hiding a nine-inch pair of scissors as she did in Washington. When I first saw those scissors, I was puzzled and asked her about them. Without a trace of emotion, she told me she'd once been raped, and if it ever happened again, the culprit would get them in his back. She was dead serious. It was a side of her I'd never seen before.

In Olivebridge, Nyoko didn't talk much about her life in Washington. But occasionally, on the front porch, our conversations turned personal.

"The right man, the elusive right man," she sighed late one night. "I meet lawyers mostly—some are nice, but straight, conservative. They don't have a clue who I am."

"What about an Asian guy?"

"Tried some Japanese guys. I freak them out. They want a traditional wife."

"Daw was Asian. He didn't want that," I pointed out.

"I still have a self-portrait of Daw. I thought he was my soul mate."
She paused. "But he wasn't."

I'd spent most of my adult life alone, so I understood Nyoko's
dilemma. But I figured she wasn't unique. Most of my friends were in
and out of relationships, divorced, or living alone. Nyoko seemed to be
just another casualty of the sexual revolution.

Not until I visited her in Washington in the summer of 1991 did I
start to recognize the depth of her desperation. As soon as I walked in
the door, I knew something was seriously wrong. The apartment was
austere in a way that seemed unlike Nyoko, the walls bare. No sign of her
flashy outfits, no Boy Scout shirts. With the exception of a full bookcase
and a haunting pen-and-ink sketch she'd done of her grandmother in the
last painful stages of cancer, there seemed to be nothing of Nyoko in the
place. Though she'd been living there for years, she was missing.

She had developed techniques that helped her survive Washington.
In winter, when she suffered from seasonal affective disorder, she wore
a visor with a light on it. For exercise, she swam regularly, roller-skated
and took walks in the zoo across the street. For sex, she had men pretty
much whenever she wanted them. For company, she had Felix, who tore
around the apartment, clawing furniture and biting her.

To fight the depression, she took four or five medications every day.
Her psychiatrist had prescribed them, she explained as she opened up
her pill chest. They helped her maintain enough equilibrium so that she
could work. Her boss had been understanding and assigned her to low-
stress jobs. It was a civil service position, and if she could still show up,
she would not be fired.

Looking at the pill chest, I finally got it: Nyoko was a drug addict.
A legal drug addict, using drugs prescribed by a licensed doctor, but an
addict nonetheless.

A few weeks later, when she came up to Olivebridge for Labor Day
weekend, I confronted her.

"You've been going to the same psychiatrist for nine years," I said.
"Do you ever talk about your problems?"

She hesitated. "Sometimes. Dating, relationships. Stuff like that."

"You know, I went to therapy for six years. We talked a lot about
my family history—my behavior patterns, where they came from, how to
change them. Do you ever do that?"

She shook her head. "Mostly we adjust the drugs and dosages."

"Nyoko, I think it's time for you to change therapists."

She seemed unfazed. "Yes, a couple of friends have told me I should find someone who understands me better. A woman. Maybe an Asian woman."

"Yes. And maybe someone who will get you off drugs and deal with the underlying problems. Because what you've been doing isn't working."

"You don't understand."

She was right. I didn't understand. I gave her the name of a psychiatrist in Washington, a student of the Sikh naturopath who'd helped me with my chronic fatigue syndrome. A couple of weeks later she called him. He told her he used a naturopathic approach and he would see her only if she'd stop taking psychiatric drugs. Nyoko never made an appointment. Nor did she look for a female or an Asian psychiatrist.

In early 1992, I had a relapse of my illness and was limited in my activities. I was concerned about Nyoko, but I couldn't travel to Washington to see her. When she came to Olivebridge that summer, she was in bad shape—lethargic, slurring her words, staggering when she walked.

The over-medication had an unexpected side effect. Late one night on the front porch Nyoko confided to Sarah and me that for many years she'd been living with a dark secret, a source of shame. There had been abuse in her home when she was growing up, she said, and for years she'd lived in constant fear. Her father, she explained, was an angry and violent man. He'd wanted to be an architect, but became a doctor to please his own father. Unhappy at work and in his marriage, he took out his frustrations on his children, abusing them both emotionally and physically. "Once I locked myself in my room to avoid him," she told us. "He started yelling, demanding I open the door. When I refused, he broke the door down and beat me again and again."

Part of me wanted to believe she was so drugged she was imagining things. But I knew the truth, or at least part of it, was finally emerging—a truth that explained the padlock on her door years before and perhaps the need for all the mind-numbing drugs she'd taken since.

The next day we drove up Peekamoose Road, and Nyoko seemed renewed, more energetic. She laughed with the springer puppies. She even picked one out and was about to take him home. But at the last minute she decided it was impractical.

When we said goodbye, I urged her to find a new shrink, quit the drugs, and deal with the issues from her childhood stone-cold sober. She didn't say anything. I gave her a big hug. That was the last time I ever saw her.

Over the next few months I talked to her on the phone occasionally and traded information with friends who'd seen her or talked to her. One said Nyoko had begun reading books on death and the after-life. She told him that she'd gone to Florida with the intention of swimming out to sea and never returning. She'd actually swum out beyond the breakers, but the exercise had so invigorated her that she decided to swim back to shore. Another said that one day she called him from her office at the FCC. She had a knife in her hand and said she was going to kill herself. But talking seemed to calm her, and by the time she hung up, she'd done no harm.

Several of her closest friends from the Santa Cruz counterculture days discussed the possibility of doing an intervention to get her off drugs, maybe even bring her to California. But in the end, scattered and disorganized, we did nothing.

I can't say I was surprised when one morning in the spring of 1993 I got a call from my high school girlfriend Kathy. Nyoko had taken an overdose of pills, but fortunately a friend had discovered her in time.

I called Nyoko in her hospital room. She sounded okay and said she was under observation in the psychiatric ward. There were group therapy sessions every day, and the psychiatrists wanted her to go into a detox unit. I encouraged her. "So much to live for, so many people who love you." Blah, blah, blah. Words that sounded empty even to me. Nyoko replied in an even voice I'll never forget.

"I'm going to do it again. I know how to do it now."

"Nyoko, go to detox," I pleaded. "You'll get into a program, start fresh."

"No. I'm going home."

"You can't be alone. Is anyone with you?"

"My mother came from L.A. They'll release me if she takes responsibility."

"Okay," I said. "As long as she stays with you."

A few days after Nyoko got home, Kathy talked to her on the phone. She sounded better. She told Kathy that sometimes this terrible incomprehensible thing came over her, like a black wave rolling in. She could see it coming, feel it taking over her body, and the depression would hit her so hard she couldn't bear it. The psychiatrist told her it was a chemical imbalance and all he could do when she felt like this was to hospitalize her.

"I want to live," she told Kathy.

Her mother was still there, shopping and cooking for her. Kathy invited Nyoko to visit her in Connecticut in two weeks, and Nyoko said she'd love to.

When another friend, Tim, talked to her, her mood had changed. The only thing that really mattered was love, she told Tim. And she'd given up hope that anyone would ever love her for who she was. Everyone saw her as a symbol or an object—lawyer, exotic Asian, hip artist, sexy temptress. They saw what they wanted to see. But nobody saw who she really was. And worst of all, it had reached the point where she herself couldn't see who she really was. Her job was in jeopardy as her mental faculties slipped away, and she had been treated with electro-shock, which further impaired her ability to function. Time was running out for her to have a baby. And her youthful beauty, the thing she'd always counted on to attract men, was beginning to fade. If there was no hope of love, she said, there was nothing to live for.

I tried to call several times, but got a constant busy signal. A couple of nights later, long after I'd gone to sleep, the phone rang. Dreaded sound. In a sleepy daze, I answered. It was a friend of Nyoko's from Washington. Nyoko had been stable for a while, he said. But she must have had a plan. She assured everyone she'd be okay on her own and insisted her mother return to L.A. On July 22, 1993, when she was alone, Nyoko placed a plastic bag over her nose and mouth and held it with all the strength and will she had left. Within a few minutes, she suffocated to death. She was 43.

A few of her friends arranged a memorial service in Washington. Several hundred people showed up to celebrate Nyoko's life. Kathy went and told me it had comforted her to see how many good friends Nyoko had and how deeply loved she was. Peter, an artist friend from Santa Cruz, was working in San Francisco with runaway street kids on a mosaic-tile mural for a BART-Muni station, a project that Nyoko had wanted to get involved with. In memory of Nyoko, Peter and a couple of her law school friends set up a fund to help the kids finish the mural. It's there today, at the Powell Street station, with Nyoko's name on it in a place of honor.

I was still sick and couldn't deal with the stress of it, so I didn't go to the memorial gathering. That was a big mistake. I sent a contribution to the mural project, but I grieved alone. And I've been haunted by Nyoko's death ever since. The clichés—she's out of her pain, she's at peace now—have never helped. It's hard to find anything redeeming in her suicide. I've been angry at the injustice of it, angry at her illness, angry at her. I've despaired. I've wept for her and for my own loss.

Someone once asked my mother what her philosophy of life was. She said: "People are important." I would add that plants, animals, earth, oceans, stars are important too. We're all connected. What each of us does—or doesn't do—matters beyond ourselves.

Suicide is an individual act that affects many people. But is the individual alone responsible? I ask myself, if our modern American society weren't so impersonal, or if Japanese traditions weren't so strict, or if the counterculture hadn't disappeared, would it have made a difference for Nyoko? What if there had been no internment camps? What if our health care system treated depression in a more holistic way? If Nyoko's friends or family had done more, would she still be alive? Maybe. Maybe not.

All I know is that when Nyoko died, a piece of me died with her. The innocent piece that believed things work out in the end, that there is justice, that we create our own destiny, that peace and love will prevail, that our generation would change the world. That's why I go up Peekamoose Road every July 22nd and sit in front of that abandoned dog shelter. I'm looking for something long lost.

Sometimes for a brief moment I can see Nyoko. She's young, vibrant, exquisite, wearing jeans and combat boots and a Boy Scout shirt. She approaches the shelter and gets down on her knees. A dozen yelping springer spaniel puppies rush to her, jumping all over each other in a mad scramble, licking her face, cuddling her, their joyous excitement tingling in the air. Nyoko gathers as many of them in her arms as she can, laughing, her face beaming. Her long black hair glistens in the sun.

In those moments, Nyoko still lives, I am young again, and everything is possible.

Ellen Ray (left), Bill Schaap, and Bambu, Occupy Wall Street, 2011

BILL AND ELLEN VS. THE CIA

The most satisfying and joyous years of my career were spent editing books about the CIA for Bill Schaap and Ellen Ray, publishers of Sheridan Square Press. Little did I know that they would one day ask me to edit former New Orleans District Attorney Jim Garrison's book about the Kennedy assassination—or that Ellen's chance meeting in a Havana hotel elevator would lead me to collaborate with Oliver Stone on the screenplay of one of the most controversial movies ever made.

THE FIRST TIME I MET BILL SCHAAP AND ELLEN RAY I was hooked. It was the fall of 1981, and I was attending the American Writers Congress at the Roosevelt Hotel in New York. Victor Navasky, editor of *The Nation* magazine, had organized the Congress to bring together progressive writers to fight the sharp rightward turn the country had taken with the recent election of President Ronald Reagan.

I was 33 and had been a magazine editor and freelance writer in New York for seven years, but I'd been so busy trying to establish myself in a mainstream career that I'd never had time or opportunity to connect with other progressive journalists. This was exactly the kind of community I had been yearning for.

There was another more personal and romantic reason I'd been looking forward to the Congress. My father, a Communist playwright in the 1930s when social protest drama was considered a weapon in a broader revolutionary struggle, had been one of the featured speakers at the first League of American Writers Congress 46 years before. In a strange way I was hoping that this renewal would be a sort of homecoming for me—a journey back to my roots, to a place where I belonged.

The first couple of days I felt lost and overwhelmed. I knew only a handful of the couple of thousand in attendance, and my left-wing credentials were scanty. I'd graduated from Columbia Journalism School and taught there as an adjunct. I'd edited *Juris Doctor*, a magazine for young lawyers. And I was proofreading part-time at *Time* and *Life* magazines to pay the rent. Hardly a resume that would interest anyone in the progressive journalistic community.

On the last day of the Congress, I was about to leave, disappointed and lonely, when I spotted Robert Friedman, former editor of *More* magazine, sitting in the bar. When I was editor of *Juris Doctor*, I had asked Robert to write a cover story on notorious Republican powerbroker Roy Cohn. The litigious former counsel to Senator Joseph McCarthy and mentor to Donald Trump had threatened to sue us, so I'd gotten to know Robert as we jousted with Cohn over a couple of months.

I waved to Robert, and he invited me to have a drink. At his table were a dashing pair in their early 40s, whom Robert introduced. Ellen Ray, energetic, outgoing and warm, was talking pretty loud and drinking pretty hard. Dressed in an elegant silk scarf and pants suit she had bought for a song at an Upper East Side thrift shop, she was tall and lanky, with a long, thin face and a mane of flaming red hair. Her partner, Bill Schaap, had dark hair and a thick mustache, and was dressed conservatively in a sports jacket and tie. He was drinking pretty hard too, and like William Powell in the movie *The Thin Man*, he was witty, easygoing and had an aura of unflappable, calm confidence about him, as if he could handle anything that came up.

I hadn't met either of them, but a few years before, Bill and I had corresponded and he had written a cover story on military law for *Juris Doctor*. From his writing, I knew that Bill had a brilliant mind. He had been both a lawyer and the editor of the *Military Law Reporter*. But I had no idea that his real passion was a Washington-based magazine called *Covert Action Information Bulletin,* which he co-founded, edited, researched, and wrote along with Ellen and Louis Wolf.

I'd never heard of it, so Bill and Ellen explained that their mission was to expose the nefarious activities of the CIA, including covert assassinations, destabilization, overthrowing of governments, and disinformation. *Covert Action Information Bulletin* had a small but fervent following, and had appeared every couple of months for the last three years.

But Bill and Ellen were sick of Washington—"a company town where everyone thinks you can make the sun rise in the West if you know the right congressional aide," said Bill. So they had recently moved back to New York City. They said they would continue to publish *Covert Action* as a quarterly, but they also planned to start a small publishing house specializing in books about the CIA.

I asked how they knew Robert Friedman. Bill laughed and said, "We were arrested together."

"Bill," Ellen said, frustration in her voice. "You need to tell the whole story."

"Yes, dear." He turned to me and whispered, "The two most important words for making a marriage work."

"Well, it was 1970, and Bill and I had just gotten together," said Ellen, "and I got arrested for shoplifting at Lord & Taylor. Bill was my lawyer and he got them to let me go. I said to Bill, 'It's time for *you* to get busted. I can't have a boyfriend who's never been arrested.'"

So they went to Washington to protest the Vietnam War. They met up with Ellen's friends Paula Weinstein and Louise Yellen, and with them was Robert Friedman. Each of them carried a small tape recorder to the Capitol building where Congress was in session. They stationed themselves at different spots. At a given signal, they all played their tapes, and the sounds of bombs echoed all through the Rotunda.

Bill interrupted: "And Ellen starts yelling, 'This is the sound of bombs that are dropped every day by U.S. warplanes on poor Vietnamese peasants.' And in less than thirty seconds we were all arrested. They hauled us to a huge prison in the basement of the Capitol, and then they took Robert and me to a cell in Virginia. We're sitting there, and I say to Robert, 'It's disorderly conduct, nothing much can happen to us.' But the other inmates overheard and figured out I was a lawyer. This big Black guy comes over and says, 'I got a problem. Me and my best buddy were having this argument and it got a little heated and I grabbed this 2x4 and I whupped him upside the head and the sonofabitch went and died on me. And they had the nerve to call that murder. What should I do?' I said, 'First thing, keep your mouth shut. Never mind about the whupped upside the head part…' So Robert and I spent the rest of the night giving legal advice to the inmates."

"And while that was happening to them," said Ellen, "Paula and Louise and I were driven to a D.C. jail. They made us take showers and put on these flimsy gowns. The matron tried to scare us. 'They're gonna love this, you're gonna get raped.' We held hands and went inside. There were hundreds of poor Black women, mostly prostitutes. They saw us, and they started cheering and clapping. 'Right on, sisters,' they said. 'We been watching your protests on TV.' They were wonderful, and we spent the entire night talking non-stop."

"The next day," said Bill, "the judge pointed at me and Robert and said, 'Bring up the Philadelphia Garden Society. Which one is the lawyer?' Clearly he wasn't used to this kind of criminal in his courtroom. Gave us a $25 fine, and we left."

That night at the Roosevelt Hotel bar, we drank more, and Bill and Ellen told more stories. I listened and kept wondering, who are these people? I knew leftists. I'd grown up in the McCarthy era in Hollywood, and my father was blacklisted. I remembered the FBI agents spying on our house, my parents' warnings never to talk to anyone about their politics, dear friends suddenly disappearing to Mexico or Europe, fear in the air. Virtually all my parents' friends were blacklisted too—an extended family of 1930s radicals and Communists, my surrogate aunts and uncles. But like my frightened parents, none of them were still active in politics.

Bill and Ellen were different. Progressive political people who didn't seem to be wed to any ideology, who had a sense of humor, who liked to drink and laugh and have fun while doing their work. Leftists who hadn't given up on their youthful ideals, who didn't hide their views, who weren't afraid to walk right into the halls of Congress and confront the power of the federal government. To me, they were irresistible. And though I didn't know it yet, I had finally found what I'd been looking for at the Writers Congress.

A few weeks later, Bill called. He and Ellen had an eye-opening manuscript by a former CIA agent and wanted to publish it, but it needed heavy editing and they were too busy with their other projects to do it themselves. They couldn't pay much. Was I interested? You bet I was.

The manuscript was a memoir by Ralph Mc Gehee, who had worked for 25 years as a case officer for the CIA in Thailand, Indonesia, and Vietnam and also at CIA headquarters in Langley, Virginia. He had recently retired and wanted to tell the truth about his experiences and his gradual disillusionment with the Agency—in particular about how intelligence was falsified to fit policy handed down from Washington. The chapters about Vietnam were jaw-dropping—CIA officers dreaming up body counts to make it seem like the U.S. was winning the war, creating phony horror stories about the Viet Cong to stir up anti-Communist fervor, and lying under oath to Congress to continue to receive funding.

I agreed to work with Ralph on rewriting the book as a personal odyssey so it would be more accessible to readers. I was paid as a freelance editor—$15 per hour. Bill and Ellen lived near Washington Square in the Village and wanted that to be the name of the new publishing house, but it was already taken. So they settled on the next square to the west—and Sheridan Square Press was born.

Ralph was a quiet, hulking man. He'd played tackle on a legendary undefeated Notre Dame football team and had been recruited by the CIA straight out of college. "The Agency targeted Catholic schools like Notre Dame," he told me, "because it wanted agents who fit their ideal profile—obedient and loyal to authority."

Ralph was not a natural or experienced writer, but he was smart, a hard worker and a dogged researcher. We worked on the manuscript for more than a year before it was ready. But there was a big problem. As all CIA agents must, Ralph had signed a secrecy agreement that required him to submit anything he was going to publish for prior approval by the Agency. When he submitted the final manuscript, the Agency wanted to censor large portions of it—397 deletions in all. Ralph depended on his CIA pension, and he was not willing to risk losing it by breaking his agreement.

Fortunately, Ralph had gathered a voluminous library of books and articles by and about the CIA. Bill and ACLU lawyer Mark Lynch figured out that if we could prove that the information had already been published elsewhere or that equivalent information had been approved for publication in other books by writers sympathetic to the Agency, then similar information could not be censored in Ralph's.

For example, the Agency wanted to delete any reference to Ralph's extensive work in Thailand. But Ralph proved that a memorandum by Gen. Edward Lansdale that discussed CIA liaison programs with Thai organizations had already been published in the *Pentagon Papers*. So the Agency backed off.

Similarly, the Agency insisted on deleting an entire chapter of Ralph's book that discussed his tours in Japan and the Philippines. Ralph searched his files and found a book called *Undercover* by ex-CIA agent Howard Hunt dealing with his assignment as a case officer in Japan. It also mentioned the Agency's base at Subic Bay in the Philippines. That book, sympathetic to the CIA, had been approved. So again the Agency had to allow Ralph's equivalent chapter.

The approval and appeals process took more than two years, but in the end most of the manuscript was approved for publication. The big exception was that Ralph's experiences supporting the military junta in Indonesia in the early 1970s were censored out of the book. More than a million people had been slaughtered there by the Indonesian military in its successful attempt to overthrow the elected leftist government of Sukarno, but the CIA refused to allow its role in providing the names of those targeted to be exposed. In place of a chapter on Indonesia, we added an appendix explaining the laborious process Ralph had to go through to get the manuscript approved at all.

Deadly Deceits: My 25 Years in the CIA was published in 1983. It was the first of four books I edited for Sheridan Square Press. Mc Gehee's book joined a growing list of exposés by what Bill called "the formers"— whistle-blowing ex-CIA agents who had turned against the Agency. These included John Marks and Victor Marchetti's *The CIA and the Cult of Intelligence,* Philip Agee's *Inside the Company,* and John Stockwell's *In Search of Enemies.*

Ralph became persona non grata in his home town, the CIA retirement haven of Herndon, Virginia. But he created a CIA database widely used by researchers, and he began to lecture at colleges. In 1986, when former President Jimmy Carter's daughter Amy and a group of students at the University of Massachusetts, Amherst, sat in to block a CIA recruiter from entering campus, police arrested them. At their trial, attorney Leonard Weinglass called Ralph Mc Gehee as an expert witness to testify that the student sit-in was justified because the CIA was "a criminal enterprise," which was barred from recruiting on campus. The jury acquitted the students.

Although *Deadly Deceits* was hardly a best-seller, it received a lot of attention in the alternative media. Bill and Ellen were happy, and they offered me a bonus for my work: a trip to Cuba. Of course, it was illegal for a U.S. citizen to spend any money in Cuba at the time because of the

U.S. government's ongoing embargo, but Bill and Ellen had their ways around that. There were flights from Canada and Mexico, which I would have to pay for, but the Cuban government's U.N. delegation, big fans of *Covert Action Quarterly*, offered to arrange the trip and pick up the tab once we were in Cuba.

It was tempting. Back in the late '60s, a group of radicals I knew in college had joined the Venceremos Brigade, U.S. volunteers who defied the embargo to help with Cuba's sugar cane harvest. I had wanted to go, but decided not to—a choice I'd always regretted. My interest in the island's socialist experiment had only grown stronger over the years. But after thinking it over, I declined Bill and Ellen's offer.

I told myself it was because I couldn't afford the plane fare. In truth, Bill and Ellen's boldness and enthusiasm notwithstanding, I was just plain scared. My parents' warnings not to get involved with movements or actions that could get me arrested, blacklisted or worse still had a grip on me more than 20 years after the McCarthy era had ended.

The next "former" manuscript Bill and Ellen acquired was Melvin Beck's memoir *Secret Contenders*. It recounted his years as a CIA counter-intelligence agent playing cat-and-mouse with the KGB. As I worked on it, I started to hang out at the Sheridan Square office on West 4th Street.

Bill and Ellen's apartment was one flight upstairs from the office, and one night they invited me up for dinner. As I walked in the front door, I didn't know if I'd entered a museum or a hoarder's lair. The apartment was bursting with memorabilia, artwork, knick-knacks, furniture, *tchotchkes*, clothes, crafts, photos, and books brought back from their distant travels. Not one inch of empty space. On one wall a photo of them with Cuban President Fidel Castro next to a photo of them with Grenada's Prime Minister Maurice Bishop, pushed up against a wall-hanging from Namibia. On another, a weaving from Nicaragua next to an antique clock from Holland. A ceiling-to-floor, wall-to-wall bookcase sagging with first editions, aging rare books, law tomes, mysteries, cookbooks, nature books and a framed letter from Theodore Roosevelt to Bill's great uncle, Michael Schaap, who'd been a founding member of the Bull Moose Party.

This was clearly not the apartment of leftists focused solely on politics. Bill had an eclectic mind with wide-ranging interests—stamps, coins, geography, birds, mushrooms, geology, linguistics, rare books, cooking. Ellen was a compulsive reader, not just newspapers and magazines, but her first love, literature. She also collected antiques and couldn't resist a thrift shop or a yard sale where a bargain was to be had on anything from vintage clothing to art deco furniture.

An antique veiled bed they'd found in Morocco dominated their bedroom. And at the center of the well-equipped kitchen was a large, professional-quality gas range. I soon found out why. Bill was a gourmet chef, and he'd prepared one of his favorite dishes—Beef Wellington. As we ate, they told me more about themselves. Though they were inseparable, they couldn't have been more different.

"On my mother's side, my family is from Massachusetts," Ellen said, "descended from Abigail Adams, John Adams's wife. My great grandmother graduated in the first class of Mount Holyoke College. My father's family were land and slave owners in Virginia, but later they moved to Nebraska in covered wagons."

A grand-niece of novelist Willa Cather, Ellen grew up in rural Nebraska, where her father ran a farm supply business. "My parents were atheists and Democrats," she said, "but in Nebraska in the 1940s and '50s, that was like being a Communist."

By contrast, Bill hailed from a middle-class New York Jewish family. His mother, of Russian-Jewish heritage, was first-generation American. On his father's side, Bill's great-grandfather had emigrated to the U.S. in the 1840s from Holland where the Schaap lineage could be traced back 13 generations.

"My father was a traveling silverware salesman," said Bill. "My mother taught French, German, and Latin in public school in Freeport, Long Island, where I was raised. They weren't very political, they considered themselves liberals."

Bill followed his older brother Dick Schaap to college at Cornell. Dick had made a name for himself as a sports broadcaster and author. Later, on an NBC television station he stirred up a fire storm when he called Kentucky Derby-winning racehorses Secretariat and Riva Ridge "the most famous stablemates since Joseph and Mary."

After college, Bill went to law school at the University of Chicago, graduating in 1964. "I married an heiress from Shaker Heights, bought a beautiful townhouse in the Village, got a lucrative job practicing corporate law as an associate at a prestigious Wall Street firm. I was all set for a comfortable bourgeois life," he said. "But I wasn't happy."

Meanwhile, Ellen had been kicked out of Monmouth College in Illinois for participating in a sit-in against segregation. "I got radicalized in college in 1960," she said. "It was the time, you could feel it." To get her away from her deepening political involvement, her parents sent her to Europe. "In Paris I bought all of Henry Miller's books," she said. She hitchhiked to Heidelberg, where she had many boyfriends and got into drugs.

When her parents issued an ultimatum to return to the U.S. or be disowned, she moved to Boston. For a year she studied at her father's alma mater, Harvard, before settling in New York. Her first job was at Countryside Publications. "We had about a dozen movie magazines and what we called stroke magazines. The best known was *True Confessions*— of course, all of them were made up. The publisher would dream up outrageous cover lines and stories, and if one magazine got sued, he'd just start another one."

During this time, Bill and Ellen's paths first crossed at a party thrown by the satirical magazine *The Monocle*. Advertised as "Thirty Years of Guerrilla Warfare: King Kong to Viet Cong," the bash featured Andy Warhol's 24-hour film of the Empire State Building. Bill and Ellen were both at the party, but they didn't actually meet until several years later.

By then the '60s were in full swing, and Bill had been radicalized. "One of my first big cases at the Wall Street firm had an outside counsel, Dave Lubell," Bill explained. "He dragged me to the National Lawyers Guild convention where I met William Kunstler, Victor Rabinowitz, Arthur Kinoy—lefty lawyers who were handling all the big civil rights cases. They were brilliant, exciting, powerful personalities. Of course, I joined the Guild the same day."

Not long after that, in late 1967, Bill attended his first political gathering, a benefit dinner for the Emergency Civil Liberties Committee. He was sitting at a table with Kunstler, Rabinowitz, and Kinoy, among others, when a call came in. Students protesting against Vice President Hubert Humphrey and the Vietnam War had just been arrested. "I was the youngest one at the table, and they all looked at me. Kunstler said, 'They need a lawyer.' I said, 'I'm a corporate lawyer, I've never set foot in criminal court.' Kunstler says, 'It's an arraignment, it's easy, you make friends with the clerk, get a bunch of notices of appearance, and fill out the papers.'

"So I go down to criminal court, it's midnight, 200 people are there in a jammed courtroom. They call the first defendant, and it's Paul Krassner, editor of the Yippie paper *The Realist*. All his Yippie friends are jumping up and down and screaming, so the judge orders the courtroom to be cleared. And Krassner says to me, 'Am I going to get the death penalty?' I say, 'I don't think so.' He says, 'The arresting officer is pretty mad at me.' I say, 'Why is that?'

Krassner explained that at mass arrests in the early '60s, one officer would arrest 30 or 40 people and if the officer couldn't identify the individuals he'd arrested, the charges would be dropped. So the cops started taking Polaroid photos of everyone they arrested.

"What's the problem?" Bill asked.

"'Well,' Krassner says, 'when the cop started to take the photo, I put my arm in his and said, 'So sweetie, where are we going after the prom?'"

After Krassner and 20 others were given summons to appear, the judge got impatient and ordered all the cases dismissed. Nobody went to jail. That was Bill's initiation to radical lawyering.

A few months later Bill got a call from Bernardine Dohrn, an organizer at the Lawyers Guild. "'Thirty people just got arrested up at Columbia University,'" she said. 'Go down and get them out.'

"'Arrested for what?' I asked.

"'Columbia put this fence around this place where they're planning to build a gymnasium. They tore it down.'

"'This is a political thing?' I said. 'Tearing down a fence around a gymnasium?'

"'You don't understand,' she said. 'Just get down there.'"

What began with 30 students soon became a general strike, which then led to a student takeover of Columbia President Grayson Kirk's office. "They were eating chicken and throwing bones out the window, which Abe Rosenthal, editor of the *New York Times*, thought was the most horrible thing he'd ever heard of in his life. The next thing I know, they're arresting everyone, and suddenly I have 700 clients.

"Fortunately, Mary Kaufman, an elderly Guild member who'd been one of the prosecutors at the post-World War II Nuremberg trials, came to my rescue. She knew that the best way to deal with this situation was to drive the prosecutors and judge crazy. Every day I'd be down in court with 40 clients and I'd tell the judge, 'Sorry, your honor, but every one of them wants to go to trial.' You tell a judge you want 700 trials, and he knows the whole system will grind to a halt. Eventually Mary walked in and quietly said, 'Your honor, perhaps if we made a motion to dismiss all these cases, we could clear your docket for the next eight years.' And that's what happened: the judge threw out every one of them."

After that, Bill decided to leave his cushy Wall Street job and join the small radical firm of Lubell, Lubell, Fein and Schaap, which represented, among others, the Black Panthers.

While Bill was coming of age politically, Ellen plunged into an artsy scene. She lived in the last garden apartment on Park Avenue, paying $100 a month, and worked at Columbia Pictures' story department. Among the movies she recommended was Francis Ford Coppola's first—*You're a Big Boy Now*. Occasionally she'd take some time off to make a documentary, one about the Black Panthers, another about César Chavez and the United Farmworkers.

She was also taking a lot of drugs, which led to her going to California to make "a hippie-nudie political western movie about marijuana." Called *Gold*, it featured Orville Schell as Che Guevara, and was largely improvised. When the film was nearly all shot, Ellen returned to New York to raise finishing funds.

It was 1971. That was when she first met Bill Schaap.

"It was a Black Panther support committee meeting at Bill's office," said Ellen. "I was there looking for potential investors, but Bill spoke, and I videotaped him. I liked him immediately. 'Hmmm, I said to myself, *Gold* needs a lawyer.'"

"Ellen came to see me about a contract with a guy in England who wanted to bring *Gold* to Europe," Bill continued. "We went to London together to review this fantastic contract that guaranteed she would make millions. The only problem was that it was with a Lichtenstein corporation that didn't have a dime and wasn't worth the paper it was printed on. After we finished with the contract, I said good night to Ellen. We had adjoining hotel rooms, and a few minutes later Ellen crawls into bed with me. We fell in love, and I separated from my wife about two or three hours later—well, maybe 10 days later."

Ellen added, "I figured if I shacked up with a lawyer, it would keep me out of trouble."

Back in New York, they moved into a cheap apartment together. Bill worked for the Committee of Liaison, which was passing mail from American prisoners of war in North Vietnam to their families in the States. Future Republican presidential nominee John McCain was among those POWs. "One day Bill Kunstler comes into the office," said Bill, "and announces the Guild and the Center for Constitutional Rights are looking for a lawyer to go to Japan to handle legal cases for GI's dissenting against the Vietnam War. I said, 'Can Ellen go too?' He said yes—two tickets to Japan and $36 per month each."

Nixon was President, and more than 500,000 American troops were fighting in Vietnam. Much of their logistical support came from several U.S. military bases on the island of Okinawa. Bill knew nothing about military law, but he read the Uniform Code of Military Justice on the plane. He and Ellen, both then 30 years old, lived in a commune in Okinawa with several other Americans and slept on mats on the floor. In the front of the house, they set up an office, an informal people's cafe, and a room for counseling.

Word soon got out that the Guild lawyer offered free legal help, day or night. "It was the most intense time of our lives," said Ellen. Bill handled hundreds of cases. Most of them were court martials of soldiers who opposed the war. The soldiers wanted a discharge and the military was happy to get rid of them, so those cases were disposed of quickly by mutually agreeable settlements.

But there were also cases involving assault, drugs, and murder. Dubbed Della Street (TV lawyer Perry Mason's assistant) by one military judge, Ellen worked with Bill on the trials. "You didn't have to be very smart to be a step ahead of the military," Bill said. "There are a lot of loopholes that they don't expect anyone to take advantage of. In a court martial, for example, if a defendant calls a character witness, the military is required to bring that witness to the courtroom. So if we had a case in Okinawa, we routinely asked if the defendant had a good character witness stationed in Germany. The military would have to pay to bring that witness to Okinawa. The military lawyers would ask, 'Can't you call a character witness from down the street?' and I'd say, 'Oh no.' They were on limited budgets, so they almost always settled rather than spend their whole budgets to go to trial."

Initially, Bill did lose a handful of cases, but later he discovered that the military had bugged his law office, illegally recording privileged attorney-client conversations. A friendly member of the military police slipped Ellen transcripts of the recordings. Bill filed a motion to overturn all convictions in the cases he'd lost, and the judge granted it. "So over two years in Okinawa," Bill said, "we never lost a case."

After another year of counseling GI's in Heidelberg, Germany, for the American Civil Liberties Union, Bill had become an expert in military law. In 1975, he was hired as the editor of the *Military Law Reporter*, based in Washington D.C. For the next five years, the tail end of the Ford presidency and the entire Carter presidency, he and Ellen lived in the nation's capital.

"When we first went to Okinawa," said Ellen, "we didn't know what the CIA was or what they did, but when you work overseas, you learn fast." In Washington, Ellen volunteered with an obscure magazine called *Counterspy* that reported on the activities of the CIA. Founded by former CIA agent Philip Agee and several others, *Counterspy* earned notoriety by outing CIA agents working abroad. Naming their names blew their cover and made them ineffectual.

Ellen's first assignment was to travel with Agee to Jamaica to investigate the CIA's covert war on the democratically elected leftist government of Michael Manley. While she was working on the Jamaica article, a Greek underground group assassinated Richard Welch, the CIA's newly appointed CIA station chief in Athens. Welch had been outed earlier as a CIA agent in local Greek publications and in a Peruvian publication during his previous post in Lima. Having verified these reports, *Counterspy* also listed Welch as a CIA covert operator.

After Welch's death, President Gerald Ford blamed *Counterspy* for putting him in jeopardy. But documents released later under the Freedom of Information Act proved that the CIA itself had warned Welch not to move into the previous station chief's house in Athens because it was too dangerous. It was widely known as a CIA house. Welch had written back to Langley that he and his wife liked the house and were going to take their chances.

This information didn't faze President Ford or members of the intelligence community. They called for a new law making it illegal for a publication to name a CIA agent. The controversial Intelligence Identities Protection Act was first introduced in Congress in 1978. By then *Counterspy* had ceased publishing, but Agee and independent researcher Louis Wolf had continued to name agents in their two books entitled *Dirty Work* about CIA activities in Europe and Africa. Wolf had read an article by former State Department official John Marks called "How to Spot a Spook" and had used the *Diplomatic Register* and publicly available unclassified information to identify CIA agents working under cover at U.S. embassies around the world.

Agee introduced Wolf to Bill and Ellen, and in 1978, the four of them decided to launch a new publication scrutinizing the CIA. *Covert Action Information Bulletin* had a simple format, came out every two months, and continued the practice of outing covert CIA agents in a column called "Naming Names." "We started by printing 5,000 copies," said Bill, "and we never had more than a few thousand subscribers, but we covered our printing costs."

"Nobody was paid," added Ellen. "We all had other jobs to support ourselves. We ran ads, and we *shlepped* copies to left-wing newsstands. We started doing direct mail to get subscribers, but we sold much more in bookstores. Many people were afraid to be on our mailing list. But we had subscribers all over the world—lots of embassies, international NGOs, and many libraries. Of course the CIA subscribed."

Initially, the magazine focused on the CIA's illegal activities, but later it branched out to report on domestic abuses by the National Security Agency and FBI. Eventually it expanded into a glossy, source-noted magazine called *Covert Action Quarterly*. The journal's exposés from 1978 to 2005 featured in-depth stories on the CIA's destabilization, assassination, and disinformation programs in Jamaica, Chile, Grenada, Vietnam, Nicaragua, Guatemala, Panama, Spain, Greece, Turkey, Israel, Palestine, South Africa, Rwanda, Mozambique, the Philippines, and many other countries. Bill, Ellen, and Lou researched, wrote, and edited many of the articles themselves, but they also recruited prominent progressive voices like Noam Chomsky, Ramsey Clark, Alexander Cockburn, John Stockwell, Diana Johnstone, and Mumia Abu-Jamal to write for the publication.

In 1983 Congress finally enacted the Intelligence Identities Protection Act, which was aimed primarily at *Covert Action Quarterly* and Philip Agee. Bill said, "We met with Floyd Abrams, attorney for the *New York Times*. He said, 'The law is unconstitutional, and it isn't fair, but that won't stop them. They'll go after little guys like you, not the *Times*.' So we decided to stop publishing names of agents and concentrate on other things."

Working with Bill and Ellen and hearing the stories of all they had done came at just the right time for me. I was at a crossroads. After a long battle with brain cancer, my mother had recently died. I'd broken up with María, my Cuban girlfriend of three years. I'd quit my job editing *Juris Doctor* magazine to write a novel. I supported myself by working overnights as a part-time proofreader. And I was in psychotherapy for the first time in my life.

I was lonely, and I had no idea what I was doing or where I was going.

Bill and Ellen offered an anchor and work I believed in. More important, they inspired me. During the early '80s, the office on West 4th Street became my second home. It was a beehive of exciting activity, and there were always visitors from around the globe.

Because Bill and Ellen were still publishing *Covert Action Quarterly*, they had wangled press passes at the United Nations. This afforded them access to the delegates' lounge with its free drinks and hors d'oeuvres. Through their contacts in the Cuban delegation, they had befriended progressive delegates from all over the world. Ellen would invite them over to the office and then upstairs for a gourmet feast cooked by Bill. Just hanging out at the apartment, I met people from Cuba, Nicaragua, Namibia, Jamaica, Vietnam, Vanuatu, Bulgaria, Ireland, Russia, and more.

Many of them invited Bill and Ellen to their countries to lecture about the CIA. On one tour of Africa, they spoke to eager audiences in Kenya, Tanganyika, Zanzibar, Mozambique, and recently independent Angola. In Montreal, Bill's speech revealing the existence of a CIA station in Canada made front-page news. And in Grenada, Bill not only lectured at St. George's University, but also wrote speeches for Prime Minister Maurice Bishop.

At first I felt shy around all the radical international luminaries who paraded through the office. But Ellen made sure I got to know everyone, invariably introducing me—to my embarrassment—as "the best editor we've ever worked with."

Ellen's audacity impressed me. She could walk up to any stranger, share a drink, and strike up a conversation. She was the one who reached out to people, raised money by courting wealthy angels, arranged travel, wooed writers to contribute articles. Ambitious, relentless, and fearless about nudging people, she was always on the phone, talking to someone in the office, or dreaming up a new project to add to their non-stop whirlwind of activity.

Bill was more laid back, continually working, but behind the scenes. If Ellen dreamed it up, Bill made it happen. He had the brains and skills to do whatever needed to be done—from negotiating legal contracts to laying out pages, from editing and fact-checking to giving interviews and lectures, even walking the dog—all in his competent, calm, good-natured way, always with humor. It amazed me that no matter what obstacles came up, no matter who attacked them or tried to stop their work, Bill could handle it—every time. He was always the smartest person in any room.

For me, Bill and Ellen were a tonic. I found myself lightening up and laughing more. Ellen's vision and audacity coupled with Bill's brilliant competence and rock-solid strength inspired confidence. Just being part of their unique world, I felt emboldened and protected at the same time.

Maybe it was because Bill and Ellen believed in me. Maybe my therapy was kicking in. Or maybe it was because Victor Navasky asked me to take an eight-month position filling in as Executive Editor of *The Nation*. The result was that in the sub-culture of radical politics, I finally felt I'd found a home.

In late 1984, I read a report that international volunteers were going to Nicaragua to support the leftist Sandinista government against the U.S.-backed *contras*. I regretted missing the Venceremos Brigade in the late '60s and passing up the trip to Cuba with Bill and Ellen in 1983. This time I didn't hesitate. It was the best decision of my life.

I joined a harvest brigade to pick coffee for three weeks in the rain-drenched, war-plagued mountains near Matagalpa, Nicaragua. Seventeen of us from the U.S. joined volunteers from all over Europe and Latin America. We picked coffee during the day, ate rice, beans, and tortillas at every meal, and at night fell asleep on hard bunks in migrant laborers' quarters to the sound of nearby gunfire.

I came back skinny, energized, and feeling liberated. I joined the local committee to recruit more volunteers. And that's where I met Sarah Plant, who had gone earlier to Nicaragua to pick cotton. Dark-haired, friendly, and down-to-earth, she had a soulful beauty and warmth that radiated from her. When I heard her playing flute with her fusion *Nueva Cancion*/chamber group at a benefit concert, I knew she was the one I'd been looking for.

It took a while to convince her that I was the one she was looking for. But a breakfast picnic in Riverside Park with fresh orange juice I prepared on the spot with my Mexican orange squeezer did the trick. Soon we moved in together and have been a happily unmarried couple for the last 37 years.

In the mid-1980s, Bill and Ellen founded the non-profit Institute for Media Analysis and organized a three-day conference at Harvard University on The History and Consequences of Anti-Communism. It featured presentations by prominent radical activists and scholars, including Howard Zinn, Jessica Mitford, Ring Lardner Jr., Stephen Jay Gould, John Kenneth Galbraith, Daniel Ellsberg, Blanche Wiesen Cook, Cheddi Jagan, Leonard Boudin, Edward S. Herman, and Joel Kovel.

More than 1,500 people attended the conference, and given that I'd grown up in a Communist home during the anti-Communist hysteria of the 1950s, I should have been one of them. But I wasn't. A year after returning from Nicaragua, I'd suddenly come down with a mysterious illness. It felt like a severe flu—profound fatigue, fevers, chills, digestive problems, constant fog-like headache, inability to concentrate—but it never went away. I took countless tests and was poked and prodded by a dozen doctors, none of whom had a clue what was wrong with me. The drugs they prescribed made me feel worse. Finally, after a year, I was diagnosed with Chronic Fatigue Immune Dysfunction Syndrome, but no one had a cure. I had almost no savings to fall back on, so I somehow dragged myself in to work on weekends and took the rest of the week to recover. Sarah stuck with me, or else I couldn't have survived.

It was around this time that Ellen called and said she and Bill had a new book manuscript for me to edit. I told her I was too sick. I could barely read for an hour a day. But she would hear none of it. She insisted this was a special project and convinced me to come to dinner to hear her out.

There was no Beef Wellington for me this time. Under the guidance of Dr. Shyam Singha, a naturopathic doctor Victor Navasky had recommended, I had become a total vegetarian. Bill cooked a vegetarian chili instead, and as I ate, Ellen talked.

The manuscript, by Jim Garrison, former District Attorney of New Orleans, was about the assassination of President John Kennedy. I vividly remembered this unspeakable moment in our history. I was 15 then, and I'd spent the entire weekend glued to the television as events unfolded. I also remembered that five years later, in 1968, I'd read a cover story in *Ramparts* magazine about Garrison, his investigation of the assassination, and all the witnesses who had died under mysterious circumstances.

I was a sophomore in college during that year of unprecedented worldwide turbulence. Martin Luther King Jr. and Robert Kennedy fell to assassins' bullets that spring. A student uprising in Paris in May led to a general strike and riots in the streets. A few months later Soviet tanks rolled into Czechoslovakia. And at the Democratic convention in Chicago that summer, police brutally beat protestors with the whole world watching.

As I read about Garrison's charge that the CIA had been involved in the murder of John Kennedy, I was in shock. Although the greatest mystery story of the 20th century fascinated me, I was reluctant to get involved—even as an assassination buff or researcher.

Ellen, on the other hand, took the leap. After reading the same *Ramparts* article, she'd gone to New Orleans to meet Garrison. "I had to tell him about Max Jacobson," she said, almost in a whisper.

Ellen explained that in the 1960s Jacobson, a physician, had earned a reputation in the tabloid newspapers as "Dr. Feelgood" by treating celebrities with injections he concocted himself. Ellen had lived with him for several months in a semi-romantic relationship and taken the injections too. Nobody knew exactly what the ingredients were—some combination of amphetamines, narcotics, and psychedelics, she suspected—but they helped eliminate pain, provided a high and gave the patient a feeling of energetic yet serene well-being. Ellen eventually left Jacobson, who was more than 40 years her senior, without ever paying a bill.

Bill, Ellen, and Lou Wolf (left to right), *Covert Action Information Bulletin* offices, circa 1980

Ellen, Jim Garrison, and Bill (left to right) at Garrison's book launch, 1989. Photo by Donn Young

But while living with Dr. Feelgood, she had been surprised to discover that he was giving daily injections to President Kennedy. Ostensibly they were for back pain, but it is also possible that Jacobson was treating the President's Addison's disease, which was disclosed to the public only after his death. Jacobson would fly down to Washington, or Kennedy would come up to New York. Ellen was convinced that Dr. Feelgood's drugs were not just relieving Kennedy's pain and giving him energy but also changing his consciousness. She believed the drugs were a crucial factor in Kennedy's decisions to end the Cold War with the Soviet Union and withdraw U.S. advisers from Vietnam—major policy reversals that led to his assassination.

"This was before I knew Bill," she said. "My boyfriend at the time rented a blue Cadillac convertible, and we drove down to New Orleans. We knew it was dangerous. Witnesses were getting killed all over the country—even famous people like the syndicated gossip columnist Dorothy Kilgallen—so my friend hired a bodyguard and gave me a shoulder holster and a revolver, which I wore in my suit. They took me out for target practice in North Carolina.

"When we got to New Orleans, we went to see Garrison. But everyone was paranoid down there. Before he'd meet us, Garrison had us go through all kinds of tests to make sure we weren't CIA agents. We passed and got invited to a couple of Jim's dinners at Antoine's—he had a room there where he'd eat with volunteer assassination researchers like the lawyer Mark Lane and the comedians Mort Sahl and Shelley Berman. Lane zeroed in on me and arranged for me to talk to Jim in his office. The first thing Jim said was, 'They're trying to kill me.' I said, 'I know, look what I brought'—and I showed him my revolver. He told me to get rid of it. 'You could be set up to take the blame if someone killed me,' he said. 'You'd be a patsy, just like Oswald.' I started to tell him about Dr. Feelgood, but he said, 'Don't talk about it in this office.'"

Bill interrupted at that point. "Elle, enough of Dr. Feelgood, let's discuss the manuscript." He explained that Garrison had originally been commissioned by a mainstream publisher to write a book on the assassination to be published on the 25th anniversary in 1988. But when Jim submitted the finished manuscript, the editor rejected it. Jim was convinced that the CIA had intervened. He now wanted a publisher who was CIA-proof. A friend in the New Orleans Lawyers Guild, Mary Howell, had put him in touch with Bill and Ellen, assuring him that if there was one publisher in the world that the CIA could never influence, it was Sheridan Square Press.

I didn't know what to think. I'd read some of the stories in the mainstream press about Garrison—that he was a ruthless and reckless politician, an ambitious publicity seeker who played fast and loose with the facts and bribed witnesses, a corrupt DA in bed with the Mafia, a homophobe who had persecuted an innocent man. There was even a story by syndicated columnist Jack Anderson that Garrison had fondled a boy in the sauna at the New Orleans Athletic Club. Was I willing to work with this man and risk whatever small credibility I had as a journalist?

"Jim is a good man trying to do the right thing," Ellen assured me. "The CIA tried to destroy him in the press, but in 25 years he's never stopped investigating this case. Please read the manuscript."

And so I did. It was a thorough, factual, source-noted examination of the assassination, written with intelligence and eloquence. The research Jim had done, much of it from his own investigation in New Orleans, read like a riveting thriller. And the conclusion he reached— that the CIA had been responsible for killing Kennedy—was more than plausible. It was convincing. Equally important, Jim's passionate sense of outrage that the country had been hijacked by a coup d'etat came through clearly. He was still furious, and he wondered why everyone else wasn't too.

I'd always doubted the Warren Commission's conclusion that Oswald was the lone gunman. But over the last 20 years my own rage at the government's lies had faded into depressed resignation. So much had happened since the Kennedy assassination—the Vietnam War based on a fabricated Gulf of Tonkin incident, President Richard Nixon's coverup of the break-in at the Watergate hotel and other dirty tricks which led to his resignation, the assassinations of Martin Luther King, Bobby Kennedy, Malcolm X, the Iran-*contra* affair, the Church Committee revelations about the CIA's attempts to overthrow governments and assassinate foreign leaders including the Congo's Patrice Lumumba, Dominican Republic's Rafael Trujillo, and Cuba's Fidel Castro.

Like many Americans, I had become jaded. But as I read Jim's manuscript, my rage began rising up again like a powerful geyser. And it felt good—really good.

Before I answered Bill and Ellen, I talked to Henry Kellerman, my therapist. I wanted to work on the book, but how could I? I couldn't concentrate, my brain was in a constant fog, and I had no strength. "You'll find a way," Henry said. "You'll do it at your own pace, there are no deadlines." I looked at him in silence, unconvinced. "You know the definition of depression?" Henry asked. "Anger turned inward on yourself. I think it would be healthier for you to turn that anger outward to where it belongs."

And so I told Bill and Ellen I would edit the manuscript. Jim flew up from New Orleans, and we met in Bill and Ellen's apartment. He was an impressive man, bigger than life, six feet seven inches tall, with a deep rolling baritone voice. He was now a judge on Louisiana's 4th Circuit Court of Appeals and dressed the part in an elegant blue suit and tie.

It was my job to break the news to Jim that although his manuscript was excellent, I felt it needed to be rewritten from page one. It was written in the third person, like an objective history. And given his personal involvement in the case, I explained, no one would believe he was an objective historian. After all, he had brought the only prosecution ever in the JFK assassination. He was a significant part of the story. Moreover, he had been slandered for more than 20 years in the press, and he'd never responded.

"Why get into a pissing contest with a skunk?" he asked.

"Well, this book is your chance to answer all the critics."

He wasn't convinced. "During the Clay Shaw trial, the media always focused on me, and it became a circus," he said. "I don't want this book to be about me. I want it to be about the assassination."

"Isn't there a way to make it both?" asked Ellen.

I suggested that Jim tell the story of his investigation in the first person. He could take readers step by step, fact by fact, through the evidence that led him to change his own mind from accepting the Warren Commission's lone gunman theory to believing that a CIA-led conspiracy killed the President. If he did that, readers would go with him on his journey, and their minds would be changed as well.

"You mean write it like a murder mystery with me as the detective?"

"Exactly. Not a dull history book, but a thriller, a whodunit for a mass audience."

"Jim, it's the people who need to read this, not the academics," Ellen urged him.

Jim was thoughtful. "I like the idea," he said. "But it won't be a who-dunit. It'll be a whydunit."

Jim and I spent the next week hammering out a new outline. He flew back to New Orleans, and it wasn't long before I began receiving Federal Express envelopes from the Louisiana 4th Circuit Court of Appeals, each with a new chapter. Jim immediately found the right first-person voice—intelligent, personal, and sardonically witty.

After a year we had a new completed manuscript. Ellen recruited JFK assassination researcher Carl Oglesby, former head of Students for a Democratic Society, to write an afterword. And Bill took over from there, vetting for libel, fact-checking, organizing production, and making a distribution deal.

On the Trail of the Assassins: My Investigation and Prosecution of the Assassination of President John F. Kennedy was published in November 1988 on the 25th anniversary of the assassination. We celebrated at launch parties in New York, Washington, and New Orleans. But almost none of the mainstream press reviewed the book.

The CIA's orchestrated effort to discredit critics of the Warren Commission had been successful. It was outlined in a memo dated April 1, 1967, from CIA headquarters to all station chiefs. Released under the Freedom of Information Act, the memo suggested that the Agency use its "propaganda assets" in the media—writers and editors—to plant false stories about critics insinuating that they were "politically interested," "financially interested," "hasty and inaccurate in their research," and "infatuated with their own theories."

In this way the most prominent critics of the Warren Commission, primarily Jim Garrison and Mark Lane, were effectively smeared. Jim's book was greeted accordingly—with a resounding silence.

But that didn't stop Bill and Ellen. In December 1988, they attended the Havana Film Festival. In a rickety Cuban elevator, Ellen cornered Oscar-winning filmmaker Oliver Stone, who was receiving an award at the festival. "I had to get to the seventh floor, and the ride up was interminable," said Stone. "This woman was yapping in my ear, telling me I had to read this book by Garrison, I had to make a movie about Kennedy. She was loud and brassy, and I was embarrassed. I don't like people pitching me in public places. But I have to say she was fearless, and she wouldn't take no for an answer."

Ellen extracted a promise from him to read *On the Trail of the Assassins*. "When I got out of that elevator, I was relieved," said Stone. "I thought I'd never have to see that pain-in-the-ass woman again. But the next day she sent a copy of the book to my hotel room. I packed it away, and didn't read it till a few weeks later when I was on a 14-hour plane trip to the Philippines. I couldn't put it down."

Stone said the only reason he read the book was that he'd promised that insistent redheaded woman he would. Ellen and Bill were in their apartment when Stone called. He said he loved the book and wanted to option it, but the project had to be kept in confidence. He was busy preparing to film *Born on the Fourth of July,* so he needed a writer to help adapt Jim's book into a screenplay. Because I'd worked for two years on the book and knew the material so well, Ellen recommended me. Oliver talked to me briefly on the phone and when he returned from Asia, he came to Bill and Ellen's apartment for a New Orleans-style dinner. That did it. Over a plate of étouffée, he agreed to option the book and hired me to write the first draft.

I had never written a screenplay, but I followed Oliver's advice that we use Akira Kurosawa's *Rashomon* and Costa Gavras's *Z* as film models. It took a year and a half, 200 interviews, and more than a dozen drafts that shuttled back and forth between Oliver and me. Finally we had a script. After reading Jim's book, Kevin Costner agreed to star in the film, and then Warner Brothers provided the financing.

Ironically, Jim Garrison played Chief Justice Earl Warren. And Bill and Ellen flew to New Orleans to be extras in a restaurant scene where Costner as Garrison confronts John Candy as lawyer Dean Andrews. "They must have done 20 or 30 takes," said Bill, "and Candy ate a fresh Crab Louie in every one."

When the shooting wrapped, Bill and Ellen threw a party for the cast and crew at Mary Howell's house. And of course, Bill cooked New Orleans gumbo for the occasion.

Before the movie was released, Jim died of heart failure. But he'd watched a video of it in his hospital bed and was thrilled. The three-hour movie stirred up a furious controversy in the mainstream press, which viciously attacked it. *Time* and *Newsweek* ("The Twisted Truth of *JFK*") both ran nasty cover stories on the film. The *Washington Post* labeled it "Dallas in Wonderland," while *New York Times* columnist Tom Wicker asked "Does *JFK* Conspire Against Reason?"

Yet it proved a worldwide box-office success, grossing more than $220 million. Early on a freezing morning in January 1992, Ellen woke me with a call. "I just saw the news on the *Today* show," she screamed into the phone. "*JFK* was nominated for eight Oscars, including one for you and Oliver for Best Adapted Screenplay."

The night before the Academy Award ceremony, Terry Semel, co-president of Warner Brothers, threw a party at his Hollywood home for the *JFK* nominees. There were speeches and more than an ample helping of self-congratulation. I was uncomfortable with the Hollywood glamour and glitz. But I pulled myself together and stood up to speak. I reminded the gathering that none of this—the movie, the Oscar nominations, all the publicity and the controversy—could have happened without three people who weren't present that night: Jim Garrison, who for a quarter of a century never gave up on his investigation, and Bill Schaap and Ellen Ray, who had the courage and vision to publish a book that no one else would touch.

As a result of the movie, *On the Trail of the Assassins* became a hot item. But the book's popularity could not save its financially troubled distributor from declaring bankruptcy, and Sheridan Square never got a penny from the hardcover sales. However, Bill had signed a deal with Warner Books for the soft-cover rights. When the paperback skyrocketed to number one on the *New York Times* bestseller list, Bill and Ellen finally found some personal financial stability. They bought a small house in the Catskills that actor Judd Hirsch had built. On weekends and in summer, the Sundown house became a perfect place for them to escape the stress of the city, go yard-sale hopping, and enjoy nature with friends. It was not far from Sarah's and my house in Olivebridge, so we became upstate neighbors.

Barely pausing to enjoy the successes of *On the Trail of the Assassins* and *JFK*, Bill and Ellen were busier than ever. By this time, they had stopped working on *Covert Action Quarterly*, leaving Lou Wolf to continue publishing it in Washington. Their latest project, which they published and co-edited with Edward Herman, was *Lies of Our Times (LOOT)*, a monthly magazine exposing the errors, biases, and blind spots of the *New York Times* and the mainstream media. It featured a regular column by Noam Chomsky, articles by Bill, Ellen, and Edward Herman, and contributions from Alexander Cockburn, Debra Evenson, John Hess, Michael Parenti, and many others. "We were just tired of people thinking if it's in the *New York Times* or if Dan Rather said it, it must be true," explained Bill. "They lie all the time."

During the five years of LOOT's life, from 1990 to 1994, I wrote only one story for it. After my credibility as a journalist had been severely damaged by the media frenzy over *JFK,* I was writing screenplays. But when Ellen called and said Sheridan Square had just received an explosive new manuscript by a former Israeli spy that needed editing, I couldn't resist.

Born in Iran to wealthy Iraqi-Jewish parents, Ari Ben-Menashe had emigrated to Israel at the age of 14 and had worked for more than ten years as a high-level Israeli intelligence operative. His assignments were more the stuff of Graham Greene than James Bond, but every chapter of his first-person memoir contained shocking new information about key events of the 1980s. He had been an arms dealer, one of Israel's point men in the Iran-*contra* affair. He had been present at the October Surprise negotiations in Paris where Ronald Reagan's representatives, William Casey and George Bush, cut a deal to delay release of U.S. hostages being held by the Iranian government until after the U.S. presidential election of 1980. Ari had even been a bagman, at one point carrying a suitcase filled with $56 million of laundered Saudi cash and bank checks across a U.S. border in Arizona, ushered through customs by soon-to-be CIA Director Robert Gates.

Israel had also assigned Ari to stop the CIA's secret, illegal sale of nuclear and chemical materials to Iraqi President Saddam Hussein via a third party in General Pinochet's Chile. And he had access to classified Israeli intelligence files that shed new light on the Jonathan Pollard spy case, the death of media magnate Robert Maxwell, and the connection of the Lubavitcher rabbi, Menachem Schneerson, to the collapse of investment bank Drexel Burnham, to name just a few stories that had captured headlines in the 1980s.

In 1989, the U.S. government arrested Ari for illegal arms dealing. In fact, he had been selling arms to Iran to fund the *contras,* paramilitary mercenaries fighting to overthrow the progressive Sandinista government in Nicaragua. He did this with the full knowledge and support of both Israeli intelligence and the CIA. But after his arrest, the Israeli government hung him out to dry, publicly denying that he had ever worked for Israeli intelligence. While imprisoned in New York's Metropolitan Correctional Center for a year, Ari concluded that his extensive knowledge of illegal intelligence operations made him a likely candidate for assassination by either Israeli or U.S. intelligence. His only hope was to write a book and shed so much light on himself that assassinating him might be too risky for those who wanted to get rid of him.

At a federal trial in New York, Ari produced documents that proved he was working for Israeli intelligence and that the CIA supported his arms dealing. The jury found him not guilty, and he was freed. He moved to Australia, where publisher Allen & Unwin commissioned him to write a book and then sold the European rights for $700,000 to Faber & Faber, a major mainstream publisher in London. Ari had worked with an Australian ghostwriter to produce a draft, but neither Allen & Unwin nor Faber & Faber was willing to move forward to publication. The editor at Faber & Faber told Ari that Israeli intelligence had threatened to kill him if he published the book.

A friend of Ari's urged him to call Sheridan Square Press. Bill answered and told Ari to send the manuscript immediately. Ellen read it and invited Ari to come to New York. When Ari had nowhere else to go, Ellen offered him friendship, a book contract, and a place to live at the house in Sundown while he worked with me on a rewrite.

A swarthy, restless chain-smoker in his late forties, Ari spoke five languages and loved to tell stories. He was charming, funny, and smart, had traveled virtually everywhere in the world, and seemed to have total recall. The world events of the 1980s he described were familiar to me. But he viewed them from first-hand, behind-the-scenes experience—a strikingly different perspective from the official stories I had read in the *New York Times*. How much of what Ari said was true and how much was fiction was anybody's guess. The Australian tabloid journalist who'd written the first draft had a breezy and accessible style. But the manuscript needed a lot of clarification and reorganization. That was my job. It was up to Bill to fact-check as best he could against publicly available information and to have the final manuscript vetted for potential libel.

Profits of War: Inside the Secret U.S.-Israeli Arms Network, dedicated "to Ellen Ray, who changed my life," was published in 1993. Though the revelations in every chapter were jaw-dropping, the mainstream media ignored them. And although a U.S. Senate committee called Ben-Menashe to testify about the October Surprise meetings he'd witnessed in Paris, the Senators dismissed him as a liar.

I thought that at least four good movies could be based on the stories in Ari's book, but when I pitched them in Hollywood, nobody bit. Bill, Ellen, and I were disappointed that the book hadn't made a bigger impact. We moved on, or so we thought.

Then one day I trudged up the stairs to my funky fifth-floor walkup apartment on the Upper West Side of Manhattan and found a court document nearly as thick as the phone book tacked to the door. I opened it and felt a terrible knot forming in my gut. I had been sued for $1.3 billion by a colonel in the Jordanian army.

Ari's book had identified the colonel as an arms dealer who sold weapons to Palestinian guerrillas. But more important, it had also outed him as a covert Israeli intelligence agent who reported to his masters where and to whom the weapons were sold. This description, the lawsuit charged, was an untrue libel. Ari's book not only ended his arms-dealing business, depriving him of more than $1 billion in potential profits, but also endangered his life once the Palestinian guerrillas found out he was working for the Israeli government.

Freaked out, I immediately called Bill to ask why I had been sued. He explained that for a civil lawsuit to be adjudicated in a U.S. federal court, at least one of the parties had to be a U.S. citizen. The colonel was Jordanian, and Ari, the book's author, was an Israeli citizen in the process of becoming Canadian. The colonel couldn't sue Ari, so his lawyer had decided to sue me as the editor. He had also sued Bill, as publisher and fact-checker, and the angel who had financed the book's publication. All three of us were U.S. citizens.

Fortunately, Bill had foreseen something like this and had bought $1 million worth of libel insurance. He hired his friend Melvin Wulf, former legal director of the ACLU, to defend us. For several months I waited before the colonel's lawyer called me for a deposition. I worried, but as usual, Bill came to the rescue. In his own deposition he took full responsibility for fact-checking in order to have the charges against me and the angel dropped, which they were. Thanks to Bill, the two of us were off the hook.

The case against Bill dragged on for more than a year. Mel was confident that if it went to trial he would win, but the libel insurance company didn't want to leave the matter to an unpredictable jury. It offered the colonel a minuscule settlement, and his lawyer, saving face, took it.

But Ari and Sheridan Square soon faced yet another legal challenge. President Reagan's former National Security Adviser, Robert McFarlane, also sued them for libel. In *Profits of War,* Ari had accused McFarlane of being a covert Israeli agent. Worse, he'd gone a step further and charged that McFarlane had leaked the top-secret codes that U.S. naval officer and convicted spy Jonathan Pollard used to gain access to the classified information he'd illegally relayed to Israel.

Again, Bill hired Mel Wulf. "This one is easy," Mel said. "McFarlane is a public figure, and it's almost impossible to prove libel of a public figure." The court quickly dismissed the case.

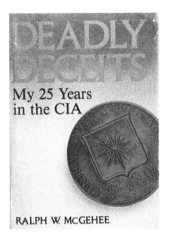
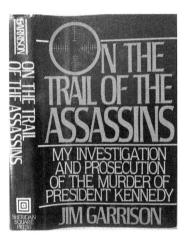
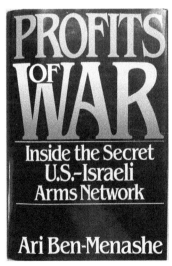

A few of the books I edited for Sheridan Square Press, including Jim Garrison's bestselling *On the Trail of the Assassins*, plus the annotated screenplay of *JFK*, published by Applause Books.

Profits of War was the last book I edited for Bill and Ellen. Though we'd successfully defended both libel suits, Sheridan Square Press lost its financial backers and never quite recovered. Somehow they kept the Institute for Media Analysis going and published several pamphlets in the late '90s and early 2000s. Eventually the Institute's office closed, but Bill and Ellen kept the space. Ellen used the front half to sell some of their antiques and collectibles. In the back, Bill opened a solo general law practice.

Bill was the smartest lawyer you could find. He handled anything—wills, entertainment contracts, real estate closings, commercial deals. He even represented our cocker spaniel Bessie when our landlord threatened to prohibit all dogs in our building. As usual, Bill prevailed. Bessie stayed and barked at that landlord till her dying day.

Bill's most important client turned out to be Ari Ben-Menashe. After his book came out, Ari had moved to Canada to start an international political consulting firm. From his days in Israeli intelligence, he had personally known Vladimir Putin, then in the KGB. When Putin rose to power in Russia, Ari had direct access. Small countries seeking financial or military aid from Russia began to hire Ari to make their case to Putin. The deals involved tens of millions of dollars, and Bill, who had handled many complicated financial transactions when he worked on Wall Street, wrote all the contracts.

Soon Bill and Ellen were debt-free and bought a small apartment in New Orleans. Because of their many trips to see Jim Garrison, they still had a soft spot in their hearts for The Big Easy. In 2005, when Hurricane Katrina destroyed the city, they were horrified by the images on TV. They decided to visit their lawyer friend Mary Howell there and help however they could. Bill ended up representing a number of homeowners who had lost everything in the storm. And as others abandoned New Orleans, Bill and Ellen moved into their new apartment in the Garden District, which Ellen had found for a bargain-basement price.

As they got older, they spent winters in New Orleans, enjoying live Dixieland jazz and Cajun pig roasts. They always took their 140-pound pure-bred white sheepdog Bambu with them. Bambu became a local celebrity when, dressed in a streetcar costume, he tugged Bill, dressed as a conductor, down Bourbon Street as part of a Mardi Gras parade.

Back in New York, the Gandhi-like Bambu was the mayor of the Washington Square dog run, where Bill walked him every day. Bambu's favorite place, though, was the house upstate in Sundown, where he loved to bellyflop and swim in the pond. While Bill and Ellen had no children, they treated Bambu like a big baby. They fed him Bill's gourmet meals, and for breakfast he often chowed down a bagel and cream cheese. Despite his enormous bulk, he curled up with Ellen on the couch as she read and at night hogged space in their bed. On Bambu's birthday, Bill even had an official U.S. postage stamp made with a photo of his sweet face, white hair flopping over his eyes.

In the last years, they spent all their summers in Sundown. The days of frantic work were over. They both seemed content to enjoy a quiet life. In 2014, Bambu died. Soon after, Ellen was diagnosed with lymphoma. And soon after that, Bill began suffering from serious pulmonary disease. For 45 years they'd done everything together––living, working, sleeping together, 24 hours a day, every day—so much so that their friends all called them "Bill and Ellen," as if they were a single unit. Now they dealt with illness together. They stopped drinking and smoking, but it was too late.

Over the next year, as Ellen's pain worsened and both of them were tethered to oxygen tanks, they never complained. But when Bill got pneumonia and had to be rushed to the hospital, Ellen was as furious as I'd ever seen her. She feared nothing more than having to live without him. "Bill, you can't die before me," she shouted at him. "I have to die first." Bill obliged, recovering from his pneumonia and coming home.

Strapped for cash, they sold the apartment in New Orleans first, then the house in Sundown. Their dear friends and fellow activists, human rights lawyer Michael Ratner and *Democracy Now* video producer Karen Ranucci, offered them a small cottage near their own farm house in Olivebridge, about five minutes from where we live. Shortly after Bill and Ellen moved in, I went over to visit. Ellen asked if we could go out on the back porch, so I dragged the oxygen tanks outside. We sat on soft chairs I brought from the living room. Both of them faced the late-afternoon sun, soaking in its warmth. They listened to the birdsong in the distance. We didn't speak.

That was the last time I saw Ellen. She went into the bathroom a couple of days later, fell over, and died. Bill was there with her.

Not a person who ever expressed much emotion, Bill was heartbroken but stoic. He moved back to the apartment in the city, and his own condition worsened. He had full-time live-in help and loyal friends visited, but he couldn't go outside. He was too short of breath to make it back up the stairs. Still, he did manage to go to the memorial celebration for Ellen at St. Mark's Church in the East Village. Their friend Evan Christopher, virtuoso jazz clarinetist, flew up from New Orleans and played with a Dixieland group put together by Bill's cousin, jazz historian Phil Schaap. This was the music that both Bill and Ellen loved. As I listened to the sad, wailing clarinet, I looked across the room. Bill, the unflappable man who could handle anything, was sobbing, great heaving sobs, as if the world had ended. For him, it had.

Bill lasted eight months after Ellen died, but his heart wasn't in it. To him, Ellen was life. Without her, little else mattered. When I visited him near the end, he was bedridden, emaciated, attached to the oxygen tank. I told him that I had fainted recently of dehydration and had fallen forward onto my face, smashing my lip and chipping one of my front teeth. He said, "You know the difference between a *shlemozel* and a *shlemiel*? A *shlemozel* falls forward when he faints, a *shlemiel* falls backward."

I left laughing, amazed that in his condition he could still tell a joke. He died two days later. Both he and Ellen were 75.

His family and friends held a celebration of Bill's life at New York University Law School, presided over by Michael Smith, friend, lawyer, and co-host of the radio show *Law and Disorder*. Again, Evan Christopher played with a Dixieland band. Again, we all wept. Bill's niece Rosie Schaap spoke, as did many others, including me.

"Bill taught me two things that changed my life forever," I concluded. "First, that you didn't have to be a super-serious ideologue to work for peace, justice, and radical social change. You could enjoy life, you could make your work an adventure, you could laugh with your friends and comrades, and eat good food and celebrate all this big beautiful world has to offer.

"The other, even more important thing Bill taught me: you could take on the most powerful and violent institutions in the world, and you didn't have to be afraid. For me, raised in Hollywood during the McCarthy era blacklist, this was a revelation. Bill Schaap and Ellen Ray, just by being who they were and doing what they did, gave me a precious gift—they gave me back my courage. For that, thank you Bill, thank you Ellen. We will always remember you, we will always love you."

March 25, 2016. A handful of close friends and relatives gathered at the Sundown house to scatter Bill's ashes. The sky was wash-water gray, and a gauzy fog hung in the air. Not a car on the road, songbirds silent. As if out of respect. Only eight months before, the same close friends and relatives and Bill, on portable oxygen, had scattered Ellen's ashes here.

We huddled together near a large oak tree on the spot where Ellen's ashes now were absorbed into the ground. Karen Ranucci had brought the urn with Bill's ashes, and one by one, each person said a few words and scattered some of the ashes under the tree. Judd Hirsch told a funny story about Bill, and everyone tried their best to laugh. But I couldn't hear it. I was too shaken.

Sarah hugged me. It was my turn. I said nothing. I reached for the scooper, dug into the urn, and poured some of the last remains of Bill into my hand. I wanted to feel him. As I walked to the tree and scattered the ashes, I found myself weeping. For Bill, for Ellen, for myself, for the terrible loss.

But as I took a moment to look at the ground where what remained of Bill and Ellen had come to rest, my mind flashed back to that first day I'd met them at the Writers Congress at the Roosevelt Hotel. How excited and vibrant they were, telling their stories and laughing. How young and beautiful, how wonderfully rebellious, and how much in love. I thought about what an extraordinary and fun adventure their life together had been and how fortunate I was to be part of it.

I felt a surge of inexplicable joy and awe at the beauty of life when it is lived the way they lived. And now their ashes, all that remained, were in the place where they belonged, dissolving and mingling together in the moist earth.

Bill and Ellen.

Bill Reuben (seated), me, Michael Ratner, Michael Smith (standing, left to right), Saratoga clubhouse dining room, circa 1998

SARATOGA BILL

William A. Reuben was one of the most colorful characters I've ever known. When I met him, I quickly realized he was a walking history of the 20th century. On our annual trips to Saratoga Race Course, he recounted riveting tales of his World War II experiences and his personal encounters with Albert Einstein, Damon Runyon, Paul Robeson, Alger Hiss, the Rosenbergs, and many more. This profile was published in *The American Scholar* in Autumn 2006.

HE LAY ON HIS BACK, EYES CLOSED, skin sallow and sagging, belly bulging under the hospital sheet. So many tubes and wires hooked into his bruised veins, I could barely recognize him.

The sterile room in the Mt. Sinai cancer ward scared me. I'd visited many hospitals, but I'd never seen anything like this.

He opened his eyes, pale blue, milky, the glasses he was always losing gone now. "Hi Zach."

"Hey Bill. How you doing?"

"Not good… Pain."

In the 20 years I'd known Bill Reuben, he'd been through spinal and prostate surgery, two cataract operations, a bleeding ulcer that had the police bashing down his door to rush him to the emergency room, emphysema, diabetes. And that didn't include three bullet wounds he got in World War II. But through all that, I'd never before heard him complain of pain.

"Don't stay," he said.

"Okay, if you don't want me to."

"Do me one favor." I nodded. "Tell the doctor… to give me something… so I can… get out of here."

"Sure, something to make you more comfortable…"

"No." He sounded irritated. "To get out."

The doctors had taken off the oxygen mask he'd been wearing for the last couple of weeks. Bill didn't want it. The congestion in his lungs was getting heavier, his heart weaker. But the resolute look in his eyes was unmistakable.

"I understand. I'll tell them."

"Look, I'm 88," he said, his breath short. "I've always believed nobody gets out of here alive." He was on a morphine drip, but his mind was lucid as ever. "I just want to say my goodbyes."

I barely nodded. When my mother died in Los Angeles in 1979 in the home I grew up in, I'd been 3,000 miles away, tied down at a Manhattan job. Same nine years later when my father died. Both had been ill for years, she with a brain tumor, he a heart condition. But both had died suddenly, the doctors' calls too late for me to get there in time. I'd never sat down with either of them on their deathbed, never held their hands, never had a chance to say goodbye. Now that moment was here for Bill, but my mind was in a fog, my nerve failing.

"Thanks for… everything, Zach," Bill continued, words coming out between gasps. "You've…been a great …friend."

My mouth was dry. I couldn't speak, couldn't swallow.

Bill's voice was quiet but firm. "We've had some…terrific times… together…"

There was silence. His mind seemed to drift into memory. So did mine…

August 1990. Our first trip to Saratoga Springs. Bill was 74, I was 41. I picked Bill up in Manhattan, we drove for three hours, got off at Exit 14 of the Northway and, as Red Smith said, entered a different century. Set on the edge of a storybook Victorian town, the race course, the oldest in North America, traces its heritage back to 1865. As we parked near the training track and walked through the stable area, watching horses being washed down and groomed, Bill said, "My father took me here when I was 15. I've been back every summer since." To him, Saratoga was a second home. "Well, except maybe a few years when my son was young and my second wife didn't want me squandering the rent money."

His step seemed to quicken as we entered the grounds of the track. Instantly I could feel myself being pulled into an insular, timeless world, operating on its own rules, honoring its sacred rituals and traditions. "Just look at this," he said, pointing to the creaking wooden grandstand with its red-and-white awnings and languid ceiling fans. "How can anyone even think of George Bush or Iran-*contra* when they're here? I keep telling you, Zach, Saratoga is the best therapy around."

I'd met Bill seven years earlier through our mutual friend Victor Navasky, editor of *The Nation* magazine. Victor had asked me to edit a pamphlet on the Alger Hiss case. Hiss's notorious 1950 conviction on perjury charges was being appealed, and the idea was to publish the pamphlet documenting more than 100 factual errors in the federal judge's opinion before the Supreme Court reviewed the case.

Hiss was one of those iconic names that every kid who grew up in a Communist home knew—like Sacco and Vanzetti, the Scottsboro Boys, the Rosenbergs, Paul Robeson—so I agreed to do it.

Victor warned me that the writer of the pamphlet, William A. Reuben, was a bit eccentric. He lived in one of the most fashionable neighborhoods of Manhattan—East 63rd Street between Park and Madison. But it was a rent-controlled fourth-floor walkup and Bill, twice divorced, had been alone for quite awhile, so the cramped interior had a shabby, decaying feel with musty books and files covering every available surface. Bill wore baggy thrift-shop clothes that smelled of dried egg and stale sweat. Rather than buy the *New York Times,* which he considered the enemy, he regularly picked it out of the garbage in the subway. "Why encourage the bastards?" he explained. He'd been studying the Hiss and Rosenberg cases for 30 years, but hadn't held a steady job that whole time. He'd briefly been a press agent for the Metropolitan Opera and the ACLU, a phone salesman huckstering land in Arizona, a taxi driver, and a plaintiff in numerous lawsuits. He'd lived on the settlement from one "successful accident" for a full year. Somehow he pieced together a living from freelance writing, Social Security, a small disability pension from his war wounds, and a few well-placed bets at the racetrack.

Victor had told me that Bill suffered from a number of maladies including diabetes, and when his blood sugar was low, he could be ornery—or worse. But I found Bill charming and gracious. Apparently my political pedigree had predisposed him to like me. As a young man, he'd seen social protest plays my father had written, and his camp counselor had been my father's best friend and collaborator, Albert Maltz, later one of the Hollywood Ten. When I told Bill I'd grown up with two of his books on my parents' shelves—*The Atom Spy Hoax,* a defense of Julius and Ethel Rosenberg, and *The Honorable Mr. Nixon,* an exposé of Congressman Richard Nixon's dishonorable role in the Hiss case—his eyes lit up and he announced to Victor that I was the man for the job.

The pamphlet proved to be a nightmare. My Columbia Journalism School training clashed with Bill's loose interpretation of what a factual error was. Bill would regularly explode and threaten to fire me, or alternatively, to abandon the project. In these conflicts, Victor became the final arbitrator. Bill protested his verdicts so often and at such great length that we missed the deadline and ended up publishing *Footnote on an Historic Case: In Re Alger Hiss* a couple of months after the Supreme Court had already rejected Hiss's appeal.

A lot had happened in the seven years since then. My father had died, I'd come down with an incapacitating case of a mysterious illness called chronic fatigue syndrome, and I'd moved to a small house in the Hudson Valley to heal. Physically unable to do much else, I spent a lot of time thinking about my father, missing him, mourning him—and exploring my anger at him. One of the things I realized was that, unlike most fathers and sons, he and I had never gone to a single sporting event together. Though the Dodgers, the Lakers, and the Rams all played regularly in L.A., I went to see them only with friends and their fathers. And although I had played competitive tennis in high school and my father had written a novel about the game, he never took me to a match or came to watch me play. In a city with an unreliable bus system, where kids depend on their parents for transportation, he never drove me anywhere. He was the only man in Los Angeles who didn't know how to drive—or so it seemed to me.

One day I was going through the childhood things I'd rescued from the house, and I found a Saratoga Springs T-shirt with a picture of horses straining for the finish line. My grandparents, who ran a small tailor shop on the Lower East Side and every August took a couple of weeks to escape to Saratoga for the fresh country air and healing waters, had sent it to me when I was eight years old. As a boy, I'd always loved that T-shirt and dreamed of the mythical place called Saratoga.

Thirty-four years later, with the worn T-shirt in my hands, I felt a longing for something—I didn't know exactly what. And then I remembered a yellowing newspaper photo I'd seen one day on Bill Reuben's bulletin board when we were finishing the pamphlet. It was of Bill in 1968, reading a *Daily Racing Form* in the paddock area at Saratoga Springs. He looked young, strong, vibrant, and slim.

Somewhere in my aching soul I felt it was time to go to Saratoga and that Bill would be the perfect guide. I called him, and here we were, strolling the grounds together—an odd couple if ever there was one. Bill was of medium height, with a balding head, long strands of gray hair flowing behind his ears, a red bulbous nose, drooping jowls, a double chin, and a protruding belly. On top of a knit shirt, he wore a stained 1950s plaid sport jacket, the pockets bulging with a racing form, sunglasses, and reading glasses. I was tall, skinny, and pale, wearing faded Levis, sneakers, and a baseball cap.

Though he was 33 years older, I'd been weakened by my illness, so we moved at pretty much the same pace as we strolled the grounds. Bill pointed out all his favorite spots—the clothing room where the rainbow-colored silks of all the stables hung, the jockeys' quarters where the diminutive athletes (mostly Hispanic and Irish) freshened up between races, the scales where they weighed in, the Big Red Spring, named for the fabled Man o' War, where we drank the mineral waters. Finally, we sat down at a picnic table in the paddock area. Here we watched the horses being saddled by their trainers and paraded before their high-society owners—beautiful women in outrageous hats and flowery dresses and aging men in white linen suits and Panama hats who smelled of money.

I knew nothing about horse racing or betting. "If you're a Marxist, you can win at the track," Bill said. "It's all dialectics." He pulled out a stack of small paper sheets with computerized numbers in graph form. Bill prepared for a day at the races by buying both the *Daily Racing Form,* which most everyone used, and also the *Ragozin Sheets,* which cost a lot and very few bettors used. "These were invented by an ex-Communist," Bill said. "He almost single-handedly supported the Progressive Labor Party with his track winnings all through the '60s."

He started to explain how they worked, but before he got very far, he was drowned out by the "Star-Spangled Banner" on the loudspeaker system. Everyone stood up, some saluting the flag. I felt my usual mixture of anger, anxiety, and fear. The flag Bill had fought for stood for freedom. But having lived through the McCarthy era and the civil rights and anti-Vietnam War movements, I had come to view it as a symbol of America's expanding imperial, military, and racist presence around the world.

I felt intimidated by the flag-wavers around me. I'd grown up in the 1950s in Hollywood, where my father had been a blacklisted screenwriter. Fear permeated our home, and my father's response to the blacklist had been to retreat. He dropped out of politics altogether, and as a boy I watched him wither, a diminished man. He still read about politics, but his dissenting voice had been silenced, his spirit crushed.

I still lived with that pervasive fear. And so I found myself reluctantly rising to my feet as that unsingable anthem blared. But Bill remained firmly seated, like a big-bellied Jewish Buddha. A heavily muscled middle-aged man with a crewcut stood nearby, his hand over his heart. He glared over at Bill.

"Hey, how about a little respect for the flag, old-timer?" he yelled. Bill didn't respond. I nervously shuffled my feet. I'd escaped Vietnam with college deferments. My father had avoided World War II by working for the movies. Patriotic military types always made me feel like a wimp.

"I said, how about showing some respect for this great country?" the man shouted, his face reddening. He was drunk. My breathing grew short and quick. "What kind of coward won't stand up for his country?"

Bill didn't budge. He looked straight into the man's eyes. "I have three Purple Hearts," he said quietly. "How many do you have?"

The man slinked away as the song ended. I was ready to follow Bill anywhere.

He led me to the horse races, and the spectacle dazzled me. Flowers everywhere, even hanging from the stables. The romantic names—Sky Beauty, Sea Hero. The sensual horses with their shining coats, flowing manes, and soulful eyes. The rituals––saddling in the paddock, the bugle signaling the horses entering the track, the regal post parade. The roar of the crowd as the horses turned for home and headed down the stretch. My own pounding heart as a horse we'd bet on surged to the lead at the finish line. For better or worse, I fell in love with horse racing that day.

Before the first race, we each put $100 in a pool, and I left the betting to Bill. By the end of the feature race, we had accumulated an astonishing profit of $1,200. As we walked through the stables on the way to the car, Bill told me his first rule of horse racing: if you win, don't give it back to the track. Treat yourself to a good meal at as fancy a restaurant as you could find.

We went to a small classy place called Eartha's, rubbing shoulders with wealthy horse-owning families like the Vanderbilts and Phippses—a temporary leveling of the playing field that gave Bill infinite pleasure.

Bill's second rule was: if you win, buy something for somebody you love. And so, after dinner, Bill and I ended up in the swankiest boutique on Saratoga's main drag, relying on the saleswoman to pick out a purple tie-dyed dress for Sarah, my life partner, who almost never wore dresses but adored anything purple.

After a leisurely drive by the luxurious Victorian homes on upper Broadway, we headed to my home in Olivebridge.

"So…three purple hearts," I said as we entered the Northway. That was all it took. Bill was off telling me stories about his war experience.

"I enlisted and went to Europe as an infantry second lieutenant," he said. "My main job was to jump out of the foxhole first and yell, 'Follow me.' The life expectancy for infantry officers in combat was about nine days. All you had to hope for was that you'd come up with what they used to call 'a million-dollar wound.' In other words, you'd get hit bad enough to take you out of combat but not maim you for life. I was the only one from my officers' training class who survived the war. Everyone else got killed. I was lucky. Got hit three times, got trench feet, which is something like gangrene. Spent seven months in hospital and got out of the army with a 30 percent disability benefit for life. It wasn't much, but it helped support me as a freelance writer."

It was late, I was tired. But Bill's stories kept me awake, and my respect for him grew the more he told me. He'd arrived on the beach at Normandy a month after D-Day. He remembered looking up and wondering how U.S. forces had been able to scale those cliffs under heavy fire. Then, when he got to the top of the cliffs himself, he saw the vast field of crosses where thousands of young men were buried, and he understood.

Right after V-E Day, he'd taken a leave and gone to Dachau with his wife Miriam, a concert violinist, and the singer Paul Robeson, who'd been entertaining the troops on a USO tour. Together they'd seen the horror of the Nazi concentration camps—an image that haunted him the rest of his life.

"The war radicalized me," he said. "Before I went overseas I was stationed all over the Deep South—Fort Benning, Georgia, Camp Shelby, Mississippi, Camp Rucker, Alabama. I was supposed to deliver lectures to the troops about why we fight against fascism. And here I was, in a segregated army, hearing the word 'nigger' every place you went. I mean, the venom that came out towards anyone whose skin pigmentation was any different—all these expressions of racism that seemed to me to be the very thing we were supposed to be fighting against.

"And then when we went to Dachau, I remember we must have stopped 15 people, and our driver spoke German, and said, 'Where is the concentration camp?' and everyone, without exception, said: 'I don't know what you're talking about. I've never heard of it.' That made such a profound impression. After the war, when I heard top-level generals saying we should go on to Moscow and finish off the Soviets, I couldn't believe my ears. As an infantryman in the trenches, I knew that these marvelous brave Soviet fighters were literally saving American lives, saving my life, by sacrificing their own against the Germans. Now I heard our generals make them into the enemy. And everyone acted like they didn't know the Soviets had been our best ally. Just like the Germans near Dachau, they didn't know anything.

"And finally, back home I went to work for the ACLU and Roger Baldwin, the orneriest s.o.b. you could ever meet. The ACLU was defending Nazis, our enemies in the war, and at the same time turning down cases of Communists, our allies in the war—this was an enormous shock that jolted me into wondering, 'Is this what we fought the war for?' And so, when everyone else was leaving the Communist Party, I joined, just to show which side I was on. But I didn't last long. Too stifling for an independent mind."

Bill spent that night in Olivebridge, marveling at the fresh air, the stars, and the quiet. The next day I put him on a bus in New Paltz. He went straight from the Port Authority terminal to Roosevelt Hospital, where he was rushed into emergency surgery for prostate cancer. He hadn't told me about the blood in his urine at Saratoga. Within ten days he had a second operation. When I finally reached him on the phone, he seemed unfazed. The doctors had told him his prognosis was good. I was relieved, but when I hung up, I said to Sarah, with more than a little disappointment, "I guess that's the last time I'll ever go to Saratoga with Bill."

For the next 13 summers, I told Sarah the same thing. And every year I was wrong. Even when Bill had spinal surgery, even as his diabetes worsened and neuropathy set in, even when he was 87 and in a wheelchair, we never missed Saratoga.

Every year the ritual was pretty much the same. I would pick him up in the city and once in Saratoga we'd head directly to the clubhouse dining room, where we would have lunch and bet on the races from a table overlooking the magnificent track with its furrowed dirt, manicured grass, and ever-present waterfowl. To conserve funds for the betting windows, we'd stay in a modest bungalow several miles north of Saratoga. At dawn we'd be up watching the horses work out in the morning mist, followed by breakfast at the concrete-block cafe in the backstretch area, where the migrant stable hands ate. In the afternoon, back to the track for more races and betting. And at sunset, win or lose, we'd drive slowly around the stable area, enjoying the smell of hay and the peacefulness as the horses settled in for the evening.

It was there in the stables near the training track that Bill took me in 1993 to visit his trainer friend Skippy Shapoff. They'd known each other since boyhood, Bill explained. Skippy's father Moe was a trainer, and a friend of Bill's father. Skippy had gone to Harvard but came back to horse training. This year he had a top three-year-old colt named Silver of Silver who'd finished fourth in the Belmont Stakes and was training for the big race of the summer, the Travers.

"Hey Billy," said Skippy. He didn't say much else. Bill asked him about Silver of Silver as we gingerly sidestepped clods of horse dung.

"Just worked in 1:12. They'll notice that."

He took us over to see the big horse, but warned us not to pet him. He was mean and could bite. Bill asked if he had any other horses we could bet on, but Skippy just grumbled. Then he looked up at Bill and said, "Y'know, I think Damon had a horse a long time ago—named him Billy Reuben."

We'd lost all our bets that day, so we went to dinner at the Four Seasons, an inexpensive vegetarian cafe that Bill didn't really like. I asked him about "Damon."

"Damon Runyon was a good friend of my father's," Bill said. "He wrote most of his best short stories at our house on Hibiscus Island in Miami. He didn't get along with his own family, but he liked me. Took me with him to the 1932 Olympics in Los Angeles. He wasn't a real hustler himself, didn't talk like the characters in his stories. In fact, he hired a friend of my father's to be his driver just so he could hear the real street talk. I forget his name—maybe Greasy Fingers Lefty or Pickpocket Harry. No, no, it was Horse-Thief Burke. He talked the real lingo."

He sniffed a seaweed casserole with suspicion. "What is this stuff? Y'know, Zach, I wouldn't come here, except I keep hoping Julie will walk in again."

Two years earlier the first woman jockey in the Horse Racing Hall of Fame, Julie Krone, a fearless 90-pound vegetarian with a squeaky voice, had sat down right next to us and talked to Bill for ten minutes about racing and diet. He was in heaven.

"So did you get to know some of these hustlers?" I asked.

Me (left) and Bill Reuben studying racing form, Saratoga clubhouse, circa 1997

"Sure, all my father's friends—con men, charlatans, scoundrels." He smiled to himself. "I remember this one guy we'd drive to Saratoga with—E. Phoshen Howard. He ran an old-fashioned shakedown operation. He'd follow the rich and famous to brothels, then he'd threaten to expose them in his weekly scandal sheet unless he was paid off."

"And your father? Was he a hustler too?"

Bill nodded as he dug into a vegetable stir-fry. "He was raised in the Cleveland Jewish Orphan asylum. A very gifted salesman, promoter, made a lot of money with his schemes. He was interested in all kinds of sporting events. At one point he owned a part of the Cleveland professional football team. And from the time I was six years old, he took me to racetracks all over the world."

"So where'd you make your first bet?"

"New Orleans. I was a teenager working at the track. A 50-1 long shot named Freedom's Call, and he won! I always thought that was prophetic. But I'll tell you, working there every day, watching the hustlers and touts and degenerate horseplayers, I figured out pretty quick the world was not what it seemed. You want to know what's really going on—on or off the track—you follow the money."

I couldn't get enough of this stuff. Like Bill, I'd been born into a non-religious Jewish home. But the world of my parents was populated by moral, honest, upright intellectuals—serious political people who believed in Marxist ideology and the nobility of the working class. Bill's Runyonesque world of scam artists hustling for an easy buck was something utterly foreign—fascinating, dangerous, and alluring.

"Through the first years of the Depression I was raised like a millionaire's son," Bill continued as he shoveled down his tofu salad. He was warming up now. "I had a governess, a chauffeur. Went to private schools. We lived on Park Avenue in Manhattan and later Hibiscus Island in Miami. Our neighbor on the next island was Al Capone."

"Hold it, hold it," I interrupted. "You knew Al Capone?"

"No, he was in prison, but I was friends with his son. Sweet, lovely boy. Every school day for a year his bodyguard picked me up in the morning and drove me and Sonny Capone to school, then picked me up and brought me back home. That ended when I was sent to boarding school in Switzerland. Then at the University of Pennsylvania, I had my own Cadillac roadster, my own suite of rooms. But I never really knew where all this affluence came from until one day at the end of my sophomore year I saw a headline in the newspaper: my father had been indicted for fraud and income tax evasion. All of a sudden there was no money. I had to drop out of college. That was the beginning of my personal disillusionment."

Although his father was eventually acquitted in a back-room payoff, whatever respect Bill once had for authority figures was now gone. The hysteria of the Cold War years further disillusioned him. "McCarthy, Nixon, Whittaker Chambers, J. Edgar Hoover—they were just lying, cheating con artists like the ones I was raised with—only on a much bigger stage. When most of America bought into their phony espionage cases, their loyalty oaths and blacklists—that completed my radicalization."

He paused, finishing his brown-rice pudding. "I guess maybe you had to be raised like me to see that was just another con game."

Bill was a walking history of the 20th century. How many other people had spent two days explaining the Rosenberg case to Albert Einstein? (Bill came back from Princeton and told his mother he'd finally met someone intelligent enough to understand him.) In the beginning, our conversations were mostly a one-way street—Bill telling stories, me listening. But over time that changed. Bill had become isolated. He was a political maverick who couldn't work with any party or organization for long. His combative personality had ended a number of friendships. He was divorced. His son lived in California. I realized that Bill needed me, not just to pass lonely hours, but to share his life, his history, his passion for politics and for horse racing.

On those long drives to and from Saratoga, we talked non-stop about politics and the deteriorating state of the world, from the frightening rise of George W. Bush to the self-destruction of the left. Always curious, Bill asked me about my family and my latest writing project. And of course, inevitably, we ended up talking for hours about horse racing—trainers, jockeys, horses, handicapping, betting strategy. We analyzed the races in detail, argued about the relative importance of factors like weight, post position, and pace, and tried to figure out where our betting should have zigged instead of zagged.

Having escaped death three times in combat, Bill considered every day an unexpected gift. After the war he lived with no fear, no caution, no plan for the future, no concern about money. He spent his time fighting for the underdog. But at the racetrack he almost invariably bet on favorites. In his view, inside information ruled the stock exchange, politics, the track, and just about everything else, and he didn't have enough money to risk betting against the big boys. His idea of a good bet was to plunk down $50 to place on an even-money favorite. When the horse won and he collected a $20 profit, he'd say with satisfaction, "Forty cents to the dollar. Now that's value."

He did a lot of homework before going to the track, carefully studying the *Ragozin Sheets,* which evaluated the past races of each horse with a numerical speed figure. By looking at the numbers and the physical pattern they made on a graph, you could, in theory, more easily predict what the horse would do on the day he was to race. If a horse had run a particularly fast race recently, for example, most likely he would "bounce" and run a poor race next time out. After sufficient rest, he might recover and run somewhere in between. Thesis-antithesis-synthesis. The Hegelian-Marxist dialectic.

Bill taught me how to read *The Sheets*, but warned me not to put too much faith in them. "The horses still have to run around the track." I learned that lesson the hard way. One day, having studied the great filly Sky Beauty's superior sheet numbers, I decided she couldn't lose. "Careful," Bill counseled. "The map is not the territory." Ignoring him, I put $300 on her to win. Sure enough, she crossed the finish line first by three lengths––but was disqualified for interfering with another horse. Bill had little sympathy.

After awhile I realized that all *The Sheets* provided was data that helped with handicapping. Whether one wanted to bet money on that horse or not was an entirely separate matter. And that depended on your betting philosophy.

Unlike Bill, I had lived a remarkably sheltered life. Growing up with so much fear during the blacklist, I had adopted a cautious approach to living. After college, I'd gone to journalism school, then got a secure part-time job proofreading at *Time* magazine while I worked on a novel. I kept my costs to a minimum and stayed out of trouble. No big risks—till I discovered the racetrack.

I found the betting part of horse racing thrilling. It was liberating not to worry about money for once, to ignore those Depression-era voices of my parents whispering in my ear to be frugal. And for someone who worked alone as a writer and editor on projects that took years to complete, there was nothing more satisfying than the immediacy of a horse race. You chose a horse, placed a bet, watched the race, and the whole thing was over, win or lose, within a few minutes.

I was the exact opposite of Bill. Whereas he had lived with reckless abandon and bet with the utmost caution, I had lived with caution and bet with reckless abandon. He usually bet favorites. I loved long shots. He liked to see the odds going down on a horse he'd bet, taking it as a sign that someone knew something. I was happiest when I saw the odds on my horse skyrocketing. He was dispassionate and scientific in his analysis. I was emotional and was even open to the predictions of a self-described psychic––something that drove Bill crazy, especially when I won with one of the psychic's picks at 18 to 1.

Once our differences became clear, we realized we could no longer pool our money and let Bill do the betting. Thus was born "The Enterprise," a reference to Oliver North's euphemism for Iran-*contra* arms-dealing. We each put $100 into The Enterprise and bet from this pool only when we could agree. That was rare, and The Enterprise generally did pretty well as a result. Otherwise, we each bet on our own. Bill never made much and never lost much. I made a lot and lost a lot. And on days when Bill did well, I did poorly and vice versa. The one thing we always shared was the horseplayer's fatal disease: optimism. No matter what happened, there was always another race, another day.

We suffered through many frustrating days when either our handicapping was dead wrong or our betting strategy was flawed and we went home with empty wallets, muttering all the gambling clichés about how you can't beat the races, the game is fixed, the horses juiced. We also basked in the glory of a few miraculous days when all of us––Bill, I and The Enterprise––won big and everything seemed right with the world. Overall, we probably lost a few more bucks than we won.

Ultimately, though, Saratoga wasn't about gambling. We'd gone to the races at Belmont Park, Aqueduct, and the Meadowlands. But Bill always said, "Losing at Saratoga is better than winning anywhere else." For Bill, Saratoga was a tonic that revived his spirit. He could leave behind George W. Bush and all the depressing news stories he followed every day on C-Span and think about nothing but horses.

Over the years, as his back, eyes, and legs began to fail, he slowed down. During that same time, I had recovered from my illness and was moving faster. Our paces were no longer in synch—which led to outbursts of Bill's temper and my patience being sorely tried. More than once, as he snapped at me or asked me to carry one more thing when my hands were full, I asked myself, "Why am I doing this?" But somehow we survived these conflicts and found ways to cope. First Bill got a cane. Then he held on to the cane with one hand and me with the other. Finally, a wheelchair. By 2000, he was having trouble seeing the odds board and I was placing his bets for him. Increasingly, it felt as if these annual trips to Saratoga were the only thing keeping him alive—except for the Hiss book.

Ever since we met, Bill had been talking about the Hiss book. In 1950, as an investigative reporter for the independent radical weekly *National Guardian,* Bill had written the first articles questioning Alger Hiss's conviction for perjury. For the next two decades he'd researched and written exposés and books on several of the most sensational espionage cases of the McCarthy era. But in the late 1970s, when Congress passed the Freedom of Information Act, he went back to see Alger Hiss. Together, he and Hiss requested all government records about the case. When the government denied their request, they sued and won. More than 200,000 pages of government documents, mostly from the FBI, were released to them.

For two decades he'd been wading through these documents, which bulged from the file cabinets in his rundown apartment. He was writing what he considered the most important work of his life: the definitive book on the Alger Hiss case. But I'd never seen a page of it. Neither had Victor Navasky. Nor Hiss's son Tony. I began to wonder if the Hiss book was Bill's equivalent of Joe Gould's Secret—the Greenwich Village legend's monumental oral history of the world that, it turned out, never existed.

In 1998, Victor Navasky and Tony Hiss, growing impatient, asked if I would work with Bill and edit his book. My career had taken a different direction in the '90s. A book I had edited, *On the Trail of the Assassins* by Jim Garrison, had been optioned by Oliver Stone, and he had hired me to adapt it into a screenplay with him. Following the release of the resulting film *JFK,* whatever credibility I once had in mainstream journalism had vanished and I had turned to screenwriting full-time.

But I found it difficult to say no to Navasky, and Bill wasn't willing to trust anyone else as his editor. So I agreed. It took no time to discover that the manuscript did indeed exist, and was hundreds of pages long. As I read the confusing chronology, I felt myself being sucked into a quagmire almost as deep as the last one I'd stumbled into in 1987— the Kennedy assassination, which had consumed my life for nearly five years. Now, instead of the endless puzzle involving Oswald, the Zapruder film, and the magic bullet, I was trying to make sense of Hiss, the Pumpkin Papers, Whittaker Chambers, Nixon, and the Woodstock typewriter.

Although Bill's prose was often like a jungle that needed to be hacked out with a machete, his main thesis was clear as day: Hiss was innocent of both espionage and perjury, and his accuser Whittaker Chambers was neither a spy nor a communist but a pathological liar. "Nixon, J. Edgar Hoover, and Chambers framed Hiss," Bill harangued me, "because he was a high-profile liberal New Dealer—big State Department official, first secretary general of the United Nations. They knew if they called him a communist spy, they'd make sensational headlines for themselves— and discredit the reforms of FDR's New Deal. The whole message they wanted to get across was: 'liberal' equals 'communist' equals 'spy' equals 'traitor.' But it was all fiction. The fact remains: of all the people accused of being spies in the 1950s, not a single one was ever convicted of espionage in a court of law. Not a single one."

Bill felt he stood virtually alone, slogging through the tedious documents and trial records to defend Hiss and expose the lies, manipulations, and half-truths of his accusers. My job was to clarify what Bill wanted to say, question what confused me, and get rid of digressions and repetitions. I was no expert on the case and the book still needed to be fact-checked, but I was persuaded by Bill's painstakingly documented arguments. And more important, all the feelings of outrage and indignation my parents had taught me to suppress during the McCarthy era were coming up and finally finding expression in Bill's book.

The work continued at a leisurely pace, in between my screenwriting jobs and our trips to the races. After several years and nearly 1000 pages, the end was nowhere in sight. Every time I thought we were approaching the final trial, Bill would add a new chapter. It became clear to me that he really didn't want the book to end. His life was pretty well set up. He didn't have much money, but he got by. He had a rent-controlled apartment. Meals on Wheels delivered a hot supper every day. A part-time housekeeper from Caring Neighbor cleaned up. Access-a-Ride took him anywhere he wanted to go. And despite all his health problems, his mind was sharp as ever. The book provided a mental challenge, something to do every day. While Saratoga and the horse races were an amusing distraction, the book gave Bill's life meaning.

Soon after we had survived Y2K, when I was delivering an edited chapter to Bill, I noticed that a new obstacle had presented itself to prevent completion of the book. Several apartments were suddenly vacant at 37 East 63rd, and Bill's landlord, Townhouse Management Company, had bought the building next door, which was already being gutted. Townhouse announced plans to create a single townhouse from the two buildings and put it on the market at a price of $23 million. While other tenants were offered buyouts, Townhouse had said nothing to Bill. He was 85 and in poor health. Relying on actuarial tables, they'd decided to wait him out, betting he would die before they had to pay him to move. But clearly they didn't know Bill.

In 1968, he had lived in a small, $72-a-month apartment on West 48th Street. The building had been targeted to make way for Rockefeller Center's new Celanese Corporation skyscraper. After all the other tenants had taken buyouts, Bill was still there, working on a book—the last holdout. Months later, when he'd finished a draft and the price reached $22,375, Bill accepted the offer to move out. He went straight to Saratoga. After he returned, he found the apartment at 37 East 63rd.

Now he was a holdout again, the only one left in the building. Every weekday for the next two years the jackhammers began at 8 a.m. Banging and thumping continued until five, rain or shine. Periodically the electrical wiring failed, and Bill was left with no lights, computer, TV, or radio. Other times there would be outages of the phone, the door buzzer, the heat, hot water, and gas for the kitchen stove. Bill rarely left the apartment, and when he did, he risked serious injury. The walls of the stairwell had been knocked down. One wrong step could send him tumbling down several flights. And the worsening diabetic neuropathy in his legs made climbing stairs painful and difficult.

But no matter how bad the living conditions got, Bill told me, "It was worse in the infantry." Besides, he said, it wasn't easy to move at his age. He wasn't budging unless he got a fair offer.

At first I was irritated by his stubbornness. But after awhile I understood that Bill's holding out was a metaphor for his life. He'd always held out for what he believed. He'd never given in just because it was easier or more comfortable or more convenient.

And then it struck me. As different as he was from Bill in so many ways, my father had been exactly like him in this most important way. When he was named before HUAC, my father suffered, he lost his work and his nerve, he got an ulcer. But he never compromised his principles. He never went for money or security, and he never lost his natural gentleness, kindness, or sense of humor. Like Bill, he found the strength and resolve to hold out. And along with my mother he managed to support the family and pass on to me, my sister, and my brother the values that now guided our lives.

I'd gravitated to Bill in the first place because he seemed so unlike my father. Now I realized how alike they actually were. Bill never knew it, but just by holding out, he'd given me the most precious gift of our 20-year friendship: he helped me let go of years of anger and regain my respect, admiration, and love for my own father.

Finally, in December of 2001, Townhouse offered Bill a spacious apartment in an elegant elevator building on 66th Street just east of Fifth Avenue. He could live in it rent-free for the rest of his life. In addition, Townhouse would give him $150,000 as a buyout fee, plus moving and furnishing expenses. "It's better than hitting the Pick-6," he told me. Even Bill couldn't hold out any longer.

They say all horseplayers die broke. But at the age of 87, Bill had more money than he'd ever dreamed of. He and his son Howard, who'd moved back to New York, bought a big-screen TV, a Macintosh computer, and all new furniture for the apartment. To thank his closest friends who'd supported him through the hard times, Bill threw a lavish party at Shung Lee Dynasty East. He sat there beaming as I and nine others feasted on Chinese delicacies and told stories about him. I'd never seen him so happy.

By early 2003, the manuscript had passed the 1200-page mark. To finish, Bill just had to write a final summary chapter and an introduction. But there were more distractions. In February 2003, it was clear that George W. Bush was misleading the United States into a disastrous war in Iraq. "If Bush had ever bled in combat and smelled the stench of death on a battlefield like I did, he couldn't possibly do this," Bill railed at me. "Take me to an anti-war demonstration. Any time, anywhere, I want to be there."

On February 15, more than 30 million people around the world poured into the streets to protest the imminent war in Iraq. It was a bitter-cold day in New York. But the demonstration was on the east side, only 20 blocks from Bill's apartment. We bundled up in our warmest clothes, I lifted Bill into his electric wheelchair—he called it his "scooter"—and we headed toward the crowd.

It was so massive that police had barricaded every street below 72nd, from Third Avenue to the East River. There was no way to get through. These kinds of situations— big crowds, lots of heavily armed cops—had always brought back my deepest fears from the blacklist days. I was ready to go home.

But Bill would not be denied. He steered his scooter right up to a young cop manning a barricade and pulled out his medals and purple hearts from World War II. "How about letting a disabled veteran through?" The cop stared at the purple hearts, and then pulled back the barricade. For the next couple of hours we joined the crowds marching in the streets, Bill weaving his way on his scooter, I on foot next to him. When we got home, we were frozen and exhilarated. Though we'd been to several memorial services together, including one for Alger Hiss, this was the only demonstration I ever went to with Bill. I'd never been to any with my own father or mother.

The war began in March. Bill was glued to the TV all spring and into the summer. By August he was ready for our annual escape to Saratoga. I couldn't fit the scooter into my car. Instead, we took a collapsible wheelchair, and Bill was just as happy for me to be pushing him around. His eyes had deteriorated badly. He could barely see the track and the horses through his binoculars. We had our usual ups and downs, our victories, near-misses, "woulda, shouldas, if I'da's." I don't remember if we won or lost. It didn't matter. We were in Saratoga.

At the end of the second day, we took our ritual drive around the stable area, watching the horses being groomed, hot-walked, washed down, fed. We stopped near the Phipps stable of trainer Shug McGaughey. It's the most secluded and beautiful part of the backstretch, overlooking the Oklahoma training track. The horses were all settled in their stalls now.

The sun inched lower, orange against a luminous blue sky. The only sounds hooves shuffling, gentle snorts. We looked out at the track and shared a moment of contentment. Late summer. Warm. All peaceful. In harmony. We didn't say a word. Somehow we both knew: this was the last time we'd be at Saratoga together.

One day that autumn Bill called. He'd awakened unable to move his left leg. His doctor told him he'd probably had a small stroke. He spent the next two weeks at Lenox Hill, taking dozens of tests and seeing specialists. He loved the attention. "If I was 40 years younger," he said, "I'd have proposed marriage to four nurses and three therapists."

He came home without a diagnosis, but with pain in his right shoulder and difficulty breathing. He talked about writing that last chapter of the Hiss book, but since he was now hooked up to an oxygen tank, didn't have the strength to do it. All winter he was in and out of the hospital. The shoulder was broken, fragile from a spreading cancer. Breathing impaired by a weakening heart. Legs almost gone now. In spring, the doctors said there was nothing more they could do.

...He blinked his weary eyes. The hospital room's lights were bothering him.

"Did that Smarty Jones win the Triple Crown?" Bill asked. On TV he'd been able to follow the exploits of the little horse from Philadelphia who'd won the Kentucky Derby and the Preakness.

"Not yet. The Belmont is this Saturday," I replied. "I'll be there rooting for you. Should be one to two. Your kind of horse."

He didn't respond. His strength was fading. I put my jacket on. "I'll make sure your book gets published."

He nodded. "Touch my hand." His voice shook.

I groped for a spot with no needles or tubes, then leaned in and gave him an awkward hug and a kiss on the cheek.

"Have a good journey... the rest of the way," he said.

"You too." My voice was trembling more than his. "Goodbye, Bill."

Bill died that night.

A few days later I went to Belmont Park to see Smarty Jones run for the Triple Crown. Surrounded by 120,000 people, I felt an aching loneliness. I bet $2 to place on the 2-5 favorite—for Bill. When a 36-1 shot passed Smarty in deep stretch, the crowd lapsed into stunned silence and I found myself weeping. But then the payoffs were posted on the big board—$3.30 for the place bet—and I had to smile. I could hear Bill's voice: "Sixty-five cents to the dollar. Now that's what I call value!"

Xolo by Francisco Toledo. Courtesy of Francisco Toledo estate

THE WORK

This is a true love story about two women and a mangy street dog in Oaxaca, Mexico. Together, they touched my heart. The essay was originally published in *The Bark* magazine in Spring 2003.

"THE *ZÓCALO* IN OAXACA, MEXICO, is one of the few utopian public spaces left in the planet, *que no?*" The poet Guillermo Gomez-Pena said that a few years ago. It's still true today.

The *zócalo* is really two adjoining squares. The upper one, bordered by the post office and a decaying stone church, is lined with street vendors selling hand-embroidered clothes, rainbow cotton candy, fanciful balloons, Indian beads, and steamy tamales. The lower one, lined with sidewalk cafes, is bigger and has an old-fashioned circular bandstand in the center where a brass band regularly oom-pahs through Latin standards and Beatles tunes. Day or night, live music floats on the breeze—guitar, accordion, flute, the state orchestra.

In the heat of the day, ancient trees cast cooling shadows. Lovers sit on wrought-iron benches and hold hands. Dogs roam, scavenging for food. Legless beggars sit on the ground, hands out. Magicians, acrobats, and jugglers do their tricks for crowds of laughing kids. And on Wednesdays at dusk elderly pensioners dressed in white, with green bead necklaces, do the elegant, restrained steps of *danzón* to a live marimba band.

At the south end of the lower square a protest against the government's treatment of Indians in Chiapas and Oaxaca has been going on for years. Today hundreds of *campesinos,* farmworkers from the countryside, are camped out there, demonstrating about stolen elections, Indian farmland taken for airport development, and wages so low that no human being can live on them. At night they curl up on the hard cobblestones of the *zócalo*—dark-skinned men in dusty cowboy hats, barefoot Indian women cradling hungry babies in their *rebozos*.

The *zócalo* turns away no one. Any time you go, Oaxaqueños are there, sitting, strolling, chatting, listening, eating, enjoying the dry air and each other. It is the center of the community. And it was here, in the *zócalo,* that the work began.

Sarah, my *compañera,* and I were in Oaxaca for a Sundance workshop for screenwriters from all over Latin America. For four days I'd been discussing scripts. With the workshop over, Sarah and I began our vacation time with a leisurely walk down the narrow streets to the *zócalo.* It was 80 degrees, clear—a typical February day. I was savoring doing nothing, soaking in the warm sun and gazing at some bougainvillea climbing the walls of a church at the edge of the *zócalo,* when I heard a voice.

"Help me, please help me." There in the street, on her knees, was a woman with sun-burnt skin, wire-rim glasses, and shiny hair spilling down to her shoulders. She must have been in her mid-30s. A young Mexican man on a bicycle was shaking his head and trying to speak to her.

"I can't speak Spanish," she cried in a New England accent. "There's this dog, it's suffering..."

I hadn't noticed the dog. It lay at her feet, an emaciated mutt with clumps of matted, scraggly dark hair. It was streaked with mud or grease, so filthy it looked black—except for the raw patches of red, oozing cauliflower skin where there was no hair at all.

"All he does is scratch himself," the woman said. "He's got mange, worst I've ever seen. I've been watching him for four days." Her voice faltered.

The dog looked up at her as if trying to understand. He had soft gray eyes.

"I'm leaving tomorrow. I promised God if I saw this dog again, I would do something about it. I was going to write postcards, but then... here was this dog. I need to find a vet, but I can't speak and this guy just keeps asking if I've seen Monte Alban. I don't care about Monte Alban. This dog needs to be put down."

I looked at the dog. He was a mess, and his floppy ears were covered with nasty-looking tumors, but he was lying there calmly, tilting his head up at the woman. For the moment he wasn't scratching.

"Y'know, dogs in Mexico, it's different," I said. "We saw one like this in Valladolid, it seemed to get along."

"I know dogs, I'd take this one back to New Hampshire if I could, but they'll never let him through customs. And nobody here is gonna care for him. This dog is suffering, he never gets a moment of peace. He's always in the *zócalo*, nobody feeds him, the other dogs won't go near him, he's an outcast."

She burst into tears, and I wondered how long she'd been in Mexico, how long it had been since she spoke English to anyone.

"Please," she cried, "I can handle the dog, but my Spanish…I need your help…"

Back in my real life in New York City, street situations like this come up all the time. It's not something I like about myself, but my usual impulse is not to get involved, to move on, to let someone else deal with it.

Sarah is just the opposite. She can't stand by and watch. She talks to homeless people, jams with street musicians. She gets up into the face of a white cop who's beating a Black kid for jumping a subway turnstile and demands his badge number, then writes countless letters to the police commissioner. She's not a person who hesitates. Except once, when we first met. I was the one who leaped. But that's another story.

So back on the street in Oaxaca, Sarah, who speaks Spanish, started explaining to the man on the bike why this woman was so upset. It had never occurred to him that the dog presented a problem; Oaxaqueños have other things to worry about. But he was friendly and told Sarah there was a vet six blocks away—Dr. Vargas.

Sarah is a sucker for all animals, dogs in particular, and this one won her heart as soon as he looked up at her, his ears half-flopped over, and wagged his threadbare tail. So she was game to take him to the vet. And I was willing to go along. Some of the best things in my life have come from following Sarah.

But it wasn't so easy. The dog had no collar, and who knew what diseases he might be carrying. Sarah thought perhaps we could lure him six blocks by offering him food along the way. So she went off to a store and returned with some waffle crackers that the dog happily started to devour as we led him down the street. But pretty soon, the dog stopped at the limit of his turf and would go no further.

Sarah disappeared to find some string we could fashion into a leash, and the woman—Diane was her name—thanked me. "I know this isn't what you had in mind for your vacation," she said.

I started to explain that Sarah and I weren't keen on shopping in upscale stores or whatever it is that most people do, that we just liked to wander around and see life as it is in another place. But Diane wasn't listening. She was talking to the dog. Soon he lay on his back and let her pet his belly. By the time Sarah got back, Diane had picked him up and was cradling him like a baby. The trusting dog didn't fuss or fight. He lay there, his head on Diane's breast, his sweet eyes fixed on her face.

We piled into a taxi with Diane holding the dog. In the enclosed space for the first time I could smell the sewer stench rising from the animal. The driver, an elderly gent with a gold-toothed smile, tolerated it in silence and dropped us off at Dr. Vargas's.

As we waited in line, Diane was adamant: the dog had to be put out of his misery. I became increasingly uneasy. What were we doing here? Imposing our values on a culture that had a different relationship to street animals? Playing God? Did Diane really know enough about this dog to decide whether he should live or die? How much was he suffering? And was suffering enough to warrant a death sentence anyway?

I'd seen my share of suffering. I'd watched my mother deteriorate steadily for three years after surgery to remove a brain tumor. A professional dancer all her life, she'd ended up bedridden, unable to walk or talk. And yet, some of the most important and honest moments between us happened during those three years. I'd never danced with my mother till she had her surgery. Then, as therapy, we danced together. I'll never forget swaying unsteadily with her to a recording of Judy Garland singing "When you're smilin', the whole world smiles with you." Maybe a few moments like that weren't worth three years of suffering for her and the rest of our family. But I wasn't so sure.

And now the dog. While Diane was absolutely clear about what needed to be done, Sarah said she wanted to hear the vet's opinion. She talked to a middle-aged woman behind the counter who explained that this was a veterinary pharmacy, not a clinic. She could sell us a syringe and something to inject into the dog ourselves, but it would take a long time. She suggested we go to a clinic four blocks away.

"Tell her to wash herself thoroughly," she said, pointing to Diane, who'd been holding the dog the whole time. "She can get sick."

As Sarah translated, Diane held the dog even closer. Then we headed through busy streets to the clinic. Sarah led the way past crowds of pedestrians, who looked up in surprise at Diane and the dog. I walked behind, watching the dog's innocent face bobbing up and down over Diane's shoulder. His mouth was a bit crooked so he looked as if he was smiling, enjoying the view. Diane never wavered or asked for a rest. Her arms were strong, her body solid. She looked like she knew what physical labor was all about.

The clinic was on a small street in a shabby industrial neighborhood, nothing like the lovely *zócalo* or the restored tourist area we'd stayed in. Trucks roared by, spewing diesel exhaust. Between a garage and an oil-drum distributor, a hand-painted sign identified the veterinarian's simple storefront. A Mexican man wearing glasses and blue scrubs appeared from the adjacent parking lot, glanced at Diane and the dog, and pointed to a tiny room. He held up his hand, indicating he'd be there in a minute.

Dr. Gonzalez, the vet, was around 30 years old and had a kind face. "Can this dog be cured?" Sarah asked. As Dr. Gonzalez carefully examined the dog, I knew what was coming. I looked at Sarah. She was explaining to the doctor that we'd found the dog in the *zócalo*.

"Are you Mexican?" Dr. Gonzalez asked. Sarah's Spanish is pretty good, but I knew that wasn't why he asked the question. Sarah has that dark kind of beauty that passes most everywhere. People always think she's one of them—Puerto Ricans, Italians, Arabs, even Indians. Actually, she's what I call a Jewish beauty. But her beauty is not conventional. It comes from inside—her soul, her heart. It radiates from her warm eyes, her smile, her laugh, her voice. People can feel it, and perhaps that's why everyone wants her to be one of their own.

Sarah explained that we were from the U.S., that we would be leaving soon.

"If you lived here," Dr. Gonzalez said, "and you were willing to spend every day for three months taking care of this dog, he might have a slight chance to survive. Even then he'd probably get sick again."

"Is there a shelter or anyone in Oaxaca that can take care of a dog like this?" Sarah asked.

The doctor shook his head. "I'm sorry, we don't have enough for people—and for street animals, nothing." He paused, trying to find the right words. "The dog has mange through his whole body. He's covered with tumors. If he goes back to the street, he'll give the disease to other dogs, he might last a couple of weeks, he'd suffer every moment."

"If the dog should be put out of his suffering," said Sarah, "we're prepared for that."

Dr. Gonzalez nodded and said, "He doesn't deserve such pain." Sarah translated, and we all looked at each other. Even I agreed now. It was the right thing to do.

Diane had never stopped holding the dog. She petted him and talked to him as Dr. Gonzalez prepared the injection. The dog eagerly took in all the love she offered. I realized that he'd probably never been touched by a human before today. He wasn't scratching now, he seemed content to give over responsibility for his life to this woman who cared enough to become a friend.

I couldn't watch, but Sarah told me the dog died in peace. Just before he lost consciousness, he was looking into Diane's eyes.

Dr. Gonzalez said he would dispose of the body. He charged ten dollars for the cost of the drugs, but nothing for his time. Diane paid, Sarah thanked him, and we stepped out into the sunshine.

As we walked together back to the *zócalo*, Diane wept quietly. She told us she lived on a farm back in New Hampshire with several dogs. She'd had to put one down recently. She was in Mexico for a cooking course.

"I know this dog wasn't the most important thing," she said as we reached the lower *zócalo*. "I know people are dying in wars, people are starving." She looked over at the *campesinos* still lying on the ground next to their signs of protest. "But those things are so big, and I can only do what I can. I know it sounds silly, but God put me here to do this, and it's no coincidence that you were here too."

We parted ways at the spot on the upper *zócalo* where we'd first seen the dog. We didn't exchange addresses or even last names. We didn't hug. Diane's shirt was black with the dog's filth.

"I don't know how to thank you enough," she said. "I couldn't have done this without you."

"I just hope someone does the same for me when it's time," Sarah said.

"Diane," I said, "that dog got more love from you in his last hour than he'd gotten the rest of his life."

Crying and waving as she walked away, she yelled back, "Something good is going to happen to you."

That night I got *turista*. Sitting on the toilet at three in the morning, desperately trying to think of anything but my stomach, I replayed the day's events. I'd felt mostly irrelevant when they'd happened, an observer. But now I realized why I'd been there. To tell the story. A story about love and work. About Diane's love for God, Sarah's love for animals, and my love for Sarah. About the work we did together.

"And what's the work?" asked Allen Ginsberg in his poem *Memory Gardens*. "To ease the pain of living. Everything else, drunken dumbshow."

ACKNOWLEDGMENTS

Many wonderful people have helped me become a writer.

I want to thank the best teachers a young writer could have: Fred Doucette, who taught me grammar in ninth grade; Ben Adelson, who taught me the fundamentals of journalism in high school; Marvin Barrett and Victor Navasky, my professional journalism mentors; Oliver Stone, who taught me more about screenwriting during our collaboration than any book or class could.

My writers' group in the Hudson Valley has contributed thoughtful suggestions, editing, and advice. My gratitude to Nina Shengold, Ron Nyswaner, Laura Cunningham, Casey Kurtti, Becky Stowe, Mary Louise Wilson, John Bowers, Mark St. Germain, David Smilow, Jai Chakrabarti.

As a creative adviser at Sundance and other Screenwriting Labs for more than 20 years, I have traveled and learned so much about writing and the world from my fellow advisers and the writers who shared their work. I am grateful to all, particularly lab directors Michelle Satter and Bertha Navarro.

The Harlem Dramatic Writing Workshop, where I've taught screenwriting since 2008, has been a source of inspiration for me. Thanks to all members of the workshop and especially to Eddie Pomerantz for making it happen.

Many friends, some of whom are no longer alive, have shared their memories of events, read drafts of the essays, and contributed in various other ways. I very much appreciate help from Jeffrey Hershey, Stuart Sender, Carol Dutton Stepick, Carroll Seron, Claudia Shafer, Lee Walters, Pat Conroy, Terry Murphree Littleton, David Morrison, Donna Healey, Tim Biancalana, Richard Fernau, Ellen Bloch, Laura Esquivel, Marcela Fuentes-Berain, Beatriz Novaro, Martín Salinas, Jo Ann Beard, Scott Spencer, Pat McNees, Mary Howell, Jenny Hersch, Sallie Ann Robinson, Margarite Washington, Ervin Simmons, Michael Smith, Debby Smith, Michael Ratner, Karen Ranucci, Mark Byrd, Ari Ben-Menashe, Tish Streeten, Jordi Castells.

Many thanks to Simi Nallaseth for her beautiful artwork and cover design and to Jennifer May for the author photo. I am very grateful to

Francisco Toledo and the estate of Francisco Toledo for permission to use the maestro's "Xolo," a beautiful depiction of his own Oaxaca dog. Many thanks to David Morrison, Kathleen Ruiz, and Janet Essley for their photos and friendship. And thanks also to Paul Cohen, Colin Rolfe, and Jerry Kalajian.

My deep respect and appreciation go to J. Herman Blake, who sent me to Daufuskie Island and provided valuable insight on my essay.

When my health failed me years ago, naturopath Dr. Shyam Singha, Henry Kellerman, Kwan Sai Hung, and John Duggan came to the rescue and enabled me to get back to writing. My deep gratitude to all of them.

Heartfelt thanks to my family who have always supported and sustained me with their love—George, Miriam, Judy, Daniel, Michael, Sonya, Oren, Toby, Miri, Abby, David, and Noa.

Special thanks to my sister Judy Sklar Rasminsky and brother Daniel Sklar, both excellent writers, who have been my trusted readers and editors over the years.

Finally, this book wouldn't exist without Sarah Plant. Not only did she line-edit every draft, but she solved tech problems, advised on fonts, photos and design, and sniffed out the slightest hint of a false note in the writing. Most important, her love over 37 years has given me a world of joy and the strength to do my small part of "the work."

ABOUT THE AUTHOR

Photo by Jennifer May

Zachary Sklar is a screenwriter, journalist, author, and editor. He is best known as co-author, with Oliver Stone, of the Academy Award-nominated screenplay for the film *JFK*. His other screen credits include *La Fiesta del Chivo* (*Feast of the Goat*) and *Hanyut* (*Almayer's Folly*).

He leads the screenwriting section of the Harlem Dramatic Writing Workshop and has served as a creative adviser for Sundance Screenwriting Labs around the world, from Utah to Mexico, Jordan, Turkey, Greece, Australia, Brazil, Ecuador, and Cuba. He also taught magazine writing at the Columbia Graduate School of Journalism for a decade.

As a journalist, he has written for *The New York Times, The Washington Post, The Nation,* and *Huffington Post,* among others. He has edited numerous non-fiction books, including the number-one-bestselling *On the Trail of the Assassins* by Jim Garrison, *Moving the Bar: My Life as a Radical Lawyer* by Michael Ratner, *Profits of War* by Ari Ben-Menashe, and *Deadly Deceits: My 25 Years in the CIA* by Ralph Mc Gehee.

He lives in Olivebridge, New York.

CPSIA information can be obtained
at www.ICGtesting.com
Printed in the USA
JSHW071521290123
36960JS00001B/7